# A
# Practical
# Guide
# to
# Church
# Planting

# A Practical Guide to Church Planting

Roger N. McNamara
Editor

Baptist Mid-Missions
Cleveland, Ohio

PRINTED IN THE UNITED STATES OF AMERICA

1st Printing June 1986

Published by
BAPTIST MID-MISSIONS
7749 Webster Rd.
Cleveland, Ohio 44103

# Acknowledgements

This book is the result of the efforts of a team of six church planters who serve under Baptist Mid-Missions.  Together they have over one-hundred thirty years of experience in starting new churches at home and abroad:

Rev. Leigh Adams
Rev. Gerald Baker
Rev. Ken Davis
Rev. Roger McNamara
Rev. David Selden
Rev. Ken Steward

In addition, valuable help in the preparation of the manu-script was received from several individuals in the Baptist Mid-Missions Home Office:

Dr. C. Raymond Buck
Dr. William Smallman
Miss Bernice Inman

# Table of Contents

Acknowledgements ................................................................iii

Foreword ...............................................................................vii

## Section I..

**Chapter**  **1.** The Mandate for Church Planting................1
**Chapter**  **2.** The Man God Uses in Church
Planting....................................................**11**
**Chapter**  **3.** The Methods of Church Planting ...............**17**

## Section II..

**Chapter**  **4.** The Place for Church Planting...................**37**
**Chapter**  **5.** The Preparations for Church
Planting....................................................**71**
**Chapter**  **6.** The Plan for Church Planting...................**87**
**Chapter**  **7.** The Public Beginning Church
Planting..................................................**105**

## Section III..

**Chapter**  **8.** The Organization of the Local
Church...................................................**121**
**Chapter**  **9.** The Oversight of the Local Church ...........**159**
**Chapter 10.** The Orientation of the Local
Church Services...................................**169**
**Chapter 11.** The Operation of the Local Church
Sunday School......................................**185**
**Chapter 12.** The Outreach of the Local Church............**197**

## Section IV..

**Chapter 13.** The Finances of the Local Church............**211**

**Chapter 14.** The Fund Raising Program of
the Local Church....................................**229**

**Chapter 15.** The Facilities of the Local Church............**247**

**Chapter 16.** The Fallacies in the Local Church............**261**

**Chapter 17.** The Finished Job–A Local Church...........**267**

Bibliography .........................................................................**277**

# Foreword

Frustration results when one is obligated to do something that he does not know how to do. Such frustration is often felt by willing but untrained Christians who accept the command of our Lord Jesus Christ to evangelize the lost and to organize the believers into local, New Testament churches. They do not know how to do what they are commanded to do.

This manual is a prescription for avoiding or reducing the frustration of planting local churches. Taken as directed, the contents will help the servant of God to know exactly what a New Testament local church is and how an ordinary Christian may be used of God to plant one.

The writers of this guide are experienced and successful church planters. The chapters chronicle the steps of their procedure in accomplishing a complicated but challenging assignment. Because the advice they give has been demonstrated, often, repeatedly, in the development of strong, self-propagating local churches, the book becomes a blueprint that others may follow.

Capable as the men are who have produced this guide, they would hasten to assure us that it is impossible to win the lost and to form the believers into New Testament churches without the direction and the blessing of the Lord. The Word of God affirms this in the words: "Except the Lord build the house, they labor in vain that build it..." (Psalm 127:1a). This manual does not ignore the importance of God's enablement, but it does make helpful suggestions as to how the church planter may create something worthy of His blessing.

It is the prayer of the writers that *A Practical Guide to Church Planting* will prove to be precisely that. May it be used to assist missionaries and all others who set themselves to the job of doing New Testament Discipleship in the New Testament way.

C. Raymond Buck, Ph.D.
President, Baptist Mid-Missions

# Section I..

**Chapter 1** .... The Mandate for Church Planting

        Why Plant Churches?
        What Kind of Churches Should Be Planted?
        Where Should Churches Be Planted?
        The Biblical Goal of Church Planting

**Chapter 2** .... The Man God Uses in Church Planting

        He Needs to Be Spiritually Mature
        He Needs to Be a Soul Winner
        He Needs to Be a Lover of People
        He Needs to Be a Leader
        He Needs to Be a Disciplined Person
        He Needs to Be Flexible
        He Needs to Be Fiscally Responsible
        He Needs to Be a Family Man
        He Needs to Be Educated and Experienced

**Chapter 3**.... The Methods of Church Planting

        Missionary Church Planting
        Pioneer Church Planting
        Associational Church Planting
        Parent-Daughter Church Planting
        Partnership Church Planting
        Bible Studies and Church Planting
        Church Splits and Church Planting
        Bivocational Church Planting
        The Man--Not the Method

# Chapter 1

# The Mandate
# for Church Planting

The term *church planting,* as commonly used today, refers to the method used to fulfill the Great Commission. This Scriptural mandate involves the establishing of local churches. Similar terms are used throughout Scripture. In the first reference to the church, the Lord Jesus said:

> ...Thou art Peter, and upon this rock I will *build* my church; and the gates of hell shall not prevail against it" (Matthew 16:18).

The Apostle Paul used the terms *build* and *plant* when he referred to those laboring in the city of Corinth:

> Who then is Paul, and who is Apollos, but ministers by whom ye believed, ...I have *planted,* Apollos watered; but God gave the increase. So then neither is he that *planteth* anything, neither he that watereth; but God that giveth the increase. Now he that *planteth* and he that watereth are one....
> ...According to the grace of God which is given to me, as a wise master *builder,* I have laid the foundation, and another *buildeth* thereon. But let every man take heed how he *buildeth* there upon. For other foundation can no man lay than that is laid, which is Jesus Christ..." (I Corinthians 3:5-11).

The Bible uses the word church in two ways: the *universal* church and the *local* church. The universal church refers to all believers from Pentecost to the rapture and is mentioned at least twenty times in the New Testament. The local church refers to a group of believers in a given locality and is referred to no fewer than ninety times.

Dr. Paul Jackson in his excellent work, *The Doctrine and Administration of the Church,* wrote:

> A local New Testament church is a body of believers immersed upon a credible confession of faith in Jesus Christ, having two officers (pastors and deacons), sovereign in polity, and banded together for work, worship, the observance of the ordinances and the worldwide proclamation of the gospel. [1]

*Church planting* then refers to the expansion of the universal church through the establishment of new local churches.

## Why Plant Churches?

• Jesus commanded it.

The mandate for church planting or church building comes from the Lord himself. We must *plant* or *build* churches because the Great Commission demands it. Our mandate is from God who commanded:

> "Go ye therefore, and teach all nations, baptizing them in the name of the Father, and of the Son, and of the Holy Ghost: teaching them to observe all things whatsoever I have commanded you..." (Matthew 28:19-20).

Jesus Christ, who stated, "I will build my church," was aware of the self imposed limitations of His earthly ministry. Luke wrote, "The former treatise have I made, O Theophilus, of all that Jesus *began* both to do and teach" (Acts 1:1). That which Christ began to do is now the privilege and responsibility of His disciples. His last words before the ascension were:

> But ye shall receive power, after that the Holy Ghost is come upon you, and ye shall be witnesses unto me both in Jerusalem, and in all Judea, and in Samaria, and unto the uttermost part of the earth " (Acts 1:8).

The Holy Spirit, as promised, came to indwell all believers everywhere. The power to carry out the Great Commission was made available at Pentecost and continues to this day. God began His work through the believers, starting at Jerusalem and spreading into all the world. He was and is building His church through those who obediently respond to His command.

Researchers estimate that at the time of Christ the world population was approximately 258 million. Considering there were only 120 people in the upper room, we are amazed at the tremendous task which God entrusted to such a small company. However, they were a very special company. They were the local church at Jerusalem.

What was their response to such a mandate? Did they consider it an impossible challenge? No, this was not the case. In giving the mandate, Jesus also gave them two promises. Preceding the

Great Commission, he stated, "All power is given unto me in heaven and in earth, go ye therefore...." At the close He stated: "...and lo I am with you alway, even unto the end of the world." Surely the promise of Christ's power and His presence should dispel any doubts, not only for the original disciples, but for church planters today.

• The disciples practiced it.

Church planting is supported by apostolic example. The book of Acts sets forth a very clear pattern of obedience to the Great Commission. Jesus Christ, in His last instructions to the disciples, stated: "Ye shall be witnesses unto me both in Jerusalem, and in all Judea, and in Samaria, and unto the uttermost part of the earth" (Acts 1:8).

It was Peter who began carrying out this commission in Jerusalem on the day of Pentecost. Crowds had gathered from sixteen different nations. When Peter arose and began to speak, there was hardly standing room. This was the first proclamation of the gospel to mankind. People were amazed— they heard the Good News— God's messenger had spoken. Many were under conviction. They asked the disciples, "Men and brethren, what shall we do?" (Acts 2:37). They were directed to accept Jesus Christ. The Scripture tells us:

> They that gladly received His word were baptized, and the same day were added unto them about three thousand souls, and they steadfastly continued in the apostles' doctrine and fellowship and breaking of bread and prayers (2:41-42).

Within a very short time, the local church at Jerusalem had increased from 120 to 3,000 souls. Did the disciples still doubt? God had begun to work. God was multiplying the lives of those first disciples. This principle of missions is called "life multiplication" through the local church (Acts 2:47; 4:4; 5:14; 6:1,7; 9:31; 11:24; 12:24; 16:5).

The Great Commission continued to be implemented by these fervent witnesses of Jesus Christ. On several occasions they were jailed for their perseverance in proclaiming the gospel of the risen Messiah (4:1; 5:17-18, 12:4-5). Local believers began to share the gospel— Stephen's message is recorded in Acts chapter 7. He died a martyr's death because of his stand for Jesus Christ.

Persecution ensued and "they were all scattered abroad throughout the regions of Judea and Samaria ...everywhere preaching the word" (8:1-4). Peter went to Samaria and then later to Caesarea to speak with Cornelius about the good news of salvation (Acts 10). Wherever they went, new churches sprang up as the gospel was proclaimed.

The Great Commission is not a cultural mandate. A missionary is not sent for the betterment of society; he has an evangelistic mandate. His responsibility under God is to evangelize and plant churches indigenous to that country or people.

Demographers estimate that in 1986 the world population numbered 4,885,000,000 souls— over four billion more than the disciples had to reach in the first century. The God who worked through the disciples in the first century is able to do the same today. God has not changed.

• The world needs it.

The local church is the instrument which God has ordained to reach the world with the gospel. In Acts 13 the local church at Antioch sent Barnabas and Saul out on a missionary assignment. Clearly we see the evidence that God is directing the beginning of foreign missions. He forbade them to go into Asia at that time (Acts 16:6) and opened the door of their ministry to the continent of Europe (16:9). The uttermost parts were being reached.

Tradition holds that the Apostle Thomas was sent by God to the Indian subcontinent with the gospel. Other missionaries went to Africa organizing local churches. Surely the gospel had spread far beyond the sixteen nations represented in Jerusalem on the day of Pentecost. The heathen heard and believed in Jesus Christ, God's sacrifice for their sin. Romans 10:13-17 was being put into action. So great was their penetration that even the secular authorities recognized their impact, "These that have turned the world upside down are come hither also" (Acts 17:6).

If we are to reach the lost and dying world around us, we must increase the number of church- planting missionaries being sent out. To do this, we must increase the number of churches which make up the home base. Only by implementing the Great Commission at home can this be done.

## What Kind of Churches Should be Planted?

We believe the church planter should establish churches indigenous to the region, congregational in polity and Baptist in name. Was the Apostle Paul a "Baptist"? This word, as commonly used today, refers not only to a mode of baptism, but also to a form of church government. In order to answer this question, we need to consider church polity or government.

In Christendom there are four basic types of church polity or government:

- **Papal**— rule by one man as evidenced in Roman Catholicism
- **Episcopalian**— leadership and authority reside in the ordained clergy
- **Presbyterian**— authority in elected sessions, presbyteries or synods, and
- **Congregational**— authority in the hands of all the members of each local church.

Local, independent Baptist churches use the congregational form of government. Paul established indigenous churches which had this form of government. The local congregations chose their own leaders (Acts 6:1-5), exercised their own discipline (I Cor. 5:1-7) and sent out their own missionaries (Acts 13:1-3). Paul baptized by immersion (Romans 6:4; Colossians 2:12). He was indeed a "Baptist."

The church planter who is faithful to the scriptural mandate will seek to plant, not transplant. His goal is to develop indigenous churches. A newly planted church must identify with the culture of the country or region in which it is being established. A transplanted church will not do that. Too often it follows the cultural pattern of the church planter. You must be just as careful not to impose a "city style" on a rural population (or vice versa) as is the foreign missionary who must not transplant an "American" church to foreign soil. This type of church is considered suspect by the community and will not reproduce readily.

The indigenous Baptist church is characterized by the winning and discipling of converts as well as the training of qualified local leadership. Ephesians 4 clearly describes the methodology of the Great Commission. The evangelist (missionary) and pastor-teacher have the responsibility of "perfecting of the saints for the work of the ministry, for the edifying of the body of Christ" (Ephesians 4:11). The missionary church planter's ministry is temporary. He is sent into an area to win souls to Jesus Christ and then to equip them to carry on the ministry of the local church. Paul achieved this in Thessalonica. He wrote, "Ye were examples to all that believe in Macedonia and Achaia, but also in every place your faith to God-ward is spread abroad; so that we need not to speak anything" (I Thessalonians 1:7-8). The church planted at Thessalonica had been equipped and/or trained to continue the work of evangelism first undertaken by the missionaries. When people responded to the challenge, missionaries were no longer needed in that area, not even the Apostle Paul.

The New Testament church evidenced other characteristics such as doctrine, worship, fellowship, prayer and discipline (Acts 2:42). These characteristics will be discussed in later chapters.

## Where Should Churches be Planted?

The answer is obvious—where the people live. Most people live in cities. A study of the missionary activity in the book of Acts clearly demonstrates the Holy Spirit's leading (16:6-10). The New Testament pattern for church planting was to concentrate on the cities, the population centers. The outlying districts were then evangelized by those local churches.

There are twenty-three cities mentioned in the New Testament. Most of them were areas in which evangelism and church planting had taken place. Biblical missions involves reaching population centers like Ephesus, Philippi, Berea, Thessalonica, Corinth and Rome—strategic cities in the Roman Empire. Biblical methodology is very important. Paul's method was to reach the city—the population center. Somehow today we have overlooked the city centers with their teeming millions and opted for the smaller towns and rural areas. We have sought to avoid the dangers and difficulties of the city. Where are the missionaries and church planters who are willing to follow God's mandate for planting churches in New York, Detroit, Philadelphia, Cleveland and Chicago?

The churches that were planted were "local" or community centered. Believers in each area met together regularly for instruction in the apostle's doctrine, fellowship, breaking of bread and prayer (Acts 2:42). The writer of Hebrews cautioned Christians: "Not forsaking the assembling of ourselves together, as the manner of some is; but exhorting one another..." (Hebrews 10:25).

In contrast, many local churches today are being replaced by media churches. Television and radio have replaced the local pulpit. Appeals are made to Christians thousands of miles away to become members of the media church. Some say, "Send your tithes and offerings to us, support our worldwide mission program." But the electronic church does not fulfill the New Testament definition of a local church. It is unable to encourage, counsel, comfort and minister the ordinances or discipline its members. It's a "comfortable" Christianity. Its lack of discipline may be the reason why some Christians appreciate the more remote church. God's program as set forth in the New Testament, however, does not endorse this type of church. It is not indigenous. It is not able to fulfill its scriptural responsibilities. In reality, it is not a church at all.

Ethnic groups must not be neglected in our church planting. These people usually locate in urban areas, the places where we have the fewest fundamental churches. Approximately 14,000 new refugees arrive in the United States monthly. *The Los Angeles Daily News* (September 12, 1982) reported that the number of "Latino residents went up 59% since 1970, bringing the official total to 2.1 million. Total [L.A.] county population is 7.4 million." The United States is currently the fifth largest Spanish-speaking country in the world. Reports estimate that the Hispanic population may reach as high as 23 million. As with most ethnic groups, you must be sensitive to the cultural and social differences which exist within the Hispanic community. Each country represented has its own national pride and character.

Cleveland, Ohio, is second only to Budapest in the number of Hungarian residents. New York City numbers 1,998,000 Jewish people. Over 6 million Jews live in the United States, almost double the population of the country of Israel. City churches, along with their congregations, often move to the suburbs, thus creating a vacuum within the city itself. The focus of modern missions should be on these city areas. Although inner-city residents are often of a lower economic status and frequently transient, making them difficult to reach, they should not be neglected. The same is true of the rural areas. What an opportunity for missions here at home!

## The Biblical Goal of Church Planting

"What is the most important aspect of your success: management, labor or sales?" Henry Ford replied, "Which of the three legs of a three-legged stool is least important?" Obviously each one is important, for without one it would fall. Similarly, the biblical goal of missions is to establish a local church indigenous to that area. This can be accomplished  only when each of the following goals have been achieved.

● **The local church must be self-governing**

From those who are won to Christ in the area, leaders must be trained for the new congregation. Paul wrote to the local church at Ephesus that the evangelist and the pastor/teacher are to "perfect (or, bring to maturity) the saints for the work of the min istry." The Great Commission very clearly sets forth this principle of training. Christ stated in Matthew 28:20, "Teaching them to observe all things whatsoever I have commanded you." The Lord spent a great deal of time with his disciples. They had been trained to plant churches. Local people are to be won to Christ, discipled and given leadership positions. They speak the language. They know and are known by those whom they are try ing to reach.

● **The local church must be self-propagating.**

Believers must learn to share their faith effectively with others or the church will die. Life multiplication is the key. For a young church to reproduce itself, it must reach the community with the gospel. Far too many churches resemble fortresses. The saints march around inside the walls, singing and praising God, but never venture forth to the battle outside. It is important for the church planter to be active in soul winning—this is expected. However, when a new Christian or church member becomes in volved in evangelism, that's news! It's like a satisfied customer replacing the salesman on his route.

● **The local church must be self-supporting..**

This is stewardship. It should be remembered that the goal is church *planting* and not church *transplanting*. All that is needed for the ongoing ministry of the local church should be provided for by its own people. This eventually includes its entire budget, pastoral salary and outreach expenses. For a young congregation to depend upon "grants" from richer Christians in other areas does a disservice to them and the Great Commission. New believers can be transformed into "rice" Christians quickly. They become mercenary, failing to trust God for that which He wants to provide for them through their own stewardship.

Why plant churches? The answer is simply that God has commanded us to plant churches. Christ said, "I will build my church." The manifestation of "His church" in any community is the local church. Only as Christians reproduce themselves (life multiplication) can we reach the four billion people in the world today. It is through the local church that the community and the world can and must be reached with the gospel. Without local churches, worldwide evangelization cannot be achieved!

## Endnotes

[1] Jackson, Paul R., *The Doctrine and Adminstration of the Church.* (Schaumburg, IL. Regular Baptist Press, 1968), p. 24.

# Chapter 2

# The Man God Uses in Church Planting

God can use anyone to establish a new church, but there are certain characteristics which stand out in the lives of those He does use for this purpose. Each church planter has strengths and weaknesses which will determine his effectiveness.

• A church planter needs to be spiritually mature.

This obviously requires a personal relationship with Jesus Christ and the assurance of salvation. If you are unsure of your own salvation, you will have a difficult time convincing others to accept the Savior you yourself have not fully trusted.

Spiritual maturity is the result of studying and applying God's Word to your life. There must be a time of daily communion with Christ which nourishes and strengthens you and your family. Set aside time each day for personal and family devotions. Without this time of Bible study and prayer, you will be powerless and frustrated.

Maturity will express itself in a number of ways in your life. You will have firmly held beliefs which you are able to communicate to others; you will have learned to look to God for your financial, family and ministry-related needs; you will be confident God is leading you to start the new church. Through faith you envision God's raising up a new congregation through you and are willing to go wherever He leads. You will not be easily discouraged by slow progress or the prospect of failure.

Having set your hand to the plow, you must not look back and wonder if you have made a mistake. Rather, keep your eye on the goal and press forward in the place of God's choosing.

God is just as big as you allow Him to be. You will find that He will bless your efforts in direct proportion to your expectations. If you expect God to do little through you, God will do little. But if you look to God for great things, He honors your faith and does as you expect (Matthew 9:29).

• A church planter needs to be a soul winner.

You must be motivated by love and compassion for those without Christ and seek to win them to the Savior. The ability to win people to Christ is essential to the church planter's ministry. If you do not win people, you will never build a church or train others to win souls.

A burden and vision for reaching people with the gospel will stimulate you to spend hours witnessing in the community you hope to reach. Initially, you should spend the majority of your time soul winning. A minimum of twenty-five to thirty hours a week should be dedicated to this pursuit in the early stages of the church-planting process. After the church is established, time must still be reserved for soul winning if you hope to see continued growth and your people becoming soul winners. After all, soul winning is not taught, it is caught.

• A church planter needs to be a lover of people.

The world in which we live is filled with people who are lonely, unhappy and without a friend. They can be hostile, they may be repulsive, they may not want anything to do with a church. But they can be reached with the gospel if you simply love them. People want to be loved and they will respond to it.

As a church planter, you must learn to express love to people. Go out of your way to be friendly. Wave to folks, speak to your neighbors. Offer a helping hand when you see someone in need. Love is not expressed in words, but in deeds. People will not believe you, until you show them in a tangible way that you really love them just as they are.

If you love people, they will listen to what you have to say and will respond to it. As D.L. Moody once said: "You catch more flies with honey than with vinegar."

• A church planter needs to be a leader.

Be a self-starter. Don't wait for others to tell you what to do. Produce the ideas, plans and programs and then motivate people to become involved. Willingly accept the spiritual and ad- ministrative oversight of the flock. Since God has led you to establish a new church, exercise the leadership necessary to ensure its success. The church will go only as far as you lead it.

As the spiritual leader of the church, set the standard through your words, deeds, dress and attitude. You cannot demand that others do what you are unwilling to do. You must set the example for them to follow.

This does not mean you do everything for the people. Your biblical role is not to do all the work yourself, but to prepare the people to do the work of the ministry (Ephesians 4:11). Leadership involves delegating responsibility. Refrain from doing anything the people are able to do for themselves. If capable helpers are not available, train them. This is part of your "equipping" ministry. Initially you may have to do many things yourself, but plan to turn that work over to someone else as soon as possible. When delegating responsibility for a job, also grant the authority and freedom to fulfill the task.

Inspect what you delegate. Inform workers that you will be meeting with them at regular intervals to review progress and to make plans for the future. This time of accounting will develop responsible leaders among your people.

• A church planter needs to be a disciplined person.

The man who gets a lot done, gets it done because he plans to. He plans his work and then works his plan. He has definite goals. He concentrates his time and efforts on reaching them. Employment, education and ecclesiastical responsibilities are not allowed to divert him. His goal is the development of a new church. By setting daily, weekly, monthly and annual objectives, he is able to keep this goal in sight.

To achieve your goal, keep your priorities in order. Many church planters find it helpful to make a list of things to do each day, arranging them in order of importance. Begin with the first thing on the list, sticking with it until finished. Then move on to each succeeding item on the list. Anything left over at the end of the day is added to the next day's list. Not only does this help keep your priorities in order, but enables you to accomplish more than would otherwise be possible.

The church planter must control his time. Since you punch no time clock, it is easy to waste time. You must guard against sleeping late, puttering around the house or spending too much time watching sports or television. It is easy to spend an hour chatting with a fellow pastor or listening to "Aunt Matilda's" latest aches and pains.

A regular schedule will help you be more efficient. Here is a sample schedule to consider:

6:00 – 8:00 a.m.
> Get up, shower, eat and have devotions.

8:00 – 12:00 noon
> Prepare message and Bible studies.

12:00 – 1:00 p.m.
> Lunch.

1:00 – 4:00 p.m.
> Go soul winning, visit hospital/shut-ins.
> Correspondence, plan programs.

4:00 – 7:00 p.m.
> Play with children, do odd jobs at home.
> Evening meal.

7:00 – 9:00 p.m.
> Soul winning, Bible studies, church services.
> Keep one night open as "family night."

• A church planter needs to be flexible.

Flexibility implies the courage to change, to discard that which does not work and replace it with something better. It may be necessary to meet in a variety of locations under less than ideal circumstances. The janitor may not show up to unlock the school door, a teacher may be absent or roads will be impassable due to a snowstorm. The church planter must be able to adjust and go on. You must improvise, using whatever and whoever is available.

Being flexible enables you as a church planter to work with people who are different from you. Not everyone is used to doing things your way. You may have to adjust to people from different cultures, with different languages and lifestyles. In spite of all your planning and discipline, there will be times when things will not go as expected. If you love people and can make the necessary adjustments, you will find it much easier to develop the church.

• A church planter needs to be financially responsible.

Before starting a church, eliminate any outstanding debts. Raise adequate financial backing so you can give full time to the work. This will eliminate much frustration.

Live within your means, do not incur debts you cannot pay or that place you in a financial bind. It is important to maintain a good credit rating in the community. You can establish credit with local banks by taking out small loans and repaying them. Larger loans are then more readily available when you have a good name and good credit. Do not "poor mouth" or complain about financial difficulties to your people. Instead set an example of trusting God for your needs.

Knowledge of bookkeeping and budgeting procedures is extremely helpful. This is especially true in the early days of the church when you may have to set up the church books and make many of the financial decisions yourself. The ability to keep accurate records, establish a workable budget and properly manage the church's finances will instill confidence in your leadership while eliminating many of the false concepts people have about church finances.

• A church planter needs to be a family man.

The Bible places great emphasis on the church planter's family. A man who has been divorced or who cannot control his children is unqualified to pastor a church, much less start one (I Timothy 3:2,3).

It is important your wife and children understand and support your efforts to start a new church. Otherwise, you will find your ministry undermined by those at home as resentment and bitterness grow.

God does not expect a man to sacrifice his family to build a church. You must not become so busy tending the "vineyards" of others that you neglect your own. Take your wife out to lunch or go shopping with her. A "family night" will provide time to play with the children or go places with them. Be careful not to cancel family plans, except in cases of genuine emergency. Even then, re-schedule the time with your family as soon as possible. A man who cares more for his church than his family is in danger of losing both.

The church planter must provide for the spiritual needs of his family. It is not enough for them to attend the services. God holds you responsible as the spiritual head of the home. As such, you must take the responsibility of leading your family in daily devotions. This should not be pushed off onto your wife. The spiritual vitality of your home is important to your success as a church planter. A strong home will produce a strong church.

## • A church planter needs to be educated and experienced.

God does not place a premium on ignorance. Your education will affect your ministry. The more tools you are able to place at the Holy Spirit's disposal, the more effective you will be.

Regardless of your education, you should be well versed in three areas: the Scriptures, methods of church planting and growth methods, and the culture of the people among whom you will be working. Keep abreast of current trends and developments in church planting through the many publications and seminars available to you.

Pastoral experience is highly recommended for anyone who plans to be a church planter. It is important to understand the inner workings of a church and how to develop lay leadership. Spend two or three years as a pastor or working in an established church before you try to establish a new one. Better yet, work with an experienced church planter and learn from him. This is not lost time, it is time invested that will pay rich dividends. The experience gained will enable you to avoid many mistakes, much frustration and possible failure.

If God has led you to plant a new church, you will experience an inner peace in doing so. This does not mean there will not be times of discouragement. There will be. But if God has called you, He has equipped you for a special ministry and will use you as you yield yourself to the Spirit's control. Your positive attitude will help your family be happy in their new surroundings and will go a long way toward inspiring people to follow your leadership.

# Chapter 3

# The Methods
# of Church Planting

Each has its own unique beginning. There is no single, "right" way to establish a church. Many methods are being blessed of God today. In this chapter we want to evaluate six basic models for church planting that have proven effective. We will also look at some of the less successful methods being used.

There are several reasons why more than one method is needed in church planting. People and neighborhoods differ. Each requires a different approach. For example, an inner-city area would need a different type of ministry than an upper-class section in the same town. Even within a given group, the responsiveness of the people will vary from one part of the country to another requiring different means to win them.

Methods of sponsorship differ. A new congregation may be backed by a single large church or by several smaller churches. Help may come directly or indirectly through a mission agency, state fellowship or denominational program. This results in a variety of church-planting models.

Finally, the personalities, spiritual gifts, experience and education of church planters differ. Each will feel more comfortable with one approach than with another. One may be an evangelist while another is a Bible teacher; still another is musically inclined while the next is good with children, youth or adults. Some church planters are effective cross-culturally, others are more suited to working with people of similar educational, regional or racial backgrounds.

There is nothing sacred about a given method. Each should be evaluated by asking two questions: 1) Does it comply with Scriptural commands and principles? 2) Does it work? Is God blessing it with the salvation of souls and the establishment of churches? Do not feel that you must use a particular method just because it worked for somebody else. Does it work for you? If not, do not use it. Too often people try to be faithful to a program that uses a church-planting method that does not work for them. The Lord of

Harvest wants us to be fruitful as well as faithful (I Corinthians 4:2; John 15:16). It is not a matter of choosing one or the other; God wants both. The book of Acts records that when the early church went out in obedience to the mandate of the risen Lord, three things were multiplied: the Word, disciples and churches (Acts 6:1,7; 9:31; 12:24; 16:5). Should we expect any less today?

## Missionary Church Planting

Missionary church planting is probably the best known method of church planting among independent, fundamental Baptists. A "missionary pastor" goes into a needy community and starts the church but does not remain as the permanent pastor. He is supported by other churches through an established mission agency. He serves as a catalyst in the neighborhood, gathering a nucleus from which to found the church. This "catalytic church planter"[1] combines the roles of pastor and evangelist. He should be an experienced man who is gifted in personal evangelism and discipling.

A missionary church planter should stay with the congregation no longer than necessary. His goal is to work himself out of a job. As soon as the church is grounded in doctrine, has trained leadership and is able to support a pastor fully, he resigns and begins the cycle all over. The time it takes for the church to become self-supporting varies from a number of months to several years.

Hundreds of churches have been established across North America by dedicated missionaries under Baptist Mid-Missions (BMM), Baptist Mission of North America (BMNA), Continental Baptist Missions, The Association of Baptists for World Evangelism (ABWE), Baptist International Missions, Inc. (BIMI), The Fellowship of Evangelical Baptists Home Mission Board (Canada) and others.

This traditional method has proven to be reliable through the years. It works well in pioneer situations where there is no nucleus or core group. A fully supported missionary can go anywhere to begin a work. He does not have to wait for a nearby church to catch the vision of "mothering" or assisting the new group.

This method usually provides strong, experienced leadership right from the start. The missionary is carefully selected and equipped by his sending churches and mission agency; he is a "professional" church planter. Normally he will accomplish more than will part-time or untrained lay people who do not have the time or training for the job.

Mission sponsored church planters are more accountable than supporting churches and give detailed monthly reports to their mission. A home-office administrator can carefully super - vise and lovingly counsel in areas of neglect or weakness. Few local churches have the time or experience to provide this kind of help.

The missionary-church planting model provides long-term financial support for the new work. The needs of the missionary's family are met through support from other churches, allowing him to give himself to evangelism and discipling in the crucial early months. No one in the community can rightly accuse him of coming with suspect motives since he is not chargeable to them. Money received in the offerings can be plowed directly into other areas of the work, speeding their development. New churches often find it difficult to secure loans by themselves. Sometimes the mission agency will co-sign or guarantee the financing at a local bank using its collective resources as collateral, or it may provide a building loan from a revolving fund at lower than conventional interest rates.

There are some disadvantages to this method of church planting. Paternalistic attitudes can easily develop through the years and permanently cripple the church. The promise of long-term support may be a detriment to the new work. It is easy for churches to become dependent on the missionary's resources. They may hold back in their own giving. New converts sometimes are not challenged to share the financial load. Churches must be taught to assume the fiscal responsibility for themselves as soon as possible. They should start contributing to their pastor's support from the beginning. Some recommend that outside support be cut back over a period of time and that the new church assume an increasingly larger share of the missionary's salary (see chapter 13).

Missionaries must periodically report back to their sup - porting churches. Their absence from the work for several weeks will hurt the church. Some works never get off the ground because their missionary is constantly away reporting to churches or trying to raise support. A missionary should not start a church until he has adequate support and should remain on the field for the first two or three years before accepting any deputation ser - vices. Supporters must understand that the home missionary cannot report back as often as they would like. Priority must be given to church planting.

Some have suggested that it takes too long for the missionary-planted church to achieve self-supporting status. This may be true in some cases. Churches do not want to lose their missionary whom they have grown to love. Consequently, they may not be as motivated as they should be to evangelize and grow numerically. Visitors are sometimes reluctant to join the new church when they learn that the missionary pastor will not be there permanently. The missionary may be satisfied to accept partial support from both the mission and the church rather than encouraging it to become self-supporting. Other factors beyond the missionary's control, such as an increasingly mobile population or local businesses laying off workers, contribute to slow growth. Each group of people has its own peculiar background and circumstances that affect the growth of the church.

The missionary approach is clearly a Scriptural one paralleling the Pauline method so prominent in the Book of Acts. A number of Bible teachers believe the modern missionary is the counterpart to the first-century apostle or evangelist found in Ephesians 4:11 That "evangelizer" was one who preached the gospel beyond the frontiers where Christ was known and enlarged the borders of "Christian territory." The Apostle Paul expressed his missionary strategy as a wise master builder: "I have laid the foundation and another builds thereon" (I Corinthians 3:10). Many people would never be won to Christ and His Church except by the efforts of these "sent ones" who lay the foundations so others can build on them.

## Pioneer Church Planting

Under the pioneering method the founding pastor is not with any mission agency. He starts a church from scratch and plans to stay with it for a lifetime. He has little or no outside financial support. If he does have any, it's only for a year or two. This forces him to "sink or swim." The initial success of the new church depends largely on his leadership and influence. These pioneers are often dynamic young men right out of college who go to a city or town without waiting for a call from an interested group. They are innovators who make things happen through aggressive evangelism.[2]

This method has been utilized by men out of schools such as Hyles-Anderson, Baptist Bible College (Springfield, Missouri), Tennessee Temple and Liberty University. Dr. Elmer Towns heads up the Liberty Baptist Fellowship for Church Planting which has as its goal the beginning of 5,000 new churches by the year 2000. Their foundational principle is: "Churches plant churches." Strictly speaking, L.B.F. is "a fellowship of Baptist pastors, not an association of Baptist churches," banded together to provide temporary assistance to pioneer church planters.[3]

There are some admitted advantages to the pioneer method. Churches can be started "against insurmountable odds with limited resources in unlikely circumstances." Experience has shown that local churches are started by dedicated men, not committees. It takes a certain personality type to be successful with this approach. A pioneer must have "dogged determination" and be a "rugged individualist" who can persevere without becoming discouraged.[4]

The pioneering method has a definite impact on the new church. The people catch the founder's zeal, faith and vision. They become involved in the outreach and give sacrificially. Since it is not dependent on outside aid, the congregation develops its own sense of responsibility and initiative. The struggle to obtain property and adequate facilities builds character into the new church.

The pioneering church planter has great freedom to lead the new church in whatever direction he desires. But with no mission agency supervising him, the inexperienced pioneer sometimes makes unwise decisions that severely hamper the work. He has no one to give him counsel when he needs it. Without encouragement from others, he may become discouraged. Both he and the church need the fellowship and reinforcing ministry of brethren of like precious faith.[5] This method is capable of great abuse and will reflect the weaknesses as well as the strengths of the founding pastor.[6]

Great stress is placed upon the pioneer and his family. At times they must make unusual sacrifices of their time and money. The wife and children may feel cheated or neglected and become bitter. Well-intentioned men who have spent long hours toiling to get a church started have been known to lose their families in the process. Some have become disillusioned when they had to seek secular employment because the church was slow in taking on their salary.

The community sometimes is suspicious of this young "upstart"; "He's only after our money" or "He's another Jim Jones." In a new church the pioneer must do practically everything. Not everyone is willing to follow his "highly structured management" style of leadership. They may feel he is arbitrary or coercive and react negatively. The aggressive leader sometimes has difficulty sharing the workload with deacons, super-intendents and other leaders God raises up. He may resist delegating authority out of fear of losing control.[7] All of these dangers exist in other church-planting models, but they are most prevalent under the pioneer-planting method. Not every man suited to be a good pioneer is gifted to be a long-term pastor. Nevertheless, the fact remains that some of the greatest churches in America are pastored by men who were pioneer church planters.

## Associational Church Planting

The Southern Baptist Convention starts over 500 churches every year in America through its state associations. The Texas Baptist Association plans to start 2000 new churches by 1990 in their state alone! So far they are on schedule. Other denominations such as the Evangelical Free Church of America, the Free Will Baptists, the Church of the Nazarene, the Christian and Missionary Alliance, the Presbyterian Church in America and the Assemblies of God have successfully utilized their home-mission departments and budgets to provide leadership and finances for church planting. They believe that by pooling their resources and know-how they can accomplish more than by working alone.

This method provides denominational churches with a joint project that motivates the missionary giving of their members. Denominational loyalty helps raise large amounts of money which are channeled through the hierarchical structure of the "cooperative program." Funds seldom go directly to the church planter. Denominational or convention missionaries do not have to trust the Lord to provide their support through local churches; they are usually guaranteed a set annual salary from headquarters.

The associational or denominational method often has a well oiled, finely tuned organizational structure that governs church-planting strategy. Duplication of services and ministries which is so common in independent Baptist circles is avoided. The financial burden is spread among many churches rather than a few. Administrative efficiency is an obvious plus. State and national leaders can provide the latest surveys, demographic materials and helps to their workers. Low interest loans are available as are traveling consultants, regional church-growth seminars, legal aid and printed materials.

There are drawbacks to this method of planting churches. What is gained by administrative efficiency may result in less involvement on the local level. Little room is left for grass-roots initiative and participation. The zeal of the new church may be weakened when everything is handed to it on a silver platter. Although rapid construction of church facilities is ensured by the associational method, it can be a drawback if done before there is actually a congregation to occupy it.

The church planter may have less freedom than he would like. Because he is obligated to work with the sponsoring churches, he may feel limited or controlled by the denomination's pre-set program. Then there is the question of the local church's autonomy. Who has the final authority, the local church or the association?

The associational method of church planting sometimes results in "provincialism." This occurs when a state fellowship loses sight of the needs in other regions and countries. Support is withheld or withdrawn because the church planter moves to an area outside the association's jurisdiction. Such associations must be ready to expand their districts so administrative structure does not actually hinder church planting.

In spite of these potential problems, this method can be adapted by independent Baptists without compromising local church autonomy. The Minnesota Baptist Association has done so through its "Planting and Watering" program. Missionaries are appointed and  their salaries are paid for one or two years. These funds are gradually phased out placing the responsibility on  the new church. Money for property and buildings is provided through the "Baptist Builder's Call," an appeal issued five or six times a year to churches and interested individuals. These funds provide a tremendous boost to the new church.[8]

A unique feature of the Minnesota plan is the use of "student/missionaries." Teams of ministerial students are sent out during the summer months to assist a missionary or to work on their own under the supervision of a nearby sponsoring pastor. The association provides a salary in addition to car and housing allowances. The students agree to spend at least forty hours each week in door-to-door calling. Accurate records of all prospects and  decisions are kept for future follow-up.[9]

The state fellowships of the General Association of Regular Baptist Churches (G.A.R.B.C.) in Ohio, Michigan, Indiana, Iowa and other states have used similar plans with great success. Often the new pastor is a man under an approved mission agency. Association churches sometimes contribute teams of laymen to help canvass a neighborhood or donate talented families to a new work for six months to a year. The state association may provide a "chapel on wheels" (a church bus or trailer converted into a traveling worship center) for areas where buildings are not immediately available. There is no limit to what churches can do when they set goals and work together.


## Parent-Daughter Church Planting

The parent-daughter church-planting method differs from the associational model in that only one sponsoring church is involved. The "mother" church selects families from its own membership to form the core group for a new church. In addition, it provides funds, equipment, advice and moral support to the new group. Under the leadership of Dr. Thomas Younger, Immanuel Baptist Church in Fort Wayne, Indiana, used this method to plant thirteen new churches. During that time the mother church nearly doubled in size and built a new sanctuary.[10] The Cloverdale Baptist Church in Surrey, British Columbia, fostered five daughter churches in this way. Churches can singlehandedly plant other churches while continuing to grow themselves.[11]

There are a number of advantages to the parenting method. It is grounded in the biblical principle of spontaneous reproduction. It is the most natural way for healthy churches to grow and multiply. Normal growth in the body comes by division of cells, not by unlimited expansion of existing cells. This method makes possible a greater participation of laymen in the outreach of the church. The parent church is motivated to new levels of evangelism and stewardship. They are compelled to develop new leaders to replace those who left. This produces a reviving effect on the mother church and keeps her from spiritual stagnation.

The new congregation has immediate visibility and stability. By transferring faithful families to the new work, the church has an instant membership with mature leadership, a sound financial footing and a strong doctrinal foundation. They are usually families who live in the target area. They are spiritually mature and willing to leave the home church to help establish a new one in their area. The nucleus should include several Sunday school teachers and men qualified to be deacons. All should be regular tithers. Visitors will be more willing to unite with the new church when they see a well planned program led by committed Christians.

Parenting creates a greater sense of responsibility. It en-courages the careful, well-planned development of the new church. It helps to ensure that the characteristics, strengths and doctrinal distinctives of the mother church are reproduced. Monthly meetings between the representatives of the mother church and the daughter church should be held. This along with joint services helps to create bridges of belonging. Combined baptismal services, joint youth activities and yearly retreats further the spirit of unity. A combined evening service where progress reports are given of attendance, visitation, and the building program tends to keep both congregations excited and motivated.

Financially, parenting makes good sense. The sponsoring church can assist its daughter church with buying land and erecting its first building. With rising construction costs, it is sometimes cheaper to plant a daughter church than to replace an existing auditorium. This is especially true of downtown churches which often find it cheaper to secure land in the suburbs than to buy adjoining property in the city. The mother church does not have to construct an expensive new structure to accommodate an ever growing membership.

Finally, more people can normally be won in a community by two churches than by one. Statistics show that new churches win and baptize more converts than most established works. Small churches tend to be more efficient. Too often a church in the midst of a large harvest field will fail to see its total respon-sibility; it is either far-sighted (seeing only the overseas mission field) or near-sighted (focusing only on the local church in-group). Daughter church planting helps to keep missions in balance.

Parenting requires a spiritually mature church with a strong pastor, a balanced ministry and active lay leaders. Timing is essential if a premature birth is to be avoided. Spiritual maturity, not size, is the key. The church needs to be united behind the project, bathing it in prayer. The needs, plans and problems involved must be understood. They must see the project as obedience to the Lord of Harvest whose plan is that we divide and multiply. Are they prepared to see the new church through to the end, i.e. until it is capable of standing on its own feet as a self-supporting, independent congregation? If so, then both churches, the mother and the daughter, can grow to the glory of God.[12]

Has the church dealt with its hidden fears? Is it ready to face competition from a new church? What about the loss of leader-ship and tithers? If deacons, teachers and musicians are given to the new church, is the mother church prepared to develop new leaders to take their places? Experience has shown that rather than decreasing the number of leaders, parenting actually expands the number of leaders. The Holy Spirit raises up people who might never have been leaders if a new church had not been started.

There are a number of variations to the parent-daughter approach of church planting. The *colonization* model involves Christians who deliberately move to another city or another part of the same city for the express purpose of founding a new church. One of their homes may be used for a Bible study from which a new church is formed.[13] Southern Baptists have seen many families voluntarily move from Texas to Chicago to be nuclei for projected churches.

The *task force* model involves loaning rather than giving families to a new work. Some of these may eventually decide to stay permanently, but most will return to the home church within a year.[14]

The *multi-congregational* model is sometimes used in metropolitan areas where several language groups live. The parenting church starts several daughter churches, each ethnically or culturally different from the others. These then share the main church facilities by staggering services on Sunday afternoons until each group secures its own building. There might be an occasional combined service bringing three or four ethnic congregations together for a service in several languages. Care must be taken not to manifest paternalistic attitudes when working with this model. Churches located in deteriorating inner cities might consider this model. Instead of simply moving out, why not start one or two ethnic churches and turn over your facilities to them before you leave?

The *satellite church* involves a large parent church which forms semi-autonomous house-churches, chapels or church-type missions across the city, all of which remain a permanent part of the sponsoring church. A satellite is thus one church meeting in two or more places, having one staff, one committee structure, and one budget. The senior pastor oversees all the satellites established. Scott Memorial Baptist Church in San Diego and Highland Park Baptist in Chattanooga use this approach. Some groups use a modified form called *indigenous satellites*. Here each church has its own pastor, budget, officers, teachers and programs. Each becomes a fully indigenous church which is no longer connected to the mother church.[15]

Occasionally a church uses the *adoption* model of church planting. In this case a church adopts a struggling work and seeks to bring it to maturity. This usually involves providing the salary for a pastor for one year. He is often one of their own staff members or "preacher boys."

## Partnership Church Planting

Partnership church planting blends the best elements of the methods described to this point. A full-time missionary joins forces with an enterprising pastor who wants to found a church but lacks the experience and know-how. They enlist the temporary support of one or more churches near the target area. The missionary's role is to stay in the background to counsel, encourage and assist the pastor. This is sometimes termed "brothering."[16] It differs from the "parenting" approach in that several churches are involved instead of just one.

The Greater Northwest Baptist Church in Indianapolis is a good example of the partnership method of church planting. This predominantly black congregation was brothered by two other black churches and the Baptist Bible College of Indianapolis. A Baptist Mid-Missions missionary assisted for the first two years. Seed families were given by the cooperating churches. The new church became self-supporting within a month and called a full-time pastor. The missionary stayed in the background, helping them write their constitution and moderating the organizational meeting. Assistance was given in the development of promotional materials, teaching of new believers, locating and rezoning of property, among other things.

The partnership model provides immediate strong leadership and visibility in the community. It divides the burden among the brother churches, the new church, its pastor and the missionary. Smaller churches which would be unable to start a daughter church by themselves are able to do so in partnership with other churches.

Partnership provides on-the-job training for a young preacher coming directly out of Bible college with little experience. He does not need to go under a mission agency nor spend valuable time raising support. He can enter right into the work, growing and maturing with the new church. There is no disruption, no search for a qualified pastor when the missionary leaves.[17]

Sponsoring churches must work together to overcome any spirit of independence, jealousy or competition. They must be willing to sacrifice families and finances. Each must be allowed the privilege of participating without unreasonable demands upon their time, gifts and resources. One church may be able to do more than another. Care must be exercised not to do for the new church what it can do for itself. A balance must be maintained. Financial support for the new work should be sufficient to help it survive, but not enough for it to become dependent. Too much for too long creates a welfare mentality. The missionary must not try to dominate or control the church from behind the scenes. This can be avoided if there is a clear understanding of their respective roles between the missionary and the young pastor.

We now move to three of the less effective methods of church planting being promoted today. We are not saying these approaches are never to be used, but that they are beset with potential problems. The church planter needs to look at them carefully before using them. Other methods are more effective than these.


## Bible Study Method

Some church planters have used a home Bible class to win and disciple people who are then formed into a local church. Sometimes they assume the leadership of a Bible study already in progress, other times they organize their own. For these men, the Bible study becomes a "half-way house," a stepping stone to the church.

"Cell groups" and home Bible classes are quite popular in some circles today. Interdenominational and Bible church groups, parachurch organizations, charismatic prayer cells and others emphasize home Bible studies. People have been saved and Christians strengthened through these meetings.

The problem for the church planter is that many home Bible studies never develop into local churches. Such studies often attract people who are unwilling to accept the responsibility of church membership or the authority of the local church. A Bible study is attractive because it makes few demands. People can come and go as they please; everyone can express his or her opinion and no financial demands are made on them. There are few restrictions and virtually no obligations. People enjoy the "fellowship" but back away when you speak of membership in a local church.

Church planters who begin with this approach often find it difficult to step out by faith or risk losing people by starting a church. With people from many church backgrounds present, there is a temptation to leave out "denominational" distinctives, such as believer's baptism by immersion, public confession, tithing and church membership, lest someone be offended. It is easier just to remain a Bible study indefinitely.

Bible-study groups often continue for months or even years. It is claimed that the people need to be taught so they can be formed into a local church. But the Great Commission implies that converts need to identify publicly with their Lord and a local church before they are taught "all things." The order is baptism, then teaching, not vice versa. For some the Bible study becomes a substitute for the local church. This is wrong. No Bible-study group can scripturally practice the ordinances. Only the local church can immerse and celebrate the Lord's supper. People need to see that they will grow more in the Word if they are obedient to their Lord in the matters of baptism and faithful church membership (Hebrews 10:25). A vital part of God's plan for the individual is the ministry of the pastor-teacher through the local church (Eph. 4:11-14). It is not enough to be *in* the Word; we must also be *under* the Word.

Although frequently advocated, a Bible study seems to be a rather slow and uncertain method for developing a church. Few of the strong, growing churches in America were organized via this route. An aggressive church planter, however, could use it as a *fusion model.* He could go into a selected neighborhood, start half a dozen or more evangelistic Bible studies and then "fuse" them together into a single congregation after a few weeks when he begins public services. This is a little different because the church planter announces right from the start that his goal is to bring the various groups together as soon as possible to form a new church[18]

Established churches can use home Bible studies as an evangelistic outreach ministry to help the church win new people. The studies should always be under the authority of the local church and have capable leaders trained by and accountable to the pastor. Converts should be fed into the sponsoring church, rather than just attending the Bible study. Bible studies can be effective tools in the local church's ministry,[19] but are one of the less effective methods for planting new churches.

## The Church Split

A number of churches have begun as the result of church splits. The causes involved vary greatly and may or may not be justified. Some new churches have arisen from splits over personality or procedural problems. Others are the result of breaking away from a church which is tolerant of false doctrine or sinful practices.

A church split is justifiable only on biblical grounds and only after every effort has been made to rectify the situation. When there are a number of evidences which when taken together would indicate that God's blessing has been removed, withdrawal from the church would be proper. These might include outright doc-trinal error, cooperation with groups which hold unscriptural positions or refusal to deal with known sin in the church. In some cases, it might even be justifiable to break away and start a new church if the old church has lost its vision and has lapsed into a "Laodicean" condition. When repeated attempts to resolve these and other problems are unsuccessful, then it may be time to separate. To stay in such a church ("infiltration" rather than separation) in order to be a godly influence, to hold on to the building or because of tradition and friends, would be disobedient to the clear teaching of Scripture (Mt. 18:15-17; II Thess. 3:6,14).

A church planter should be careful about becoming involved in a church which is the result of a split. You may find strong opposition from the old church. Bitterness and bad attitudes may be present which will hinder the new church's ministry. A poor testimony in the community could hurt the work for years to come. People who could not get along in the former church may cause you problems as well.

Be sure your motives and those of the people are right. There should be a sweet spirit. Have they followed the Matthew 18 pattern for dealing with personal and doctrinal grievances? Have they tried to make things right with those at the former church (Matthew 5:23,24)? Check to ensure that each one is saved and scripturally baptized. Do not assume they are. If the group is composed of committed Christians who have separated from another church for biblical reasons, they can be formed into a strong church to the glory of God. They must be willing to make the sacrifice of time and money necessary to get the church going and to keep it growing. Bathe the entire situation in prayer. Let the community know that you are motivated by love for people as well as the truth.

## Bivocational Church Planting

Bivocational church planting is sometimes known as the "tentmaking" approach. In this case the pastor works in a secular job while serving the new church, often for years with little or no financial remuneration. His living expenses are provided by his vocation. Bivocational church planting is seen by some as the answer to the problem of inadequate support for "home" missions. It is being used with some success in inner-city, black and ethnic communities by the Southern Baptist Home Mission Board. It also may be feasible in communities too small to support a pastor. A few independent Baptist missionaries have fallen back on tentmaking out of necessity when outside support has proven inadequate.

There are some advantages to the bivocational method. A working pastor often meets more people in the community and can better relate to them. He has many opportunities to witness to people whom the full-time church planters seldom see. Working pastors tend to be more understanding of the work schedules and stresses their members face. They sense how much to expect from people who work all day. Also a man in this dual role can hardly be accused of having selfish motives or of being lazy. There is no doubt that churches have been started by this means when there is no other way and very little financial help for a new work.

Before we cut our home-missions budget, let us remember there are some serious drawbacks to this method. The numerical and spiritual growth of the new church is usually stunted because the pastor has so little time for soul winning, sermon preparation, goal setting, discipling of new converts and other responsibilities in the church. There are times when a working pastor becomes so secure in his job and dependent upon its income that he is reluctant to resign to become a full-time pastor. Some men never step out. They have become used to a comfortable lifestyle guaranteed by a good job. If the leader's vision and faith are small, it is inevitable that the congregation's will be also.

The church may become accustomed to having a bivocational pastor and his willingness to work. They are sometimes slow to step out by faith to assume his salary. They point to the fact that the Apostle Paul was a self supporting missionary who made tents. In so doing, they fail to understand that this was by his choice and was done only in Corinth. Later the Apostle wrote back to the Corinthian church and asked their forgiveness for "this wrong" (II Corinthians 12:13). He recognized that he had robbed them of the privilege of participating in God's work and had actually hurt the church in the long run. The church was "inferior" to other churches he planted because he was "not burdensome" to them.

The Bible teaches that those who preach the gospel should live by the gospel. The church must be made aware that the laborer is worthy of his reward (I Timothy 5:18) and that their pastor is their first obligation. All it takes is ten tithing members. In many cases, the reason for bivocational pastors is the hardness of believers who are unwilling to give sacrificially to God's work. The church planter must teach his people biblical principles of giving.

Our Lord taught that no man can serve two masters his loyalties will be divided. Is not this the danger with all too many modern day tentmakers? There may be some situations which may force a man to work temporarily, but this is not the scriptural ideal and should only be a last resort. The New Testament makes it clear that Paul, unlike so many working pioneers today, was not hindered by dual professions. We admire the patience, humility and perseverance of bivocational church planters. But we are reminded that our responsibility to build churches does not depend on the economy but on the commission of the Risen Lord.

## The Bottom Line–the Man, not the Method

The prospective church planter must decide which of the above approaches he is going to use. No one method will fit every situation. Methods change; the message and mandate do not. A church planter who goes under a mission agency has a definite edge. He has the counsel of godly men who are experienced in church planting, he has the prayer backing of churches and Christians where he has spoken, and he has financial help. He is able to devote full time to the new church thus giving it a greater chance of success.

In the end it is the man, not the method, that God uses to start churches. You may pick the right method and still fail if you do not experience the power and blessing of God upon your ministry. A Spirit-filled man using the right method with the right motives can accomplish much for God.

# Endnotes

[1] Paul R. Orjala, *Get Ready to Grow.* (Kansas City, MO: Beacon Hill Press, 1978), p. 113.

[2] Elmer Towns, *Getting a Church Started* (Lynchburg, VA: Church Growth Institute, 1982), p. 105.

[3] *Ibid.,* pp. 185187.

[4] Towns, *op. cit.,* pp. 105-109.

[5] Timothy Starr, *Church Planting: Always in Season.* (Canada: Fellowship of Evangelical Baptists, 1978), p.41

[6] Towns, *op. cit.,* p. 111.

[7] *Ibid.,* pp. 107-108.

[8] Dr. Arthur Allen, *Planting Baptist Churches.* (Minneapolis: Minnesota Baptist Association, n.d.), mimeographed paper, pp. 9-11.

[9] *Ibid.,* p. 11.

[10] Thomas Minnery, *Success in Three Churches: Diversity and Originality.* Leadership Magazine (Winter Quarter, 1981), pp. 62ff.

[11] Starr, *op. cit.,* pp. 48 ff.

[12] *Planting a New Church: A Mother Church Planting Progam.* (E.F.C.A.: Church Ministries Dept., n.d.), mimeographed sheets.

[13] Orjala, *op. cit.,* p. 111.

[14] *Ibid.,* p. 115.

[15] For more information see *The Indigenous Satellite Program Manual,* (Dallas: Baptist General Convention of Texas, 1982).

[16] Orjala, *op. cit.,* p. 110.

[17] Adapted from The *Advantages of Church Planting with Mother Churches.* (E.F.C.A., n.d.), mimeographed paper.

[18] Orjala, *op. cit.,* p. 114.

[19] Write Bethesda Baptist Church, 7950 N., 650 E., Brownsburg, IN 46112.

# Section II..

**Chapter 4**....The Place for Church Planting

> Selecting the City
> Selecting the Ministry Area

**Chapter 5**....The Preparations for Church Planting

> Things to Do before Arrival
> Things to Do after Arrival

**Chapter 6**....The Plan for Church Planting

> Discovering Prospects
> Developing the Core Group

**Chapter 7**....The Public Beginning in Church Planting

> Things to Do
> People to Train
> The Day Before
> The Big Day
> The Day After
> When to Begin Other Weekly Services

# Chapter 4

# The Place
# for Church Planting

Once the church planter has decided on the basic method he will employ to start a new church, important decisions must be made as to where and when the church should be planted. Location and timing are crucial and may affect the success or failure of the venture. In some cases it may be preferable to discuss the place before the method since the latter will need to be adapted to those with whom you are working.

The question of where to plant the new church is basically a twofold one: Which city or town shall I go to and where within that city shall I begin the church? The goal is to select a ripe, responsive area where a new church will most likely take root, grow and become indigenous.

## Selecting the City

There are many ways God can lead a man to the right city. Some men make a list of needy cities and pray over them. We should not expect a Macedonian call in the form of a dream, vision or audible voice from God. God does not reveal His will by these means today (Hebrews 1:1,2). Some tend to rely more on other factors such as an inner, God-given confidence or peace, circumstances, an open door or a special burden for a particular city. Other men feel God is speaking to them through a telephone call or a letter of invitation from someone in a needy city. All of these are subjective factors which can be misinterpreted. God gives us a mind and sanctified common sense: He expects us to use them.

Be objective in selecting the city in which to plant a church. Visit the community under consideration and spend a few days surveying it. This should be done before moving your family there. The community survey form provided at the end of this chapter should be used and filled out in its entirety. The basic data required will help church planters make prayerful and wise decisions based on facts rather than hunches or guesses. God never blesses ignorance; He calls, burdens and guides our thoughts through knowledge of the facts and through His Word. Surely the Lord is pleased with the man who diligently does his homework and at the same time prays for wisdom (James 1:5) in the decision-making process!

To select a good place to begin a new church or to discern which of several communities should be entered first, the following questions are basic:

## • Is There Spiritual Need in the Community?

There is little sense in going to a place that is already evan-gelized. If the city is small and there is already a large soul-winning Baptist church or a number of smaller, growing fundamental congregations, do not go. You would only be competing with other gospel ministries and could easily become discouraged and quit. Go where there is a genuine need for the Word of God and a fundamental Baptist church which will preach the gospel. An unchurched area where there are multitudes of unsaved folk will keep you motivated in the work. A community where the people have heard the gospel repeatedly is often hardened and is not a good prospect. Some areas have greater opportunities for outreach and church growth. Churches of the same denomination should rarely be located closer than two miles from each other.[1]

Recent surveys of midwestern communities reveal that from 60% to 75% of the population either do not attend church at all or do not attend regularly. Less than 10% attend biblical churches. Over half of Canada's population has no vital connection to a church. National weekly attendance of Canadians in sects and cults exceeds attendance in Canada's mainline denominations. With so many needy communities, why start a church on someone else's doorstep?

There are three kinds of growth in personnel in churches: transfer, biological and conversion/baptism.[2] (Transfer growth is the result of Christians joining from other churches. Biological growth is the natural increase resulting from the birth of children to members of the church. Conversion/baptism growth is the result of winning new people to Christ.) The latter should be the primary source for developing the new church.

Evangelism must be the heartbeat of every new church. A religious survey will help you discover the percentage of people who are unsaved, uncommitted or who are attending non-biblical churches. It will give an accurate picture of the spiritual condition of the community you are considering.

Get a city map and pinpoint every church regardless of size or affiliation. You can secure a church directory from the Chamber of Commerce or local council of churches (ministerial alliance). Also check the yellow pages and nearby pastor friends who are acquainted with the area.

The number of churches in any given city can be deceiving. Some places have dozens of churches, but actual attendance is small. Mainline denominations sometimes have membership rolls which far exceed their actual attendance. Try to acquire the average attendance figures for their morning services. Some conservative churches are not growing and have few participating in visitation or mid-week prayer meeting. Timothy Starr rightly observes, "Three serious problems face many of the North American churches today: apostasy, apathy and absenteeism."[3] A preponderance of either type of church may indicate the need for a new church. If there are multitudes of church members whose spiritual needs are not being met, there may be good potential for church planting.

A growing community may have four or five fundamental churches which have reached the "saturation point." They are no longer growing nor reaching new families. There may be considerable biological growth and transfer growth but little conversion growth. For example, a community of 30,000 people might have five churches with a total of 700 people in attendance. What about the other 29,300? A good survey will reveal the need for additional churches. So, before deciding where to start a church, determine if there is a spiritual need which is not being met by existing churches.

● Is the Population Large Enough to Support a Church?

Be careful about locating too close to another good church or in a community which does not have adequate population to support another church. Some church-growth and home-missions experts recommend that there be a population of at least 2000 to 3000 persons per church in the community.[4] Too often new churches are started in areas which have several churches or where the population is too small to support another church.

The first-century church planters concentrated on the population centers, places like Ephesus, Corinth, Thessalonica,
Antioch, and Philippi. They recognized that a thriving church
would have a great impact on key cities which would then reach
out to outlying areas. God's agenda has not changed today.

The major urban areas of North America have often been
neglected. We have concentrated on the rural areas, the suburbs
and the small towns. Yet two out of every three Americans reside
in one of twenty-eight urban regions. These metropolises are
continually expanding, gobbling up more and more countryside.
They are becoming huge "strip cities." Growth is especially
dramatic in the Sun Belt region of our nation.

According to the 1980 U.S. Census 46% of the country's population, 103 million people, live in the 50 largest Standard
Metropolitan Statistical Areas (called SMSAs). The term "meg-
alopolitan" is now being used to refer to these population centers
(see list at end of this chapter). Altogether there are 272
metropolitan areas (50,000 or more in population) and these
contain 75% of the total U.S. population. Church planters should
seriously consider working in the urban areas where the
percentage of unchurched persons is highest and the need the
greatest.

This is not to say that there are not many other smaller areas
which need new churches. We are only saying, be sure there are
enough people to warrant a new church. The smaller population
areas tend to have a far higher ratio of churches than do our
major metropolitan communities.

## • Is the Area Growing?

The American society is highly mobile. We are constantly on
the move. Most families relocate once every five years on the
average. In the next ten years Canada and the United States will
have more family units than ever before in our history. Most will
move into the already bulging cities. Church planters have
tremendous opportunities to reach these "newcomers."

Select an area that is growing. Not all cities are expanding.
During the 1970s over thirty U.S. metropolitan areas declined in
population. The greatest declines were in the Northeast and
North Central States. The largest losses were recorded in New
York, Jersey City, Cleveland and Buffalo. The twenty-five fastest-
growing cities are all found in the Southern or Western States.
Over half of them recorded at least a 50% increase in population

between 1970 and 1980. Heading the list was Fort Myers-Cape Coral, Florida, with a 95.1% population growth rate. Rounding out the top ten are Ocala, Florida (77.4%); Las Vegas, Nevada (69%); West Palm Beach, Florida (64.4%); Fort Lauderdale, Florida (63.5%); Olympia, Washington (61.6%); Bryan College Station, Texas (61.4%) and Reno, Nevada (59.9%). The same type of growth is predicted for some Canadian cities such as Edmonton and Calgary, which are expected to double by 1995.[5]

Ascertain what the projected growth trends are for the area you are considering. What direction is the city going? How is the population distributed now and how will it be in ten to twenty years from now? Where are new hospitals, shopping centers, schools, housing developments, subdivisions, roads and utilities being planned? These are the areas where new churches should be planted. On your survey trip buy a detailed city map and familiarize yourself with it. Then deliberately drive the boundaries, expressways and main arterials to see the city as a whole. This will enable you to see the growth potential of the area.

The Chamber of Commerce can tell you how many new families are moving into the city each month. The Public Health Department is another helpful source to check: they can tell you the number of births in the area. While you are at the Chamber you should also ask them where to secure a list of newcomers. Many cities have a Welcome Wagon or civic newcomers' association which may provide you with this useful information. Purchase several of the leading metropolitan newspapers (preferably Thursday, Friday and Sunday). Read them carefully to get a better idea of where the city is going.

## • Is Property Available and Affordable?

A wise church planter will select an area where real estate can be reasonably obtained. What is the cost of land per acre? Can a small church afford it or is the price prohibitive? Are property values increasing? Is it raw or developed land? What would it cost to provide utilities and other services? Check on the building costs per square foot. Are the zoning and building codes stringent and unduly restrictive? Do they recognize what a baptistry is so it does not have to be treated as an indoor pool or Jacuzzi? You should find these things out before you begin, not after. Remember that  all the costs will be higher by the time you are ready to buy or build. It would be ideal if prime property onthe growing edge of town could be purchased  by an association or visionary church before the prices go up.

A more immediate need is for a temporary meeting place. Check to see if there are auditoriums, halls, schools or other suitable facilities available (see chapter 5). Can they be secured at reasonable rates? Also check on housing for yourself. Is suitable housing available, and can you afford to buy or rent it? Do not take this for granted. Contact the two largest and oldest real estate firms in the area. They will be the most knowledgeable. Plan to spend half a day with them and let them show you the area, the housing and the meeting places available.

## • Are There Prospects or Interested Families?

There are obvious advantages to starting with a nucleus of believers, especially mature ones. While surveying the area, did you find people who are interested in starting a new church? Are they homeowners or renters? Are they transient or settled? Do they move frequently? Are they scattered over a wide area or concentrated in the target area? Would they be willing to drive across town to come to a Bible-preaching church? For how long?

Are they interested in a Bible class, or has a home Bible study already been started? If so, what is the average attendance and rate of growth? Are the leaders Baptists or leaning toward becoming Baptists? If they are of another persuasion, they may be so settled in a traditional church they would never switch. Do your contacts have a real burden for the community? Are they willing to give, work and pray for the new church?

While it is not essential to have prospective families before deciding on where to start a church, it is helpful. If a church planter is considering several possibilities, it would seem preference should be given to the one that already has families waiting and praying.

Carefully weigh the answers to each of the five questions above. Let the Holy Spirit control your head as well as your heart in deciding where He would have you to go to plant the new church. Do not be stampeded or pressured into a situation without first adequately researching the area. Count the cost before you enter the battle (Luke 14:28-30).

## Selecting the Ministry Area

Once the city has been chosen, the same diligent research should go into selecting the target area within that city. Do not begin holding services anywhere you can obtain a building. Thoroughly study the area and its people to determine where the fertile soil and responsive people are located.

The ministry area you choose will depend somewhat on the kind of people you want to reach in building the church. No church can be all things to all men, nor reach every people-group in an area. Are you trying to reach minority groups, whites, professionals or working-class people? A church geared to everybody will be mediocre and will reach few. Concentrate on excellence in a few areas rather mediocrity in many. Know your target group and focus on how best to reach it.

Your background, education, experience and gifts will influence whom you can effectively reach. For example, to evangelize ethnics or minority groups, you need special cross-cultural training and skills. A church planter with a rural background may have difficulty relating to urban people as might a southerner to northerners. In some cities there are strong regional identities and loyalties which do not readily mix. The church planter who seeks to combine them often encounters real frustration.

Conduct a thorough survey to determine exactly where to start the new church in the community. In most cases the preliminary survey done in selecting the city will not be thorough enough to determine the best location within the city. A community survey will reveal the most fertile and responsive areas.

Gathering community data will accomplish several things. It will help you understand what the community is really like. Too many men rely on the recommendations of others, brief observations, their own hunches, rumors and preconceived ideas rather than factual information. A survey will help you discover community needs which are not being met. This in turn helps you define your geographical or basic ministry area and gives you a sense of direction and purpose.

A good survey will include such things as the geography /demographics, religious data, ethnic/cultural and socio-economic factors of the community.


• Geographical Considerations

Not every neighborhood is conducive to starting a church. It is difficult to begin in old established neighborhoods where residents are settled and have membership in traditional churches. The loyalties of the people are fixed and the soil has been worked over again and again. Care must also be taken when considering a low-income area. Such churches seldom become self-supporting since the people reached are generally poorly educated and have limited economic potential.

Avoid locating near industrial areas, stadiums and cemeteries. These often have a heavy flow of traffic but few homes from which to draw families. Also stay away from dead-end streets, excavations, gravel pits, steep hills or areas where future highways may cut through. Property which is isolated, odd-shaped or rocky is often lower in price but is not a good buy. What appears to be a "good deal" or a loving act of Christian giving may in reality be a hindrance to God's work if it lacks accessibility, visibility and growth potential. People will not search for a hard-to-find church.

Weigh the pros and cons carefully before locating in a shopping mall. While this may give you high visibility and easy access, the cost is often excessive. The mall may be surrounded by low-income, government-subsidized apartments or hard-to-reach retirees, Jewish or Catholic people. Avoid storefronts altogether.

New subdivisions and suburban developments are the most conducive for church planting. The people have not gotten their roots down yet. They are eager to make new friends and establish new patterns of life. Because they are searching for stability after leaving their previous homes, they make good prospects for both the Gospel and a church willing to meet their needs. Look for growing neighborhoods with a good mix of young families, middle-aged people and senior citizens. These new communities usually have land available for churches and some of them even set aside property for this very purpose.

Civic leaders, city building and zoning departments or public-utility companies can tell you where schools, shopping centers and developments will be built. They must plan five to ten years in advance and have already done intensive research on the area. Their distribution departments will often give you data on future community plans and population projections.

• Demographic Considerations

McDonalds is one of the most successful fast-food stores in America. This is due in part to their product and in part to their choice of locations. Before opening a new store, they carefully gather and analyze statistical projections on the area under consideration. Then they choose the sites which are most likely to produce results. Their competitors watch where the double arches are going up and build nearby.

Demographic studies can be a great assistance to the church planter in determining where to begin a new church. The statistics will help you locate unchurched homogeneous groups within your city. They can indicate which areas will be the most receptive. Once you know the socioeconomic components of your community, you can make a decision based on fact rather than ignorance. A knowledge of demographics will build up your confidence as well as that of those sponsoring you.[6]

There is much statistical information available if you know where and how to obtain it. Census data is available from regional offices of the U.S. Census Bureau, the Government Printing Office or the Population Reference Bureau. Information on census statistics in Canada is also available from the Canadian government (see list of addresses at the end of this chapter). If you are going to be working in one of the fifty largest SMSAs in the U.S., you can get detailed statistics on every block in your city. Since a national census is only taken once very ten years, the further you get from the year the census was taken, the less valuable the statistics become.

Be selective and concentrate on finding data you can utilize. Don't attempt to dig into too much raw, uninterpreted census material by yourself. Other people have already interpreted it and you can easily borrow from them. For example, the Home Mission Board of the Southern Baptist Convention (Orders Processing Department, 1350 Spring Street, Atlanta, GA 30367) has an excellent booklet entitled: "Census Data Manual for Church Planning." This 77-page manual explains the 1980 census, how to analyze it and what is relevant for churches. The cost is reasonable ($1.10 in 1983). They also have census data manuals for studying families, population life cycles, Hispanics, Blacks and others.

Obtain the latest "census tract map" from your city or county planning commission, city hall or Chamber of Commerce. Each census tract contains approximately 4000 people. Use a street map to determine which census tracts you want included. If your local planning office does not have adequate census information, try the library, the local school board, your county research and economic development office or the sociology department at a nearby university. The R.L. Polk Company, which publishes directories on many cities, also has data that show changes from previous years.

Request information that will tell you both the present and future racial, ethnic and socioeconomic makeup of the city as a whole and for the target area you are considering in particular. Tell them you are interested in the movement of people and how your church might be affected by these changes. Ask for a land-use map that shows how the land is being used now and where housing, industry, commerce, recreation and institutions will be located in the future. Some planning offices will have this broken down and analyzed by neighborhoods. Do not be afraid to ask the officials to interpret the data for your projected ministry area. Take good notes or even make tape recordings of your conversations with city officials (with their permission).

When studying demographic material, there are five things the church planter should try to learn. First, find out the socio-cultural composition of the community, noting where each group tends to reside. (You may be surprised at the number of ethnic people in your city.) Second, get an overall view of population growth by age and marital status. Is the community composed of singles, young marrieds or retirees? Third, note the internal migration patterns. Who is moving in and who is moving out? An area that is WASP (White Anglo-Saxon Protestant) may not be so five years from now. Fourth, study the traffic patterns. Since weekday traffic patterns carry over to weekends, it is best to locate a church on or just off a major traffic artery going out of the city. Fifth, study the land-use projections. These will tell you where and when highways are going to be built and new land developed.[7]

A case study illustrates how this data can be useful. Envision a white, college-trained church planter who wants to start a predominantly black (integrated) Baptist church in a metropolitan area. Where should he locate the church and begin his outreach? He would be wise to concentrate on middle-class blacks with whom he can more readily relate and minister rather than going to the biggest black neighborhood which often consists of female-headed households on welfare. By studying local statistics he can locate the census tracts with mixed black-and-white housing patterns. This would indicate socially mobile blacks. Further study would reveal the social (male heads of household), educational (high school, college graduate) and economic structure of the area under consideration. Since these people are most likely to be open to a new church established by an Anglo, the section of the city where these Blacks are concentrated should become the church planter's primary, though not sole, ministry area.[8]

● Religious Considerations

In determining where to begin a church, you should know as much as possible about the churches that are already in the area under consideration. How many are there? What denominations are represented? What are the membership and average attendance for each? What are their growth rates and ethnic composition? How many are unchurched in the community? How many attend Bible-believing churches?[9] Some of this information may have been gathered during your initial fact-finding visit, but now a more thorough study is needed.

Begin by developing the "Church Category and Directory" form at the end of this chapter. List every church under one of the headings: Evangelical, Fundamental, Holiness, Pentecostal, Liberal Protestant, Catholic, Jewish, Cult or any others you prefer. Record the address, the name of the pastor, priest or rabbi and the telephone number for each church. (This information is available from the local council of churches, the Chamber of Commerce, state fellowships and the telephone directory.) Then call each church and talk with the pastor or a knowledgeable person who will assist you. (A survey form and suggested telephone procedure with specific questions to ask is located at the end of this chapter along with other useful forms.)[10]

If you cannot get all the information you want directly from the churches being surveyed, check a nearby seminary or Christian college library for a Glenmary study which gives percentages in each county and state. If this is unavailable locally, write Glenmary Research Center, 4606 East-West Highway, Washington, D.C. 20014 (phone: 314-654-7501). You can also visit those churches for which information was unavailable and make your own estimates.

After completing the survey of the churches, tabulate the results on the "Summary Sheet." Complete the form by figuring the percentages for lines 21-39. Now you have a detailed overall view of the religious make-up and spiritual needs of the community you are considering.


● Personal Observations


Take a "windshield" tour of the target area under consideration. Drive the streets slowly and observe the housing patterns, land-use design, educational facilities, recreational areas, churches and service organizations. Become familiar with the layout of the community.

Walk through the area and talk to residents. Ask: "How long have you been a resident here? Do you intend to stay for a long time? What attracted you to this neighborhood? What was the community like when you moved in in terms of housing, family and stability? How do you feel about changes in the community? What kind of problems do people living here encounter on a daily basis? What do you feel is the future of this neighborhood? Are you familiar with the churches in the area? Have you ever been contacted by any of them? Do you belong to or have you visited any of the churches?" The more people you talk to the better understanding you will have of the area.

Visit community leaders. What political issues might affect your new church? What changes have occurred in the community in the past five years? A real-estate agent can tell you of changes in property values, age groups, family sizes and racial make-up in the area. A representative from a neighborhood association could tell you of community needs as he sees them. Gain as much personal insight as possible into the area you are considering. Get a feel for the community.

● Develop a Community Profile

When you finish your research, develop a community profile of the target area. Record the findings of your feasibility study[11] under the following headings:

1. **Ministry Area:** Define the geographical boundaries of the area in which you plan to focus your efforts and draw it out on a city map with a felt-tipped pen. The ministry area should normally be within twelve minutes' driving distance of the church. It will be more in rural areas and less in major cities.

2. **Type of Ministry Area:** Identify the kind of area you have selected as Inner-Urban (a residential area for ethnics), Out-Urban (middle to upper-middle class neighborhood toward the edge of a city), City Suburb (prestige residential neigborhood beyond the edge of the city), Metropolitan Suburb (residential area circling a city with shopping, etc.), Independent City (not more than 50,000 people and no suburbs), Small Town (village with less than 3000 population), Rural (few homes scattered miles apart).

3. **Population:** What is the total number of people living in your area? Is the population increasing or declining?

4. **Religious Characteristics:** Give the percentage of churched and unchurched people in the target community. Of those who attend church, what percentage go to Bible-believing churches?

5. **Family Income:** List the average annual income per family. How many will be needed to support a church?

6. **Housing:** Indicate what percentage of the people live in each of the following types of housing: Single-family units (owner-occupied); Single-family units (renter-occupied); Multi-family units (owner-occupied-condominiums, high rises): Multi-family units (renter- occupied: apartments, townhouses); Temporary housing units (mobile homes, trailers). Normally you want to work in an area where people own their own homes.

7. **Ethnic/Class:** Identify the social class and ethnic or minority groups which predominate in your targeted area. These will either be upper-class (wealthy), middle/upper, middle-class (white collar), or poverty-stricken; either Anglo, Black, Latinos, Chicanos, etc.

8. **Schools/Institutions:** List all elementary, junior-high, senior-high, college, and vocational schools. Include hospitals, prisons and military bases.

9. **Age-Sex:** Does your ministry area have a healthy balance and distribution of all ages and both sexes? This shows up as a pyramid when graphed. An inverted pyramid with a high percentage of elderly indicates a dying community.

10. **Occupational Profile:** What percentage of the people in your area are "white collar" (professional, management, sales and clerical)? What percentage are "blue collar" (craftsmen, operators, transport or laborers)? What percentage are service workers? What percentage are farm workers? Diversity reflects an economically secure area. It is not wise to locate in areas dependent on a single industry. A poor year could destroy the church.

• Clearing the Air

Good research is a tool the Holy Spirit can use to direct you to your ministry area. This in no way implies that you should be unconcerned with people or needs outside the target neighborhood. While no one should be excluded, you will want to concentrate your efforts on the most responsive area.

Jesus taught in the parable of the sower (really the parable of the soils) that some areas are more productive than others. In Matthew 10:14 He told the disciples to shake the dust off their sandals if the people were not responsive and go on to more fertile towns. While everyone should have opportunity to hear the gospel, the church planter should focus his attention on the ripened portions of the harvest field.

We are not advocating that church planters minister only to the upper class, the educated or the elite. Jesus warned us that it is hard (not impossible) for the rich to be saved (Matthew 19:23,24). Money sometimes insulates people from their real-life needs. It is also true that the less affluent people may be more responsive to the gospel.[12] But at the same time the church needs a core of people with steady finances if it is to become self-supporting. Seek to develop a healthy economic cross-section. If you start too low on the socioeconomic ladder, it will be difficult to move up later.

Is it right for the church planter to target a specific cultural or language group? Doesn't this smack of racism or segre-gationalism? A good church planter will not discriminate against anyone, regardless of his or her color, race, language, age or sex. But at the same time he must recognize that the vast majority of growing churches are basically homogeneous (of the same group). People do not like to cross racial, linguistic or class barriers in order to become Christians. To require people to do so creates a stumbling block which may keep them from coming to Christ. Let the mature Christian be the one to cross the barriers to the unbeliever rather than forcing him to leap over hurdles to get to Christ.

America is not a "melting pot" but a giant "stew pot." It is a beautiful mosaic, a multicultural, multicolored tapestry. We are a pluralistic society. Man exists in social structures, and if we are to reach him, we must communicate through his cultural channels. God created the various ethnic groupings and loves each one. He wants them all to be evangelized.[13] He tells us to make disciples of all peoples (*panta ta ethne* meaning every ethnic and language group). The best way to do this is to plant congregations in every segment of our society; so that people can hear about Christ among their peers without being asked to renounce their cultural distinctives.

# Summary

Good surveys are essential in determining where new churches should be planted. Intensive research will indicate the following:[14]

1. New churches should be planted in relation to the number of unsaved and unchurched in a community. Second and third generation "Christians" need to be evangelized as well as new residents. Evangelism must include the established communities as well as the high-growth areas.
2. As a church grows, it tends to level off and becomes less effective in reaching its community. New churches are needed to evangelize those not reached by the large church. A cluster of churches working together will reach more people than a single large church.
3. The existing churches may be reaching only one socio-economic group. A careful analysis might show that the neighborhood is in transition, changing from white to black, from white collar to blue collar, from English to Hispanic (Americans speak 157 different languages). New churches are needed to reach these people in their cultural settings.
4. Natural barriers such as highways, railroads, rivers and lakes create geographical pockets of unchurched people. Also mobile-home parks, apartment complexes, resort or military-related housing may be isolated from the main population. These need new churches nearby to reach them for Christ.
5. New housing developments are being planned and built. Each will need a Bible-believing Baptist church. Ideally, potenial church sites should be purchased before prices rise.
6. Cities will need churches in every section. Research will help you develop a ten- or twenty-year master plan for effectively evangelizing an entire area.

Casual assumptions about the community and its religious conditions may be deceiving! Once a church planter has done his homework and understands his community, he will be better equipped to plan prayerfully how to reach it for Christ. Lack of proper data may hinder him and keep him from being as effective and fruitful as he could be.

52

## Endnotes

1 Roy Thomas, *Planting and Growing a Fundamental Church.* (Nashville, TN: Randall House Publications, 1979), p. 129.

2 Donald A. McGavran, *Understanding Church Growth.* (Grand Rapids: Eerdmans, 1970), p. 87.

3 Timothy Starr, *Church Planting: Always in Season.* (Canada: Fellowship of Evangelical Baptist Churches, 1978), p. 28.

4 Elmer Towns, *Getting a Church Started.* (Lynchburg, VA: Church Growth Institute, 1982), p. 130.

5 Starr, *op. cit.*, p. 26.

6 C. Peter Wagner, "How To Plant a Church Seminar." (Pasadena, CA: Charles E. Fuller Institute, n.d.), author's notes.

7 Wagner, *op. cit.*

8 *Ibid.*- adapted from Wagner Case Study of Morningside Baptist Church in Inglewood, California.

9 *Ibid.*

10 Forms adapted from "Developing a Community Religious Profile," mimeographed sheets distributed by the Evangelical Free Church of America, Church Ministries Department, n.d.

11 Adapted from "Church Planting Community Profile Survey," mimeographed sheets distributed by the Evangelical Free Church of America, Church Ministries Department, n.d.

12 Towns, *op. cit.*, p. 131.

13 Charles L. Chaney, *Church Planting at the End of the Twentieth Century.* (Wheaton, IL: Tyndale House Publishers, 1982), pp. 30-31, 152.

14 Adapted from J.V. Thomas, ed., *How to Start New Mission/Churches: A Guide for Associational Mission Leaders.* (Dallas: Baptist General Convention of Texas, 1979), pp.5-7.

## U.S. Megalopolitan Areas

| | |
|---|---|
| 1. New York | 9,119,737 |
| 2. Los Angeles-Long Beach | 7,477,657 |
| 3. Chicago | 7,102,328 |
| 4. Philadelphia | 4,716,818 |
| 5. Detroit | 4,352,762 |
| 6. San Franciso-Oakland | 3,252,721 |
| 7. Washington, D.C. | 3,060,240 |
| 8. Dallas-Fort Worth | 2,974,878 |
| 9. Houston | 2,905,350 |
| 10. Boston | 2,763,357 |
| 11. Nassau-Suffolk | 2,605,813 |
| 12. Saint Louis | 2,355,276 |
| 13. Pittsburgh | 2,263,894 |
| 14. Baltimore | 2,174,023 |
| 15. Minneapolis-Saint Paul | 2,114,256 |
| 16. Atlanta | 2,029,618 |
| 17. Newark | 1,965,304 |
| 18. Anaheim-Santa Ana-Garden Grove | 1,931,570 |
| 19. Cleveland | 1,898,720 |
| 20. San Diego | 1,861,846 |
| 21. Miami | 1,625,979 |
| 22. Denver-Boulder | 1,619,921 |
| 23. Seattle-Everett | 1,606,765 |
| 24. Tampa | 1,569,492 |
| 25. Riverside-San Bernardino-Ontario | 1,557,080 |
| 26. Phoenix | 1,508,030 |
| 27. Cincinnati | 1,401,403 |
| 28. Milwaukee | 1,397,143 |
| 29. Kansas City | 1,327,020 |
| 30. San Jose | 1,295,071 |
| 31. Buffalo | 1,242,573 |
| 32. Portland | 1,242,187 |
| 33. New Orleans | 1,186,725 |
| 34. Indianapolis | 1,166,929 |
| 35. Columbus, Ohio | 1,093,293 |
| 36. San Antonio | 1,071,954 |
| 37. Ft. Lauderdale-Hollywood | 1,014,043 |
| 38. Sacramento | 1,014,002 |
| 39. Rochester | 971,879 |
| 40. Salt Lake City-Ogden | 936,255 |

4 9
asegment

454

41. Providence-Warwick-Pawtucket 919,216
42. Memphis 912,887
43. Louisville 906,240
44. Nashville-Davidson 850,505
45. Birmingham 847,360
46. Oklahoma City 834,088
47. Dayton 830,070
48. Greensboro-Winston Salem-High Point 827,385
49. Norfolk-Virginia Beach-Portsmouth 806,691
50. Albany-Schenectady-Troy 795,019

***According to the 1980 U.S. census, 103 million people or 46 per cent of the country's population lives in the 50 largest standard metropolitan statistical areas.

### Bureau of the Census Regional Offices

| Atlanta, GA | 30309, | 1365 Peachtree Street, N.E. |
|---|---|---|
| Boston, MA | 02116, | 441 Stuart Street |
| Charlotte, NC | 28202, | Suite 800, 230 S. Tryon Street |
| Chicago, IL | 60604, | 55 E. Jackson Blvd., Suite 1304 |
| Dallas, TX | 75242, | 1100 Commerce Street |
| Denver, CO | 80225, | 575 Union Building |
| Detroit, MI | 48226, | 231 W. Lafayette, Room 565 |
| Kansas City, KA | 66101, | One Gateway Center, 4th & State St. |
| Los Angeles, CA | 90049, | 11777 San Vincente Blvd., Room 810 |
| New York, NY | 10007, | 26 Federal Plaza, Room 4102 |
| Philadelphia, PA | 19106, | 600 Arch Street, Room 9244 |
| Seattle, WA | 98109, | 1700 Westlake Avenue, North |

Further inquiries and/or orders of census data should be directed to:

Government Printing Office
Superintendent of Documents
Washington, D.C. 20402

Population Reference Bureau
1337 Connecticut Avenue, NW
Washington, D.C. 20036

** Data on Selected Racial Groups is available from the Bureau of the Census Booklet "DAD NO. 40" ($1.00).

## Canadian Census Information

Information on census statistics in Canada is available from

Statistics Canada
Use Advisory Services
Data Dissemination
Ottawa, Canada
K1S 5A4

Statistics Canada
Ottawa, ON
Canada
K1A 0T6
(613) 992-4734

## Sample letter requesting information needed for a survey

Chamber of Commerce

Dear Sirs:

I would like some information concerning your city and county. Please send me what information you may have about your city. I am especially interested in the following areas:

1. Maps of the city, county and state
2. Map showing the density and increase or decrease of population
3. List of the different races of people and the approximate number of each
4. Average income per person
5. Cost of renting a one-bedroom home
6. Cost of land
7. List of the churches and their addresses
8. List of the clergymen
9. List of industries, factories, and other places of employment with the approximate number of employees
10. List of the schools and colleges in the community
11. List of doctors in the community
12. List of the major newspapers
13. List of hotels and motels

Thank you for your cooperation in sending the materials which you have available.

Sincerely,

# How to do a Community Survey

I. Purpose of the Survey
   A. To reveal spiritual needs of a city or area
   B. To assist the Church Planter in setting priorities and
      selecting potential sites

II. Sources of Information
   A. Municipal Offices or City Halls
        Planning Office
        Zoning Office
        Building Department
   B. Local Utilities
   C. Chamber of Commerce or Board of Trade
   D. School District Office
   E. Government Statistical Reports–Taxation Statistics
   F. Local Real Estate Board
   G. Housing Project Developers
   H. Newspaper Offices
   I. Travel or Visitors Bureau
   J. Local Ministerial or Pastors' Fellowship

III. Tips on Completing Survey
   A. Try to be as accurate as possible often estimates of trends
      vary a great deal. Try to obtain various figures or
      estimates and then record the average. Be sure to note the
      date of research data.
   B. For areas over 15,000 in population, survey with the
      intent of developing a master plan for more than one
      church over a ten-year period.
   C. In metropolitan areas, do a separate survey for each
      community within the metropolitan area.
   D. Try to discover and use the advice of impartial Christian
      businessmen within the area being surveyed (contractors,
      developers, bankers, real-estate people,    municipal
      employees).
   E. Recognize and provide for ministries to ethnic groups in
      the area. A separate survey focusing on the possibility of
      an ethnic church may be warranted if population is large
      enough.
   F. Try to assess the possible interest of nearby Baptist
      churches in "mothering" or providing people, finances
      and moral support for an extension pastor.

## BAPTIST MID-MISSIONS
## CHURCH PLANTING AND DEVELOPMENT
## CITY SURVEY FORM

Completion Deadline _____ Date Sent _____
I. General Information
    1. City _____ Subdivision _____
       State/Province _____ District_____
    2. Person making survey_____
    3. Date of survey _____ 19_____
    4. Attach a map of the city showing churches, educational institutions and hospitals

II. Demographic Data

    1. Population Breakdown
       a. Central city _____
       b. Suburbs _____
       c. Surrounding area _____
       Total Metro Population _____

    2. Population Growth

    (For cities under 15,000 give only figures for entire city.) (For cities over 15,000 give figures for both city and the subdivision you are considering entering.)

| | CITY | SUBDIVISION |
|---|---|---|
| a. Population 10 years ago | _____ | _____ |
| b. Population 5 years ago | _____ | _____ |
| c. Population 2 years ago | _____ | _____ |
| d. Population at the present | _____ | _____ |
| e. Projected population in 2 years | _____ | _____ |
| f. Projected population in 5 years | _____ | _____ |
| g. Projected population in 10 years | _____ | _____ |

    3. Population Trends

    a. Is Population: Increasing _____ Decreasing_____
    b. Is the area: City _____ Suburban _____ Rural _____
    c. What percentage are:
       Young _____ Middle-aged _____ Elderly _____
    d. What percentage are: Homeowners _____ Tenants _____

e. Is this a Family or an Adult community? _____
f. What is the average size of family? _____
g. What percentage of families are single parent? _____

4. Sociological Data

   a. What is the occupational composition of the adult
      community (indicate percentages)

      _____ Craftsmen, equipment operators, farmers,
              service workers
      _____ Professional, officials, clerical, self-employed,
              sales
      _____ A general mixture
      _____ Other (write in) _____

   b. What is the occupational composition of any existing
      nucleus of people interested in the proposed new work?
      (Indicate percentages)

      _____ Craftsmen, equipment operators, farmers,
              service workers
      _____ Professional, officials, clerical, self-employed,
              sales
      _____ A general mixture
      _____ Other (write in) _____

   c. Are any of the core group families homogeneously
      matched to the area under consideration:

      _____ race            _____economic status
      _____ language        _____ social status
      _____ ethnic background

   d. What major ethnic groups are located in the city?_____
      _____
      _____

   e. What significant changes have taken place in the
      neighborhood in the last five years? _____
      _____
      _____

f.  With which of the above groups do you intend to work?

_____

## III. Ecclesiastical Data

1. What percentage of the population is:

    Catholic: _____
    Protestant _____
    Jewish: _____
    Other: _____
    Non-churched: _____

2.

| Fundamental Churches | Date of Origin | Av. A.M Attendance | Condition of the Church ** |
|---|---|---|---|
| 1._____ | ____ | ____ | ____ |
| 2._____ | ____ | ____ | ____ |
| 3._____ | ____ | ____ | ____ |
| 4._____ | ____ | ____ | ____ |
| 5._____ | ____ | ____ | ____ |

Evangelical Churches

| | | | |
|---|---|---|---|
| 1._____ | ____ | ____ | ____ |
| 2._____ | ____ | ____ | ____ |
| 3._____ | ____ | ____ | ____ |
| 4._____ | ____ | ____ | ____ |
| 5._____ | ____ | ____ | ____ |

** For "Condition of Church" put   G — Growing
                                   S — Static
                                   D — Declining

60

List the Major Cults in the Area

| _____ | _____ |
| _____ | _____ |
| _____ | _____ |

3. List the three closest independent Baptist churches

| | Church | Miles | Affiliation |
|---|---|---|---|
| a. | _____ | _____ | _____ |
| b. | _____ | _____ | _____ |
| c. | _____ | _____ | _____ |

4. Is there a local Fundamental Pastors' Fellowship? _____

   Is it strong? __Weak? ___How many members? _____
   What is their attitude toward your starting a new
   church?
   _____

5. How many local people are interested in helping you start a
   church in this city? Adults _____ Children _____

6. Has a "Get-Acquainted" meeting been held? ____ If yes,
   how many attended? _____ When was the meeting
   held? _____

7. Has a home Bible study been started? ____When did it
   start? _____ What is the average attendance? _____
   Who is leading it? _____

IV. Real Estate Data

   1. What auditoriums, halls, or other facilities are available that
      can be used for a temporary meeting place? _____
      _____
      _____

   2. What is the average rental for these? _____
   3. List the schools in the area and distance from proposed
      location:
      _____
      _____

4. List the names of any vacant church buildings available for rent or purchase (include approximate cost): _____

_____

_____

5. Are property values:  Increasing?_____  Decreasing?_____

6. What is the average cost for housing? (2 - 3 bedroom)
   Rental _____Purchase _____

7.Are churches taxed? _____ Parsonages? _____

8. What is the cost per acre for:  raw land __
                                  developed land___

9. What is the average cost per square foot for commercial construction in the area? _____

10. What is the most desirable location for a church in the next 20 years? _____

11. Attach a copy of the zoning requirements for church construction in your area.

V. Economic Data

1. What is the median family income in the area? _____

2. Is the job market:
   Stable? _____Hiring? _____ Laying off? _____

3. List the major industries and the number each employs:

| Industry | Employees |
|---|---|
| _____ | _____ |
| _____ | _____ |
| _____ | _____ |
| _____ | _____ |
| _____ | _____ |
| _____ | _____ |
| _____ | _____ |
| _____ | _____ |
| _____ | _____ |
| _____ | _____ |

62

## Church Directory Form

List the name, address and phone number for each church and
pastor in the survey area.

| NAME | ADDRESS | PHONE NUMBER |
|---|---|---|

**Fundamental**
church _____
pastor _____

church _____
pastor _____

church _____
pastor _____

**Evangelical**
church _____
pastor _____

church _____
pastor _____

church _____
pastor _____

**Pentecostal/Holiness**
church _____
pastor _____

church _____
pastor _____

church _____
pastor _____

**Protestant**
church _____
pastor _____

|        | NAME | ADDRESS | PHONE NUMBER |
|--------|------|---------|--------------|

church _____
pastor _____

church _____
pastor _____

church _____
pastor _____

church _____
pastor _____

**Catholic**
church _____
priest _____

church _____
priest _____

church _____
priest _____

**Jewish**
temple _____
rabbi _____

temple _____
rabbi _____

temple _____
rabbi _____

**Cults**
church _____
pastor _____

church _____
pastor _____

church _____
pastor _____

64

| | NAME | ADDRESS | PHONE NUMBER |
|---|---|---|---|

**Other**

church
pastor _____

church
pastor _____

church
pastor _____

church
pastor _____

church
pastor _____

church
pastor _____

church
pastor _____

# COMMUNITY CHURCH SURVEY**

Name _____ Address _____ Phone Number_____

Church: _____
Pastor: _____

Fundamental _____    Evangelical _____    Protestant _____    Cult _____
Pentecostal _____    Catholic _____    Jewish _____    Other_____

"Hello, my name is _____ , and I am with_____(name of mission or church)____ . We are trying to determine the areas of greatest need for new churches. To do this we are conducting a survey of all area churches and synagogues to develop a religious profile of the community. I would like to ask you some questions concerning attendance, membership and constituency. Would you mind helping us by providing this information concerning your church?...... Thank you very much.

## I. Attendance

1. What is the total number of the persons who attend your church? _____

2. What is the average Sunday-morning attendance at your church? _____

3. Small Town:
   Approximately what percentage of the persons who attend your church:
   live in town? _____ %
   drive in from the country? _____%

   Larger City:
   Approximately what percentage of the persons who attend your church:
   live in the area of the church? _____ %
   commute in from outside the area? _____ %

4. About what percentage of those who attend your church are:
   over 18 years of age? _____ %
   under 18 years of age? _____ %

## II. Membership

5. What is the present size of your membership? _____
   What was it 5 years ago? _____

6. What percentage of your membership is resident in the area? _____ %
                                              Non-resident_____ %

7. Approximately how many of your members commute 20 minutes or more to get to your church? _____ %

8. What is the predominant ethnic group(s) in your church?
   _____
   _____

Thank you for all your help. I deeply appreciate it very much... Goodbye.

** This form may be used for either telephone or personal interviews.

Try to obtain the above information for every church listed on your "Church Directory Form"
(Note: Copies of this form are avilable from Baptist Mid-Missions.)

66

## Summary Sheet

Tabulate your survey sheets of area churches and record your findings on this Summary Sheet.

1. The geographical area being studied includes:

   a.Urban Area _____
   (city, suburb, town)
   b.Rural Area _____
   (county, school district,towns)

2. The current population of the survey area:

   a. Urban Population _____
   b. Rural Population _____
   c. Total Population _____

3. _____ % of the population are adults (over 18 years)

   _____ % of the population are children (under 18 years)

4. _____ Total number of people who attend church

   _____ % of those who attend church are adults

   _____ % of those who attend church are children

5. _____ Total average Sunday morning attendance
6. _____ Total membership of all area churches
7. _____ Total number of members who commute 20 minutes or more to attend church
8. _____ Total who attend fundamental churches
9. _____ Total membership of fundamental churches
10. _____ Total who attend evangelical churches
11. _____ Total membership of evangelical churches
12. _____ Total who attend Pentecostal/Holiness churches
13 _____ Total membership of Pentecostal/Holiness churches
14. _____ Total who attend Protestant churches
15. _____ Total membership of Protestant churches
16. _____ Total who attend Catholic churches
17. _____ Total membership of Catholic churches
18. _____ Total who attend cult churches

19. _____ Total who are members of cult churches

20. _____ % of the population who attend church (Subtract line 7 from line 4 and divide by line 2c)

21. _____ % of the population who do not attend church (Subtract line 20 from 100%)

22. _____ % of the population who attend church regularly (Subtract line 7 from line 5 and divide by line 2c)

23. _____ % of the population who attend church occasionally (Subtract line 5 from line 4 and divide by line 2c)

24. _____ % of the population who attend fundamental churches (Divide line 8 by line 2c)

25. _____ % of the population who attend evangelical churches (Divide line 10 by line 2c)

26. _____ % of the population who attend Pentecostal or Holiness churches (Divide line 12 by line 2c)

27. _____ % of the population who attend Protestant churches (Divide line 14 by line 2c)

28. _____ % of the population who attend Catholic churches (Divide line 16 by line 2c)

29. _____ % of the population who attend cult churches (Divide line 18 by line 2c)

30. _____ % of the population who are members of area churches (Subtract line 7 from line 6 and divide by line 2c)

31. _____ % of church members who commute 20 minutes or more to church (Divide line 7 by line 6)

32. _____ % of church members who reside near their church(Subtract line 31 from 100%)

## Instructions for Church Planting Priority Score Sheet

1. Select those communities in your area which you feel have the greatest need for a new fundamental Baptist church.
2. Write the names of those communities in the blank space on the Scoresheet.
3. Following the example in column one, proceed to evaluate and thereby determine the order of priority of the communities for church planting outreach.
4. Your evaluation of the first ten items will be based on the surveys and intensive research completed on each potential community.
5. On a scale of 1 to 10, rate each community you have selected according to its
   a. Population Factors (size, growth, etc.)
   b. Area Potential (Geographically is the community located in an area which provides future growth potential?)
   c. Ethnic Make-up (Is the population dominated by one or more major ethnic groups, and what is your evaluation of the potential of a fundamental Baptist church to evangelize these people?)
   d. Economic Factors (employment, income factors plus your evaluation of its economic future)
   e. People's Responsiveness (based on sociological factors of age, education, values, and other characteristics)
   f. Area Churches (Based on the Religious Profile, is the community a spiritually needy area in comparison to other communities?)
   g. Sponsoring Potential (What is the potential for direct sponsorship of a new church in this community by the nearest existing fundamental Baptist church in the area?)
   h. Nucleus Available (Is there in the community a nucleus of people who desire a fundamental Baptist church be started there, and are they willing to get involved and support it?)
   i. Resources (What are the available resources for starting a new church in this community on a local, state and sponsoring church basis?)
   j. Strategic Area (is the starting of a church in this community of strategic importance to our over all church-planting program for reaching out from this community into the surrounding areas?)

## Score Sheet for Church Planting Priority

# A R E A S

| | A | B | C | D | E | F | G | H | I |
|---|---|---|---|---|---|---|---|---|---|
| Population Factors | 5 | 8 | | | | | | | |
| Area Potential | 8 | 9 | | | | | | | |
| Economic Factors | 7 | 9 | | | | | | | |
| Ethnic Make-up | 6 | 6 | | | | | | | |
| People's Responsiveness | 5 | 7 | | | | | | | |
| Area Churched | 5 | 7 | | | | | | | |
| Sponsoring Potential | 8 | 10 | | | | | | | |
| Nucleus Available | 8 | 3 | | | | | | | |
| Resources | 5 | 10 | | | | | | | |
| Strategic Area | 4 | 7 | | | | | | | |
| TOTAL | 61 | 76 | | | | | | | |
| Score Number | 2 | 1 | | | | | | | |
| Rating | H | VH | | | | | | | |

1. List communities under consideration A, B, C, etc
2. Rate each item on a scale of 1 - 10; 1 = lowest,; 10 = highest
3. After totalling each column, determine the priority by placing #1 on the Score Number line for the highest score, # 2 for the next, #3 for the next, etc.
4. Use this guide to fill in the Rating line: 1 - 25 low (L), 25 -50 medium (M), 50 - 75 high (H), 75 - 100 very high (VH)

# Chapter 5

# The Preparations
# for Church Planting

While determining where God wants you to plant a church, there are some important plans and preparations you must make. These are crucial. Experience has shown that careful plan - ning will enable you to build a better, stronger church.[1]

## Things to do Before Arrival

There are a number of matters you should attend to before moving to your selected city. These will speed up your ministry and free you for meeting and winning people once you arrive.

### • Prepare Enough Messages for the First Six Months

Before moving, prepare enough messages (approximately seventy-five) to last for the first six months on the field. By studying and developing your messages beforehand, you will be able to give the majority of your time to visitation, soul winning and discipling. You will still have to spend some time each week reviewing messages to keep them from being dry or stale.

The very nature of the new church calls for simple Bible teach - ing. In-depth material should be kept for later. Include messages on salvation, the local church, prayer, how to study the Bible, witnessing, separation, stewardship and surrender. There are many people who are hungry for old-time gospel preaching. If you feed them, your church will grow. Shoddy preparation and pre - sentation will not attract nor hold people. Give them the best you have right from the beginning, even while the number is small, if you want to have an opportunity to preach to larger crowds at a later time.[2]

Plan ahead for your Sunday school. Secure samples of pub - lished materials to be sure they are acceptable and can be adapted to your use. Regular Baptist Press provides surplus Sunday-school materials free of charge to missionaries through its Gospel Literature Services.

### • Carefully Plan your Initial Church Program

Make plans for effective youth, evangelism and follow-up programs to be used during the first six months. Changes will have to be made later, but broad, workable plans should be made before you begin the church. Develop weekly lessons for new converts or order published discipling materials. You also need to secure tracts and other gospel literature.

Develop plans for training your people to witness. Talk with pastors who have successful outreach. Find out what they are using and how to implement it. You might want to contact First Baptist Church in Elkhart, Indiana; Bethesda Baptist Church in Brownsburg, Indiana; Calvary Baptist Church in Grand Rapids, Michigan; or Emmanuel Baptist in Toledo, Ohio. They all have excellent evangelism training courses for missionaries and pastors.

Plan for a regular youth night. Teens enjoy being together. It can be held in a private home or rented quarters. Divide the program into three segments: 1) fellowship and games (table games, ping pong, singing, etc.); 2) Bible study and Scripture memorization (Books of the Bible, Sword drills, etc.); 3) food (supplied by families). At first you will have to lead this weekly fellowship time. Plan periodic specials such as trips, hikes, bowling, skating, hayrides, and ball games.[3] Two excellent, inexpensive youth programs designed for new churches called "Bible Seekers" and "Bible Teens" are available through Baptist Mid-Missions.

### • Prepare a Church Constitution, Covenant, and Doctrinal Statement

Before starting a new church, you should prepare the constitution, covenant and doctrinal statement. Think through very carefully what you want to include in these documents. Talk with other pastors; collect and compare their church documents for ideas on what should be covered. Be sure your constitution is scriptural, legal and workable. Do not make it so complicated that people cannot understand it. Keep it simple. A constitution and bylaws should simply provide guidelines for the smooth functioning of the church, not be a detailed guide to handling every problem that comes up in the future. (See chapter eight for more information concerning how to develop these documents.)

## • Have Publicity Pictures Made

You will need sharp, black-and-white glossy photographs to use in newspapers and other promotional materials. Go to a good commercial photographer who will give you quality work. You will need a good photograph of yourself and another of you and your family together. Order at least twenty copies of yourself. It is far less expensive to purchase them in quantity than to reorder later.

## • Design an Attractive Visitation Brochure

You will need an attractive brochure to hand out during your door-to-door calling. First impressions are often lasting, so it is essential that your literature be first-class. Take time to develop carefully the basic layout and wording in advance. Details such as meeting place and telephone numbers can be added once you arrive in your target area. Collect good brochures from other churches to get ideas, then make up your own by combining the best features. Do not use someone else's brochure.

When you develop the brochure 1) be sure you gear it to the unsaved since they will be the primary ones receiving it–use terms they will understand; 2) design the brochure primarily as an invitation to interest people in your new church; 3) make it informative, telling people the vital details they need to know if they want to visit.

The front cover should give the name, address, and phone number of the church. It should also include the pastor's name. A picture or silhouette of your church or meeting place may also be included. The second page should give a description of your services and their times. The third page should tell why you are starting the new church and list its ministries. It could also include your picture or a brief doctrinal statement. The back should give a brief plan of salvation. Most people automatically turn over any piece of literature they are given to see what is on the back. Sample brochures may be obtained from sources listed at the end of this chapter.[4]

When you are ready to print the brochure, have it typeset and printed by a professional printer. Never mimeograph it. Use sharp photographs, quality paper and the right color ink. The extra expense will bring rich dividends in the end.

## • Develop a Survival Budget

Lack of proper financial planning is one of the major causes new churches do not survive. Sit down and realistically count the costs involved in starting the church (Luke 14:28,29). Develop a "survival" budget showing the amount the church will need each week to function during the first six months of the church's existence. (See chapter 13 for a sample survival budget and details concerning what to include.)

The survival budget can be used as a prayer challenge for potential sponsoring churches and friends and will be passed out at the first public services of the new church. People respond more readily when they can see why their money is needed and how it is being used. After all, "money is ministry. The way you handle the money is the way you handle the ministry."[5]

## • Send Out an Appeal Letter

Send the survival budget and an explanatory letter to friends, relatives and churches you want to support your ministry. Give basic information concerning the targeted community, your goals, the name of the proposed church, when you plan to move to the community, the cost of moving, equipment needs and the projected date for the first service. You may want to include a letter of recommendation from your home pastor.

There will be some Christians who will respond to your appeal if you ask them to consider prayerfully supporting you on a monthly basis for six months to a year. Church planters with a mission agency would not need to do this since they already have outside support pledged to them. They should however inform their supporters of their plans for developing a new church and seek to enlist their prayer support.

## • Raise any Remaining Financial Support

Ideally you should be fully supported before you move to the community you have selected. You should not be away from the church at all during the first year. Working part-time or traveling to secure funds will cause the work to suffer and grow much slower. Ask churches of like faith for the opportunity to share

your burden with them. Even if they cannot give monthly support, a one-time offering will help to pay for supplies, equipment
and moving costs. Missionary church planters should not try to
begin a new church until they have raised adequate support to accomplish it.

### • Secure Office Equipment and Church Supplies

Good office equipment will help you to be more efficient and
effective in your church-planting ministry. Don't wait until you
arrive on the field to determine what your needs will be. Plan
ahead and begin securing the equipment in advance. Share the
need with your supporters. (Any equipment purchased from the
gifts of others will belong to the church, not to the church
planter.)

You will need a typewriter which produces a good quality type
style. Electric typewriters which use carbon ribbons are best
because their copies can be readily used with photocopy ma-
chines. If at all possible, get a dry photocopier rather than a
mimeograph or liquid copier. Mimeographs are messy, and it is
becoming more difficult to get supplies for them. A paper-folding
machine can save you many man-hours. Don't forget to get a
desk, bookcases and filing cabinets.

A label addressing machine can be useful for mass mailings.
However, addressing can be done on the dry copier if you have
one. Consider seriously a computer for word processing and
mailing lists. Include the supplies for your equipment (paper,
ribbons, labels, etc.). Some church may be willing to donate
hymnals for you to use. Be sure the songs are doctrinally sound
and not filled with liberal or liturgical music.

Acquire tracts, a financial ledger, a clerk's book, visitor's
cards and offering envelopes. They should be available for your
very first public service. Most of them can be purchased at a
Christian bookstore. Don't be afraid to make your needs known.
James 4:2 tells us: "Ye have not because ye ask not," so ask. Many
of God's people are willing to help if they know of your need.

### • Find a Suitable Place to Live

Arrange housing before you move to your field of service.
Locate in the area where you will be working so you will not need
to pack and unpack twice. Your home will probably be used as the
church office, for prayer meeting and youth activities; so choose

one with plenty of room. If you are buying a home, you will need to pick it out far enough in advance to allow for the loan to be processed before you arrive.

There are a number of advantages to buying a home rather than renting one. Owning a home conveys a sense of permanence to those with whom you work. It will keep you from leaving in times of discouragement and will give your family a sense of security.[6] In the long run, owning a home is better stewardship. You will recover most or all of your investment when you sell. When you rent, you recover nothing. You will also gain valuable insight on locating property, securing financing and arranging mortgages. A man who has never gone through this experience may find it difficult later to lead his church in acquiring land and undertaking a building program.[7] Those serving with a mission agency like Baptist Mid-Missions should secure home-office administrative approval before buying a home.

The time spent in preparation will pay rich dividends when you actually locate on your field of service. You will have adequate support raised, messages prepared, programs planned, supplies collected, church documents written, a budget ready and a home to move into. Now you can concentrate on reaching people and discipling them for Christ. After all, that's why you are there.

## Things to do After Arrival

Do not make the mistake of plunging directly into the work as soon as you arrive on your field of service. There are still a number of things you should do before you begin.

• Take Time to Get Settled

Arrange to have the utilities turned on by the time you arrive at your new home. There is nothing worse than moving into a house which has no water or electricity. Take a few days to unpack and to get settled in your new home. Your family needs the security this will provide. They will support your church work more readily if they are happy. Moreover, you do not want people to begin visiting your home if it is cluttered with boxes or in a state of disarray. Take care of this now because there will be little time for it when you begin planting the church.[8]

You will need to pick up your telephone from the local phone center. Be sure they list your name as "Pastor" or "Reverend" in both the white and the yellow pages. If you have moved into a new state, get a new driver's license and car tags as soon as possible. You do not want to visit homes with an out-of-state plate on your automobile. That would be a poor advertisement. Enroll your children in school and meet their principal and teachers. Plan to participate in the PTA or PTF meetings. These will give you valuable contacts.

Secure a good map. Drive around to become acquainted with the major expressways and streets. Encourage your family to call this new area "home." Avoid public references to "back home" lest people get the impression that you are an "outsider." Make this your permanent residence as soon as possible, in every way possible.

Seek to develop good community relations by making contact with its leaders. You need to establish your credibility as a min - ister and trustworthy leader. If possible, make brief, friendly visits to the mayor, councilmen, newspaper editors, broadcasting managers and civil leaders. Cultivate a working relationship with those whose expertise you may need in the future.

Accept speaking opportunities from worthwhile civic func - tions which do not place you in a compromising position. As you do so, you will build bridges to the community that will pay rich dividends in the future.

## • Choose a Name for the Church

Before you can print any literature, you will need a church name. Select the name carefully. It will remain long after you and the charter members are gone. Some men prefer to choose a name which identifies the church with the geographical area in which it is located such as "Northwest Baptist Church." Avoid naming the church after the street on which it is located. The church may move some day. Whatever name you choose, check the phone book or your survey sheet to be sure no other church is using the same name.

All church planters who are Baptists will naturally include the word "Baptist" in the church name. (This is required by mission agencies such as Baptist Mid-Missions.) The word "Baptist" tells people that this church is dedicated to carrying out the Great Commission including immersing converts, committed to teaching Bible doctrine and the fundamentals of the faith, and believes in congregational authority and New Testament church polity.[9] By contrast, the use of terms such as "Community" or "Bible" church communicates that the new church probably will not take a clear stand on important issues. Don't be afraid to identify yourself and your position. People will support the church if the power of God is there.

As soon as you have selected a name for the church, open checking and savings accounts in the church's name at a local bank. Initially you may have to sign checks and handle the funds, but you should train someone else to do this just as soon as possible.

Once you have opened an account for the church, you can begin to place your tithes and any gifts from friends and supporters in this church fund. Keep accurate records of all income and expenses. These will become part of the church's permanent financial file. However, until the church is organized, it cannot issue tax-deductible receipts unless it is under a mission agency or mother church. Missionaries should remember to channel all gifts through their mission agency.

## • Get a Mailing Address for the Church

You will need a mailing address to print on your checks and literature. As soon as you have picked a name for the church, rent a post-office box rather than using your own address. This way the church's address will not change every time you or the church relocate. You may also need it to incorporate. The local address will help residents identify you as a part of their community.

## • Set a Date for Your First Sunday Services

Regardless of the method you use to start the church, you should have a definite date in view for beginning public services. Set a specific time and work toward meeting that goal. Schedule the first public services four to six weeks from the time you begin your intensive visitation in the area. This will give you time to advertise, find a meeting place, and collect a core group. If you start without adequate preparation, you may find that you will have a "premature birth."

You want your first service to be well planned and well attended. Grant Rice says, "It takes a crowd to draw a crowd." It is important that people get the impression that the church is going to succeed. Otherwise, they will not be back. So allow enough time to plan and prepare for this all important first public service. You may wish to invite some people from nearby sister churches to visit the first service to enliven the singing and increase the attendance.

### • Secure a Suitable Meeting Place

One of the first problems you must solve is, "Where will we hold our meetings?" Initially, Bible studies and get-acquainted meetings may be held in private homes, but these will not suffice when you begin holding regular Sunday services. A private home usually does not have adequate space or parking. People are reluctant to attend "church" in a private home. In some areas, zoning laws prohibit the use of homes for religious services.

You need to find a suitable meeting place before beginning public services. The location and size of this meeting place will have a critical effect on your success or failure. First impressions are often lasting impressions. Look for something that has good visibility, easy accessibility and plenty of parking. It should be located in your target area and ideally have enough room so that you will not need to relocate until you move into your own building.

Be sure it has adequate heating and cooling. Are there rest rooms for both men and women? Can you have the building on the days and at the times you want? Is the cost within your means?

Public and private schools make excellent meeting places. They are visible, easy to find and have ample parking. Most have auditoriums that provide all the space and seating you need. Classrooms are usually available for Sunday school and nursery activities. They may even let you use the piano and P.A. system.

You might also consider community or civic centers, the YMCA and the YWCA, recreational halls, day-care centers, libraries, lodge halls, banks, funeral homes, firehouses, veterans' halls, mobile homes, or any number of other facilities that might be available. Try to avoid being boxed in by the limitations of your location. Strive to get the best possible location so that you can begin with an image of excellence. Then make the building as attractive as possible by cleaning, painting and repairing it if necessary. Every church is judged to some extent by the appearance of its meeting place.

It is important that you have a signed contract. It should spell out the terms of lease, such as the hours of use, the cost involved, and who is responsible for maintenance, breakage and utilities. You may be required to pay for insurance and the services of a custodian. Check to see if you need a certificate of occupancy from the city before you sign the contract. Also be sure you can post identifying signs on the property to inform the public of your presence. Schools may allow this only on Sundays.

Be careful about acquiring church buildings. They are not always the blessings they may first appear to be. Find out why the church is available. Would the new church be associated with a bad reputation from the former occupants? Is it in a declining neighborhood? Is it in a deteriorating condition? It may be so unattractive and run-down that visitors will not attend. Repairs may be prohibitive. Look before you leap into something you may be sorry about later.

Investigate all the possibilities, weigh the pros and cons of each and then choose the one which will best meet your needs and financial situation. If this is God's place for you, He will provide you with the facilities you need. Just look around until you find them.

### • Acquire Church Signs

You will need a well-lettered sign to place outside your facilities. A permanent sign which can be seen all week long is ideal, but you may have to settle for something which is more temporary. A large, portable sandwich board works well. It should include the church name, times of services, a telephone number and the pastor's name. It should be set near the driveway or entrance to the property where it can be easily seen.

Enlist the help of a professional sign painter unless you are very good at lettering and painting. You want the sign to be as attractive as possible. It will be money well invested. Check with local officials to be sure you comply with local sign ordinances.

You will also need smaller signs inside to guide visitors to the rooms you are using. You can hand-letter or stencil these yourself. Be sure there are no misspelled words.

You may want to include a church logo or slogan on your signs and literature. These help people identify you more easily. For example, McDonalds is instantly recognized by its golden arches. A well chosen logo or slogan will do the same for your church. Collect letterheads from other churches for ideas. You may find one you like or can adapt for your own purposes. A slogan communicates your purpose and priorities. You might use some-thing like: "Founded on the Word, Focused on the World" or "Preaching Christ Crucified, Risen and Coming Again." There is no limit to what you can do if you try.

## • Print Your Visitation Literature

As soon as you have an address, phone number and a meeting place, you should complete the church brochure you began before you arrived. The brochure should be first-class because people will judge you and the church by it. If you do not have the expertise to design a brochure properly, seek the advice of a printer or lithographer. Be sure to have it  professionally typeset and printed. Order several thousand copies so you can begin visiting door to door as soon as possible. Ask for the best price possible. Let the printer know that you will have more business for him as the church grows. When he sees the quality and quantity of work you are bringing, he should be glad to cut his prices to gain your business.

You may also want a special flyer printed to invite people to your first service. It should be colorful and informative, giving pertinent details of the time and place. Finally, secure an attrac- tive calling card you can give to professional and business people.

## • Visit Every Available Hour for Four Weeks

Once literature has been printed, begin extensive door-to-door visitation in your target area. On a map, draw a circle around the area that would be within fifteen minutes' driving distance of your meeting place. Divide this circle into four sections. Begin visiting in the neighborhood nearest your meeting place and work outward. Concentrate on a different section each week. This will enable the church to have a healthy cross section of the pop- ulace and keep it from being composed of just one class or group of people.

Begin visiting about 9:00 o'clock each morning and continue throughout the day, spending eight to ten hours in visitation. If you work hard, you should be able to average 150 homes per day. These are not necessarily soul-winning calls, but are designed to introduce yourself and to inform people about the new church and its first service. Keep the calls short and friendly. Leave a brochure or flyer and invite them to a "get-acquainted meeting" the following Tuesday (see the next chapter). When you find some- one who shows interest, jot down his or her name and address on a three-by-five card and plan to call back in the evening when the husband is more likely to be home. Add their names to your pros- pect and mailing lists.

If you will concentrate on visiting people in this way for several weeks, you will find several who will respond to your invitation. There is no substitute for personal contact when trying to plant a new church.

● Publicize Your First Service

Begin publicizing the new church as soon as a date is set for its first service. A well written press release telling about the new church and a picture of the pastor should be taken to the religious editor of every newspaper within a thirty-mile radius. It should be typed with double spacing on good quality paper. Include all pertinent information: who, what, when, where, why and how. Always include your name and phone number in case the editor needs to contact you for some additional information. Label any photos with a soft-tip pen and provide a self-addressed, stamped envelope if you want them returned.

Place a large paid ad in the newspaper announcing your first service. It should be well laid out and include the church's name, meeting place, time of service and pastor's picture. This could be done in the form of a letter to the community explaining the church's affiliation and plans.

Send "public service announcements" to the radio, television and cable stations in your area two to three weeks before your first service. Hundreds of free advertising spots are given out each week by stations to non-profit, charitable organizations. Check the yellow pages and compile a list of media names and addresses you can use in the future. You might even visit station managers to see if they would be interested in interviewing you.

Post invitational flyers in grocery stores, laundromats and convenience stores. Ask the manager if you may place a flyer in the window. Finally, send a personal letter of invitation to each of the prospects you have met through your visitation. Include an attractively printed announcement as well. Your goal is to saturate the community so that as many people as possible will know that a new church is starting. Use every available means to notify every available person.

Prepare a follow-up letter for first-time visitors to your services. These letters can be printed beforehand so that you only need to type in the name and address. (Several sample letters are found at the end of this chapter.)

Finally, prepare a visitor's packet containing your church brochure, a doctrinal statement, a visitor's card, and a salvation tract. It should be given to all first-time visitors who attend the church.

## Endnotes

1 Grant G. Rice,"Church Planting Pre-Planning"(pamphlet).( Rockvale, TN: Grant G. Rice, n.d.).

2 Elmer Towns, *Getting a Church Started*. (Lynchburg, VA: Church Growth Institute, 1982), p. 120.

3 Grant G. Rice, *Church Planting Primer*. (Louisville, KY: Tabernacle Press, n.d.), pp. 87 - 89.

4 For sample brochures, write to

Evangelistic Press                     Tabernacle Press
P.O. Box 25285          Jeffersonville Baptist Tabernacle
Charlotte, NC 28229                    P.O. Box 99141
                                   Louisville, KY 40299

5 Towns, *op. cit.*, p. 134.

6 Roy Thomas, *Planting and Growing a Fundamental Church.* (Nashville, TN: Randall House Publications, 1979),p. 58.

7 Towns, *op. cit.*, p. 133.

8 Thomas, *op. cit.*, p. 59.

9 Towns, *op. cit.*, pp. 61, 62.

## Sample Letter to Visitors

Dear_____,

It was our privilege to have you visiting in our services at (name of church). We trust you found God's people to be friendly and that you received a spiritual blessing from the Bible teaching and preaching ministry of our church. We are excited about what God is doing through our people. We are convinced there is a great need for this type of ministry in our community.

I hope you visit with us again in the near future. We meet for Sunday School, with classes for all ages, at _____; Morning Worship is at _____;Evening Service at _____ and our Wednesday Bible Study and Prayer Service is at _____.

We look forward to having you with us again. May God's richest blessing be upon you. If I can ever be of any help or counsel to you, feel free to call. It would be a joy to be of service to you. You are someone special and we are interested in you.

Sincerely in Christ,

## Sample Letter to a New Resident

Dear_____,

Welcome to (name of community)! We are glad that you have chosen to make our community your home and hope you will find it as enjoyable as I have.

Perhaps in getting settled you have not yet found a church home. I would like to invite you to worship with us this Sunday at (name of your church). We are located at (state community or town).

We have a full range of services including Sunday School for every member of the family at _____; our Morning Service is conducted at _____ and an Evening Fellowship at _____. There is also a special Bible Study and Prayer Time on Wednesday evening at ____ p.m.

Come and enjoy the friendliness of our people. We want to become your friends. If I can ever render any spiritual assistance to you, please do not hestitate to contact me.

Sincerely in Christ,

## Sample Letter to a Prospect Contacted through Visitation

Dear _____,

Recently, members of our Friendship visitation team had the pleasure of meeting and introducing you to the ministry of (name of your church.)

We sincerely hope that you will visit and worship with us in the very near future. As the pastor of (name of your church), let me assure you that I am personally interested in you and your family. Please do not hesitate to contact me if I can be of assistance to you.

We extend our hand of fellowship to you. I look forward to meeting you soon.

Sincerely,

## Sample Letter for New Converts

Dear_____,

I am so glad you have asked Jesus Christ to be your Savior and have been born into the family of God. Many things will happen in your life during the coming months, but just remember you have a Savior who loves you so much that He gave His life for you and He will *always* be there to help you.

I am praying for you and your family as you begin your new life in Christ. Let me encourage you to read your Bible and pray every day. This will provide spiritual nourishment for you. You also need to attend a good Bible-teaching church where you can find strength and encouragement from other believers. Please accept my personal invitation to attend the services here at (name of your church). You will find a warm welcome awaiting you.

Anytime you need me for any reason, please feel free to call. I love you, and I am so proud to have you as a member of the family of God.

Your Friend,

## Sample News Release

A new church will be "born" on Sunday morning, (date). The (name of your church) will hold its first services this Sunday at (time) A.M. in the (location). Several months of preparation, planning and prayer have gone into the development of the new church. The founding pastor, (pastor's name), will be speaking in both the morning and the evening services.

The new congregation will be an independent, fundamental, Bible-teaching church with a family-oriented ministry. There will be Sunday-school classes with trained teachers for each member of the family. A supervised nursery and transportation are also available.

Sunday School will begin at (time); Morning Worship at (time); Sunday Evening Service at (time). Mid-week Prayer Meeting and Bible study will be held Wednesdays at (time).

The public is cordially invited to attend all services. For more information call (your phone number).

# Chapter 6

# The Plan for
# Church Planting

Upon moving into an area, the church planter must locate people who are willing to help him establish a new church. Where will he find them and how can he get their cooperation? If he knows no one, how can he discover prospects and develop a nucleus of believers with whom to start the church?

## Discovering Prospects

There are two basic types of people in the world: resistant and responsive. "Resistant" people are those who are hostile to the gospel and either refuse to listen to it or reject it outright. "Responsive" people are those who will listen to Christ's message or who are favorably disposed toward it. These responsive people are the prospects the church planter is seeking. Everyone is a prospect until proven otherwise.

Prospects include both saved and unsaved, active and inactive church members, mature and immature believers. In a sense, everyone in the community is a prospect until proven otherwise. The church planter must sort out the good prospects from the poor ones and develop a list of potential core-group members. There are a number of ways to do this:

• Ask for names of friends, neighbors and relatives

Visit area pastors to see if they will loan one or more of their families to help the new church get started. If a group of believers has invited the church planter to help them develop the church, they can give him names and addresses of people they know who may be interested. Church-growth studies indicate that 70% of people begin attending church because a friend or family member invited them to come. You will never know who is interested if you do not ask.

- Locate prospects through door-to-door visitation

Get a map of the area and systematically visit every home. Go street by street, visiting different sections each day until you have covered the entire area. Keep the visit brief. Do not go in. Simply inform people about the new church, giving them a brochure and an invitation to a "get-acquainted" meeting on Tuesday evening. Jot down the name and address of anyone showing interest and call back in the evening when both husband and wife are at home.

As you visit you will meet other believers. Not all of them will be prospects. Some will be active members of good churches and should not be encouraged to leave. This would be unethical. Others may have dropped out of church because of a critical spirit or an unresolved sin problem. If they would not follow another pastor's leadership, they may be just as rebellious toward yours. Caution needs to be exercised in including them in your core group.

Still other believers will be located who have not found a church home since moving into the area. Then there are those who are dissatisfied in liberal churches. These folks need to be encouraged to help start a new church in their community.

- Use bulk mailings to locate prospects

Secure a bulk mailing permit from the post office as soon as possible. It will enable you to contact hundreds of people at very little cost. You are required to mail at least two hundred (5,000 in Canada) identical letters each time you use the permit. The letters must be the same size and weight and be presorted by zip codes. There is an annual fee, but this will be offset by the substantial savings on postage. Send a letter, a church brochure and a gospel tract to each resident and newcomer in your target area. Be sure all letters are printed or well typed. Personalize the letters by putting the individual's name and address on each one. Do not send to "resident." Tell about the church and invite them to attend the services or a "get-acquainted" meeting.

One of the easiest ways to get the names and addresses of the people living in your target area is to purchase a copy of the "Haynes Criss-Cross Directory" or "Polk's Directory."[1] These directories list the names of every person in the community by street address and telephone number. They can be purchased directly from the publishers, or you may be able to get last-year's edition from a local realtor or businessman. Check the local library for a loan copy. The directories are expensive, but worth their weight in gold. In Canada, there is a census before every federal election which lists the names and addresses of all residents. Copies may be purchased from the president of the electoral district.

Watch for families moving in. Secure a monthly "newcomers" list for your community. It can be obtained from utility companies, welcome committees, city hall, realtors or commercial companies which specialize in locating new residents. Also mail to all prospects you meet while doing door-to-door visitation.

Learn to use the mails to advertise your church. Send out a weekly church newspaper from the very beginning of your public services. Once the church is established and growing, you can cut back to a monthly newsletter. Regular mail contact keeps your new church before the community so they can see what God is doing. Share the excitement of the new work, and they may get excited and decide to visit. People identify with success.

In your newsletter include attendance figures (compared so growth can be seen), offerings (show accumulations so strengths can be seen), conversions, baptisms, new items purchased, new ministries begun, special days coming, Sunday-school campaigns, films, special speakers, retreats, banquets, summer camps, land purchases, building plans and anything else that might be interesting. The newsletter should be informative and not be used to preach. If you are too busy to prepare your own, you might want to mail out the "Fellowship" paper.[2]

### • Conduct a telephone survey

The telephone is an excellent way to reach apartments and condominiums where access is restricted. It is both economical and effective. Many people will talk with you by phone who will not speak to you at the door. (See the end of this chapter for details.)

### • Watch the newspapers for special events

Births, deaths, weddings, graduations and special honors are often announced in the paper. Contact these families with an appropriate call, letter or visit. Share their joy or grief, and they will often respond to your invitation to visit the church. (See sample letters at the end of this chapter.)

- Visitors in the church service are prospects

Visitors are your best prospects. They have already shown enough interest to attend at least once. Their names and addresses may be obtained by distributing visitor's cards during each service. Plan to visit them before the following Sunday.

The innovative church planter will find many other ways to locate those interested in seeing a new church developed in their area.

Develop and maintain a good prospect file. Put the name, address and phone number of each prospect on a file card. Arrange the cards according to the degree of interest. Those who show the greatest interest should be visited weekly, the others every two to four weeks. Update the file regularly by adding new names and removing those who are no longer considered good prospects. This file will provide the church planter with an unlimited source of potential church members, both before and after a church has been started. (See the end of this chapter for a sample prospect file card.)

## Developing the Core Group

The term "core group" refers to a nucleus of people who have committed themselves to organizing a new church in a given area. It may consist of a few or many and be made up of both new and mature believers. The larger the number, the stronger the group will be.

Not everyone who shows interest in the new church or who attends its services will become part of the core group. Commitment of time, resources and self are essential to becoming part of this select group. It will become evident as the work progresses which ones are willing to pay the price to be a part of the nucleus of the new church. Be sure to state clearly from the outset that this fellowship will become a Baptist church.

Developing the core group can take anywhere from a few weeks to several months depending on the circumstances. It often takes longer to begin a church in areas with high Jewish or Catholic populations than in the Bible Belt. Progress is measured in terms of changed lives, not in months and years. Generally, however, a core group should take shape within the first year of the church planter's ministry. Once the church is officially organized, you no longer have a core group, but church members with whom to work.

There is no single method for developing a core group. What works in one community will not work in another. The church planter must determine which methods are most effective for him. Since people's responses vary according to culture, religion and social background, he should study the people in his community and then use whatever approach is best. A variety of methods may have to be tried before he finds the right one.

Four of the most effective methods for developing the core group are described below:

• Community Survey

The community survey is an effective tool for discovering prospects and developing a core group. It involves using a pre-printed form as you visit from door to door. It will help you locate prospects for the church, children for the Sunday school and will enable you to witness to those who would not otherwise listen to you.

Prepare yourself physically and spiritually for the occasion. Your appearance attracts or repels people. Be neat and well groomed. Brush your teeth, comb your hair and put on a clean shirt or dress. Men should wear ties. Remove your sunglasses when approaching a door. Eye contact is important. Pray and ask the Lord to empower you through the filling of the Holy Spirit. Be confident. Expect God to use you today.

Take a pen, a small New Testament, tracts, church brochures, a clipboard and a supply of the survey forms with you. (A sample survey form is located at the end of this chapter. These forms are available in quantity from Baptist Mid-Missions.)

"Secure a good map of the area and number each block. Make a 3x5 card showing the street and the four sides of the block, with the top of the card being north.

"Give each card a number, being careful that the boundaries agree with the number on the map. Always start on the northeast corner and go completely around the block. If you have to stop in the middle of the block, just note the last house you visited. Block in the area on the map with a red pen as soon as it is finished."[3]

As you approach a house, conversation should be kept to a minimum. Women are reluctant to open the door if they hear the voices of strange men outside. Knock loudly (door bells often do not work). Take a step backward and wait for the door to open. Have a smile on your face. If no one comes, knock again. If no one is home, leave a gospel tract and a church brochure. Record the address on the survey sheet with a note to return later. Go on to the next house.

When the door opens, introduce yourself and your partner (if you have one) with a smile and say:

> "Hello, my name is _____ and this is_____. We are from (name of your church) and we are trying to determine the religious thinking of the community. Will you help us by giving your opinion on a few brief questions?"

Many people are willing to help, especially since you want to know *their* opinion. However, if someone is unwilling to co-operate in answering the questions, pleasantly thank him for his time, give him your literature and go on to the next house. Do not stand there and argue with him.

If the person is cooperative, read the questions quickly and record his response to each one. Do not argue or show disapproval of his answers. You are there to gain information for future use. If he shows interest or is a good prospect, ask for his name and phone number as well.

When you have completed the survey form, thank them for their help and give them a tract and church brochure.

If your purpose is evangelistic, you may say:

> "Before I go, I wonder, did you know there is a verse in the Bible that says you can know you have eternal life? That you can be sure you will go to heaven when you die?"

Regardless of their answer, continue:

> "I'm concerned that you know for sure that you will go to heaven. Just before I go, could I show you that verse in the Bible? It'll only take a minute."

Take your New Testament from your pocket or purse as you speak. Normally the person will allow you to show him the verse. If not, thank him and leave graciously.

If the person allows you to show him the verse, say:

> "Thank you, I appreciate the opportunity to share this with you."

Hold the Bible where he can see it and slowly read First John 5:13 to him. Then explain:

> "The Bible was written to tell us how we can have eternal life. It begins by revealing that heaven (eternal life) is a free gift that cannot be earned nor deserved...."

You are now on your way to presenting the plan of salvation to the person. Not everyone will allow you to present the gospel to him. However, by using the survey form you will have more opportunities to witness and will see more people saved than would otherwise be true.

If a person is a good prospect, record pertinent information on a permanent prospect card. One copy of this should go to the pastor and the other to the visitation secretary.

## • Get Acquainted Meetings

Many church planters have found that holding three or four consecutive "get-acquainted" meetings is an effective means for gathering a nucleus. These meetings are informal, relaxed get-togethers in a private home where you explain your desire to build a church. Preferably, the meetings should take place in the home of an interested person other than the church planter. They should be held on an evening which does not conflict with the regular mid-week prayer services of area churches and when the most people can attend. We recommend the three Tuesday evenings prior to the first public service.

A number of preparations need to be cared for before hosting a "get-acquainted meeting." Literature must be prepared and print-ed, a constitution and doctrinal statement written, a weekly bud-get developed and contacts made. Visit forty to sixty hours each week, inviting people to attend the meeting.

**At the first meeting,** introduce yourself and your family. Tell about your background and experience. Have each person introduce himself or herself and share a little about his or her family. Keep the atmosphere relaxed and informal. No pressure should be placed on anyone to do anything.

Share with the group how God has burdened your heart to start a new church in the area. Tell of your desire to preach the gospel, see people saved, families restored and young people helped. Carefully present the plan of salvation, explaining how a person can be saved. Do not preach, just talk with them in a friendly manner. The invitation should be low-key, with those wanting to know more being asked to remain behind after the others are dismissed. Encourage the people to return the following Tuesday when you will tell them more about the new church. End the meeting by serving refreshments. Permit the guests to stay and chat with each other as long as they want.

The next day begin visiting for the next "get-acquainted" meet-ing. Again spend forty to sixty hours during the week knocking on doors and inviting people to come.

**At the second meeting** introduce the new people. Then explain what kind of church you plan to start. Emphasize that it will be one where the Bible is taught in every service, missions will receive high priority and people will be encouraged to trust Christ as their personal Savior.

Hand out a brief printed doctrinal statement and explain each point. Do not debate the doctrines, simply inform the people that this is the position of the new church you are starting. (See sample at the end of chapter 8).

Distribute a weekly budget. It should include funds for rent, advertising, supplies, missions and pastor's salary. Briefly review the budget and explain the principle of tithing. Ask the people to pray about what God would have them do to help the new church get started. Do not ask for any commitments at this time. You do not want people to misunderstand your motives and think you are only after their money. Dismiss the meeting with prayer and serve refreshments.

The next day, begin visiting for the final "get-acquainted" meeting. Again spend forty to sixty hours during the week seeking additional prospects.

**At the third "get-acquainted" meeting,** introduce the new prospects who have come. Give them copies of the doctrinal statement and weekly budget. Again explain that you are starting an independent Baptist church that will emphasize Bible teach-ing, soul winning and missions. As you make your doctrinal and denominational position clear, there will be a natural "weeding out" process. Some people will not remain with you when they learn the kind of church you plan to build. Do not be discouraged, this is a part of planting churches.

In a positive manner, explain your goals and the ministries you plan to develop. Share the challenge and sacrifice needed to make the church succeed. Tell them you need people who love the Lord, people who will be faithful, who will tithe and work to make the new church a reality. Challenge them to help you do a great work for God. Finally, invite everyone to be present for the first service on Sunday morning. Be sure they know the time and place.

By this time some people will have decided to join the work. Others will adopt a wait-and-see attitude, and some will drop out. Those who stay will form the core group. Select two or three men and teach them how to usher (greet visitors, hand out visitor's cards, and take offerings). Also appoint two or three responsible ladies to take care of the babies in the nursery when services begin.

In the weeks following the beginning of public services, main-tain a regular schedule of visitation, soul winning and discipling. This effort, coupled with solid preaching on basic doctrine and Christian growth, will further strengthen and enlarge the core group.

## • Home Bible Studies

As you survey the community, you will find people who are interested in attending a home Bible study. This can be an effective tool in gathering a nucleus for a new church. There are a number of advantages in this method: unsaved and unchurched people will come more readily, any size group can be accom-modated, it can be tailored to meet individual needs, costs are minimal and it provides a foothold in difficult areas.

Care must be exercised, however, to avoid the common pitfall of the home Bible study. Too often it becomes an end unto itself rather than a means to an end (see chapter 3). The goal of the home Bible study is to channel people into the church-planting ministry, not to build a perpetual study group meeting in private homes.

Set specific limits on what is to be taught and how long the classes are to last. It is recommended that each class period last no more than an hour or an hour and a half and that the study group meet for no more than three or four weeks. Keep the material simple and easy to understand.[4] You are only trying to whet their appetites, not create gourmet cooks. If people want more, invite them to attend the public services you will be starting.

Conduct your Bible studies in various locations around the community. This allows for smaller, more personal classes while giving you greater exposure. It is preferable that the studies not be held in your home. Find someone who will allow you to teach the class in his or her living room, providing a more neutral setting. Tell them you will be conducting the class for only three or four weeks and then stick to your word. Encourage class members to invite friends and neighbors to attend.

Inform each group of your plan to start a new church. Then channel the interested participants into the public services of the church. You should begin holding public services by the time the first home Bible study has completed its classes. You can continue to use additional home studies to channel new prospects into the church throughout its history.

## • Telephone Surveys

The telephone can be the church planter's best friend or his worst enemy. It all depends on how he uses it. Many apartments, condos and retirement communities are off limits to the home visitor. The phone removes the barriers and allows you to visit in every home. Care must be exercised, however, that this does not become a substitute for other methods which may be more effective.

There are definite advantages in conducting a telephone survey. It is economical and efficient. There are no fuel costs, no transportation problems and weather does not interfere. Virtually everyone has a phone and will answer it. It does not matter what they are doing, how they are dressed or what the house looks like. They will talk to you by phone when they will not open the door.

There are a few things to remember when conducting a telephone survey. First of all, identify yourself and explain why you are calling. Be friendly and courteous. Show genuine interest in the person you are talking to. Listen to what he has to say. You do not win people by talking to them, but by listening to them. They have problems, they are lonely and will share those feelings with a stranger over the phone if you take time to listen.

Speak slowly and distinctly into the phone. Do not rush the call. If you speak too fast, the person will not understand you or it will sound as if the call is a "canned" speech being read from a script.

Call at the right times. Avoid early morning and late night calls. Be careful about interrupting meal time. The best time to call is between

9:30 a.m. to 11:30 a.m.
1:00 p.m. to 3:00 p.m.
7:00 p.m. to 9:00 p.m.

Do not get sidetracked or drawn into an argument. Remember why you are calling. Use a printed form such as the "community survey" form at the end of this chapter to get the information you want. It will help you stay on track.

Obtain a phone directory that lists numbers according to the street address, rather than by name. The "Haynes Criss-Cross Directory" or the "Polk Directory" are excellent. They will enable you to cover the area more thoroughly as you call each home on the street. Begin with the streets nearest your meeting place and work out in all directions.

Using the survey form, fill in the name, address and phone number before placing the call. These are listed in the directory. If no one answers, try again later.

When a person answers the phone, introduce yourself immediately and tell them why you are calling:

> "Hello, my name is _____. I'm calling from the _____ Baptist Church in Coconut Creek. Our church is conducting a survey to determine the religious thinking of the community. Will you help us by giving me your opinion on a few brief questions? It will take only a moment or two."

If they refuse to anwer the questions, do not argue or be unpleasant. End the conversation on a high note. Simply say:

> "Thank you, I can appreciate how you feel. If we can ever be of service to you, please feel free to contact us or visit our services. Goodby for now."

Then hang up and record their response on the survey sheet.

In most cases, however, people will answer your questions. Read the questions in order, enunciating each one clearly and slowly. Check the appropriate response. Do not argue or show disapproval of their answers.

Invite each person contacted to your church. If they are already attending a church say:

> "Mr. Jones, that's fine, but I would still like to invite you to attend one of our services sometime. We have Sunday School for all ages, including adults, at 9:30 every Sunday morning.
> The morning service is at 10:30 when our pastor preaches right from the Bible and shows us how it applies to our lives. In the evening we have a special service at 6:00 o'clock with good singing and fellowship. We would love for you to pay us a visit sometime soon."

Many people in dead or liberal churches are looking for a church like yours. By telling them about your church, you are giving them the opportunity to choose something better. Be careful not to encourage people to leave good Bible-teaching churches.

Simply provide people with the information and leave the rest to the Holy Spirit.

If a person does not attend church, say:

> "Mr. Jones, since you are not now attending a church, let me extend a special invitation to you and your family to visit the services at our church this week. You will find a warm welcome there. We have Sunday School for.... (continue as you did above)."

Tell them you are looking forward to seeing them in church. If any interest is shown, offer to pick up the family or invite them to come to your home for the meal following the service. People need to know that you are really concerned about them.

You can even use the phone survey to create an opportunity to witness to people. After completing the survey form and having invited them to your church, simply say:

> "Mr. Jones, before I go, I wonder, did you know there is a verse in the Bible that says you can know you have eternal life? That you can be sure you will go to heaven when you die? Let me take just a moment to share that verse with you. It's found in I John 5:13."

Read the verse to them slowly, emphasizing the words "know" and "eternal life." Then continue:

> "Isn't that great! The Bible says that it is possible to know that you have eternal life. You see, God says that eternal life (heaven) is a free gift...."

You are now on your way to explaining the plan of salvation. Keep it simple and uninvolved. When you have completed the plan of salvation, ask:

> "Mr. Jones, does this make sense to you?" (Yes, it does.)

> Would you like to receive God's gift of eternal life right now by placing your trust in Jesus Christ who died for your sins?"

If the person is willing to accept Christ, lead him in the sinner's prayer right over the telephone. After leading the person to Christ, set up a time when you can go to visit him.

Not everyone you call will answer the survey questions or be a prospect or allow you to witness. Regardless of the response you receive, always end the conversation on a pleasant note, thanking the people for their help and cooperation. Leave a good impression when you hang up.

Note on the survey form which families are good prospects. Later in the week, send them a letter and plan to visit them soon. The letter might read like this:

Dear Mr. & Mrs. Jones:

During our recent telephone survey of the community, one of our members contacted you. They related to me how pleasantly you responded. As pastor of this church, I want you to know that I deeply appreciate your courtesy and interest.

I want you to know that, if as a pastor I can be of assistance to you, you may call on me at any time. Thank you for your kindness.

Sincerely yours,


Signed

Enclose a gospel tract and church brochure with your letter. Add the names of those you consider prospects to your prospect file and visit them as soon as possible. Do not let the contact grow cold through neglect. Churches in areas with restricted access have found the telephone to be an effective tool for reaching people. You can, too, if you will work at it.

## Endnotes

[1] The Polk Directory may be ordered from

R.L. Polk Co.
6400 Monroe Blvd.
Box 500
Taylor, Michigan 48180
(313) 292-3200

The "Blue Book" Cross Reference Directory may be ordered from

City Publishing Company, Inc.
118 South 8th
Independence, Kansas 67301
(316) 331-2650

[2] Order from

Brethren Missionary Herald Press
P.O. Box 544
Winona Lake, IN 46590
(Toll Free 1-800-348-2756)

[3] Grant G. Rice, *Church Planting Primer.* (Louisville, KY: Tabernacle Press. 1985), p. 49.

[4] Excellent home Bible study materials are available from

Baptist Mid-Missions
4205 Chester Avenue
Cleveland, Ohio 44103

Bethesda Baptist Church
7950 N., 650 E.
Brownsburg, IN 46112

# COMMUNITY SURVEY FORM

1. Do you attend a church or synagogue?    ☐ yes    ☐ no
2. (If yes) How often do you attend?
   ☐ weekly    ☐ occasionally    ☐ seldom
3. What denomination does your church or synagogue belong to?
   ☐ Baptist
   ☐ Catholic
   ☐ Church of Christ
   ☐ Episcopalian
   ☐ Jehovah's Witnesses
   ☐ Jewish
   ☐ Lutheran
   ☐ Methodist
   ☐ Mormon
   ☐ Non-denominational
   ☐ Pentecostal
   ☐ Presbyterian
   ☐ Seventh Day Adventist
   ☐ Other _____
4. Do your children attend Sunday School?    ☐ yes    ☐ no
5. Are you certain you will go to heaven when you die?    ☐ yes    ☐ no
6. In your opinion, how does a person get to heaven?
   ☐ baptism
   ☐ good works
   ☐ church membership
   ☐ Ten Commandments
   ☐ trust Christ (born again)
   ☐ love your neighbors
   ☐ live a good life
   ☐ other _____
7. Would you be interested in a Bible study in a private home in this neighborhood?
   ☐ yes    ☐ no

Name: _____    Date: _____

Address: _____    Phone: _____

Baptist Mid-Missions CPD Form No. 105

### Sample letter responding to a new baby announcement in newspaper

Dear _____,

It has come to my attention that the Lord has blessed your home with a new baby. I know these are days of excitement, thrill and happiness. We at (name of your church) want you to know that we enter into your joy during these days. We join the many others who have expressed congratulations to you.

I wish several things for the child: First, a healthy body; then strength of character and a good mind; and then most of all, spiritual perception and growth. It is certainly a tremendous obligation to be a mother or a father. May God give you wisdom to lead your children in spiritual matters.

May we invite you to attend the services of (name of your church) if you are not already attending a church? In any case, let me offer you our assistance if we can ever be of help to you.

Again congratulations and God bless you.

Sincerely,

### Sample letter responding to a wedding announcement in newspaper

Dear _____,

We have noticed in the local paper the announcement of your wedding. Upon behalf of me and the entire congregation (name of your church), we want to congratulate you and wish God's blessings upon you as you begin life together.

There is nothing as sacred as the marriage vows. God Himself is the author and the founder of the home. We trust that you will include Him in your new home.

Oftentimes such experiences bring us to recognize our need of Christ. We at the (name of your church) would like to offer our services to you if we can help you in any way. I, as pastor, or any of our members would be happy to be of service to you. If there is anything we can do, please feel free to contact us.

Again, may we say congratulations and God bless you.

Sincerely,

### Sample bereavement letter responding
### to a newspaper announcement

D e a r_____


  We have noticed in the local paper an announcement concerning the death of your loved one. On behalf of the entire membership of (name of your church) I extend to you our heartfelt
sympathy.
  It is always the desire of our church to be helpful in times of
sorrow. If we can help you in any way, we would be honored for
you to contact us.
  May God bless you in these difficult days! With warmest
personal regards, I am


                              Sincerely,

104

| BAPTIST MID-MISSIONS | | | | | | | |
|---|---|---|---|---|---|---|---|
| **VISITATION CARD**<br>**PERMANENT FILE** | | | | | | | |
| FAMILY NO | LAST NAME | | ADDRESS | | CITY | PHONE | MAP NO. |
| MEMBERS OF FAMILY | BIRTH | CLASS NO.<br>(PENCIL) | STATUS<br>S–Saved<br>M–Member | | GENERAL INFORMATION | | |
| | | | | | | | |
| | | | | | | | |
| | | | | | | | |
| | | | | | | | |
| | | | | | | | |
| | | | | | | | |
| | | | | | | | |
| | | | | | | | |
| | | | | | | | |
| | | | | | | | |

| | VISITOR | | | | | | | | | | | | | | | | | | | | | | | | | | | | |
|---|---|---|---|---|---|---|---|---|---|---|---|---|---|---|---|---|---|---|---|---|---|---|---|---|---|---|---|---|---|
| | DATE | | | | | | | | | | | | | | | | | | | | | | | | | | | | |

# Chapter 7

# The Public Beginning in Church Planting

How many people do you need in the core group before you begin holding public services? In the past some denominational leaders have maintained that a new church needed no fewer than a hundred families.[1] J.V. Thomas, noted church planter among Southern Baptists, believes a minimum of 12 to 24 committed adults is required. His experience has shown that this size core group properly prepared can produce at least 100 people in attendance at the first Sunday service.[2] On the other hand, some men have started with as few as one family, although this appears to reflect inadequate preparation and planning.

Since local circumstances differ greatly and there are always exceptions, no arbitrary minimum number can be established. As a general rule, however, you will need a higher number of people if you are seeking to reach those high on the socioeconomic scale and fewer if you are working with people on the lower end of the socioeconomic scale.

The ultimate test is faith. "The eye of faith is sometimes greater than the mind of reason."[3] Are you willing to trust God? Set a date for opening day and then work hard to see it brought to fruition. If you will pray and ask God for wisdom to select a realistic starting date and do the practical things recommended in this manual, you will be surprised at what God will do.

Before beginning any public services, implement the "preplanning" steps discussed in chapter 5. Use the following checklist to ensure that you have not overlooked anything:

1. Have you chosen a church name?
2. Have you established a checking account and mailing address for the church?
3. Have you located and rented a suitable meeting place?
4. Have you secured professionally lettered church signs?
5. Have you printed church brochures and letterheads?
6. Have you held at least three "get-acquainted" meetings?

7. Have you prepared promotional letters and literature for church visitors?
8. Have you made yourself known in the community?

The church planter who diligently cares for these eight items will discover that he is able to attract and retain the people he needs to start the church. Visitors will come, be impressed, and often stay with you. However, if you are unorganized and things are hastily thrown together, people will not come back. To organize a stable, self-governing, self-supporting church, you must have "detail people." These will be attracted if they see these qualities in you from the beginning.

As the date for starting public services approaches, you may get "itchy feet" and be tempted to begin before you are ready. To avoid starting prematurely, make yourself two more check lists–one for *things to do* and the other for *people to recruit* for the first service. These checklists will enable you to prepare adequately for a successful beginning.

## Things to do

• Saturate your community with advertisements and flyers.

Run ads in the local papers a few weeks prior to the beginning of public services to arouse curiosity and capture attention.

"Services will begin soon. Old-fashioned preaching and singing, Bible-centered curriculum designed to help face today's problems. For more information write: _____ Baptist Church, P.O. Box _____."

Then place a large ad in the most widely circulated newspaper in the area one week prior to your first Sunday service. A half-page ad is best. While this will be expensive, it will be money well spent to acquaint a large segment of the city with the church. Make the ad say something that will arouse interest. First impressions are important. Include who, what, when and where. Be sure the church name, date and location of the first service are in large letters. Include your picture and name as "pastor" (not "missionary" or that you are sponsored by a "mission").

Place a smaller paid ad in the newspaper each week thereafter. Let people know you are still there, what you believe and where you are going. Each week change the wording and placement of your ad, but not your picture. This gives the impression the church is growing. People go where they know to go; they cannot go to your church if they have never heard of it. Announce the title of your Sunday message and all special speakers. You might ask the newspaper office *not* to put your ad on the church page, but on the sports or movie page. Why? Because the kind of people (sinners) you want to reach usually do not read the religious section of the paper.

To further advertise your first public service, deliver a well written "press release" to all the newspapers in your area. Mail out "public service" announcements to local radio and television stations, post flyers in public places, and mail a personal invitation to everyone on your mailing list.

* Prepare your meeting place.

Once you have secured a suitable meeting place, it is essential that you make whatever improvements are needed to make the building attractive and as much like a church as possible. Vacuum the floor, dust the furniture and paint the room if necessary. You may have to do some remodeling. Do not be afraid to get your hands dirty. With a little bit of effort even an old building can be made to look nice.

Secure a pulpit and chairs. Check to see if a sponsoring church will loan or give you these. If you have to make the podium, be sure it looks nice. Natural wood grain, stained and finished, would be best. Chairs should be neatly arranged in an orderly fashion with a wide center aisle and side aisles so people can get in and out easily.

Prepare a room for the nursery. Cribs, a changing table, sheets, blankets, extra diapers and a container of pre-moistened baby washcloths should be available. You will find that in most areas the parents will be more willing to attend the services if they do not have to keep their baby with them during the service. This will vary, however, if you work with minorities and ethnic cultures.

Obtain a small organ or a piano which has been tuned, and position it so that the pianist or organist can see the songleader. Check to see if a sponsoring church or a friend will loan an instrument to you. If not, local music companies will often loan or rent you an instrument for a few months on consignment if they see you are interested in purchasing one in the near future.

Do not accept an instrument in poor condition since it most likely will be difficult to keep in tune.

Make your building appear as nice as possible. You might place a banner across the front welcoming the people. Prepare a nice display stocked with literature about the new church and the fel- lowship of churches with which you will be affiliated. Finally, erect a church sign in front of the building so people can locate you easily.

● Prepare for the offering and finances.

If you do not have offering plates, you can buy inexpensive wooden salad bowls from a discount store and glue a piece of felt in the bottom of each bowl to muffle the sound of coins. Usually two to four offering plates are sufficient. Purchase check-size of- fering envelopes from a Christian bookstore. You can have the name of the new church imprinted on them for a small fee.

Purchase a good bookkeeping system and a financial ledger for recording individual contributions. A good bookkeeping system not only ensures accuracy but helps to gain the confidence of prospective members. You can use the simple system described in chapter thirteen, or purchase the "McBee System." This is actual- ly a simple form of double-entry bookkeeping. As checks are written, the figures are automatically entered into the ledger. The system can be expanded as the church grows. Since few church planters or their members have accounting experience, this is an excellent investment. (For more information write McBee Systems, P.O. Box 948, Newark, N.J. 07101.)

● Prepare a bulletin and information cards

To ensure a smooth-running service, prepare a bulletin listing the order of service, times of future services and announcements. Do not mimeograph it. It is best to have it quick-printed on standard bulletin stock which can be ordered from Cathedral Press, Box A, Long Prairie, MN 56347. If you have a number of future events listed in the bulletin such as special speakers, camp (with nearby sister churches), youth activities and a visitation night, visitors will be impressed that this new church has a full program.

Have a good supply of visitor's cards to distribute to all visitors in the services. They can be purchased at a Christian bookstore or you can have your own printed by a quick-copy printer.

Also prepare salvation packets for those who will be saved. They should include a decision card, tracts on salvation and baptism and a copy of the Gospel of John. Set aside a designated place for counseling and keep a supply of packets within easy reach of the counselors.

## People to Train

In order to begin the church, you need a few dependable workers. Pray to the Lord of the Harvest for laborers. Ask God for them. From the "get-acquainted" meetings you have held and the list of interested people you are making, you should be able to secure the cooperation of five or six adults before your first service. If you cannot, you are not ready to start. Some people will be able to fill more than one area of responsibility. The following workers are essential for a good first service.

### • Nursery Workers

You need someone who is cheerful and responsible to register the babies, care for them lovingly and keep the nursery clean. Several ladies can share this responsibility. However, your wife may have to oversee the nursery until someone can be trained to take over. Young couples who are your best prospects will see that they are welcome and wanted if this is properly done.

### • Ushers

The number of men you will need is determined by the size of your meeting place and the crowd you expect. After enlisting several for this task, carefully go over with them the list of responsibilities at the end of this chapter. Explain how you want them to perform each task. Do not assume they know how. Often they do not.

Show them how you want them to seat visitors, to walk the aisle, where to begin passing the offering plates, how to bring the offering forward. Explain to your ushers where to get the visitor's cards, when to distribute and collect them and how to keep the building properly ventilated or heated. Ask them to be present at least fifteen minutes before each service. Stress the importance of their job. If they do their job smartly as a team, people will sense that you have your act together as a church. (Judson Press has published a helpful book, *The Work of the Usher*, by Alvin Johnson.)

## • A Song Leader

Unless you have an experienced song leader, it is best for you to lead the song service until you can train someone to fill this vital role. This person need not have a great deal of musical talent, but he does have to be able to carry a tune and have some leadership potential. Be sure he understands the only thing you want him to do is lead the group in singing; you do not want him to tell stories or give a testimony before each verse.

Practice the songs with him ahead of time so that there will be no surprises during the service. Teach him the proper way to an-nounce a song (the number is given at least twice–before and after the title–in a voice loud enough for everyone to hear). Select songs which are well-known, enthusiastic and doctrinally sound. As time progresses, teach him to recognize and conduct songs ac-cording to their time patterns (2, 3 and 4 beats). Your song leader will either make or break your service.

## • Musicians

Ask God to give a good pianist or organist. This will be a real asset to starting the church. If your wife does not play and no one can be found, you can still sing a cappella by using familiar hymns. Be sure the instrumentalists know the order of service and how you want the music played.

Arrange to have special music for your first service. If you do not have any in your core group, invite someone from another church, Bible school or special singing group. Be sure that the music meets your standards and is well rehearsed. Since the music in your first service sets the precedent for the future, it is better to have little or no special music than to have music that is poorly done or that dishonors the Lord!

## • Personal Workers

Before the first service, train some people how to deal with those who respond to the invitation and how to lead a person to Christ. Show them how to fill out a decision card and where you want them to counsel with those who come forward, whether at the altar or in an adjoining room.

## • Special Guests

If you are working in a small city or town, you might consider inviting several local personalities to your first service. Among these could be the mayor, city councilmen, state representative, your banker, the police chief, firemen and any other public figures or businessmen you have contacted. Explain to each one what will happen and that you will recognize their presence. If they consent to come and bring words of welcome to the new church, this could be included in the newspaper and media announcements.

You can also invite out-of-town relatives and friends from your school or home church. Do everything possible to get a good crowd there for your first service. Remember, it takes a crowd to draw a crowd.

After completing the "things to do" and "people to train" check-lists, you are ready to begin public services.

## The Day Before

The Saturday before the church's first public service should be spent doing two things: canvassing and praying. Assemble as large a team of workers as possible to aid you in distributing the flyers you have had printed. These flyers should invite folks to your "inaugural services." Secure the help of students from a nearby Bible college, supporting churches and local believers who have indicated their commitment to the new church. Have them spend the entire day going door-to-door passing out flyers.

Begin working out from the immediate location of your meeting place and cover as many residences as possible. If your team of workers spends 8-10 hours, you should be able to distribute 2,000 - 3,000 flyers quite easily. Do not spend a lot of time at each house, just enough to give a cheerful hello, hand them a flyer and invite them to come Sunday.

Late that afternoon or early evening, plan to have all the workers meet together at your meeting place for a prayer meeting. Emotions will be running high by now. Trust God for a great day on Sunday and ask for His blessing. Expect God to work in that first service. Nothing of eternal value will be accomplished apart from the power and blessing of God. If you are going to bring a true New Testament church into this world, you will need to bathe all your hard work in earnest prayer.

## The Big Day

You should be the first to arrive early Sunday morning. Be sure everything is set up and ready to go: envelopes, hymn books (or song sheets), visitor's and decision cards, musical instruments, pulpit, chairs, bulletins and copies of the printed budget.

Have the ushers arrive fifteen minutes early and go over their job responsibilities again. Have them greet the people at the door as they arrive. You should personally meet people with a smile and a handshake. Be sure everyone gets a visitor's card.

Begin the service promptly at 10:30 or 11:00 (or whatever time has been announced) with a rousing congregational song. Greet the people and thank them for coming. Make them feel glad they came. Take time to tell briefly what you are doing and what you hope to accomplish. Share some of your goals and vision. This really should be the only hint that you are a new church: everything else should look as if you have been doing this for years! It's important that you not wear people out with long speeches or try to squeeze out a commitment in this first service. That will come in time.

The song leader should then lead another song. As it closes, while the pianist is still playing, have everyone turn, shake hands and greet their neighbors. In future services this is a good time to greet visitors. Make the church warm and friendly from the start.

As the folks sit down, ask them to fill out the visitor's card they have received. Explain that you want a record of their visit on this important occasion. Instruct them either to pass the cards to the center aisle or to drop them into the offering plate when it is passed. Remember, these are your best prospects for future calling.

Special music or another congregational hymn should be next in your order of service. This will be followed by the announcements and offering. Don't be reluctant to receive one on this first

Sunday, even if the crowd is small. What you do now establishes the pattern for later.

To prepare for the offering you might say something like this: "We will worship the Lord now in the giving of our tithes and offerings. You will find a printed offering envelope in your bulletin. If you have not already prepared your offering, you may do so at this time. Make your checks payable to (church name). We do not believe in any kind of fundraising, sales or pressuring Christians to give. It is our conviction that God will provide for His work through the giving of His people. We appreciate the financial help you give through your gift to this ministry. Your gifts are tax deductible. Ushers, please come forward at this time."

As the ushers stand at the front, introduce the man who is serving as the treasurer. Explain that all money received is counted and deposited in the church's bank account and will be used for the furtherance of this ministry. Explain that each month the church will distribute a complete financial statement listing all receipts and expenditures. Encourage them to pick up a copy of the monthly church budget from the back table before they leave.

This detailed explanation at the first service is designed to instill confidence in the minds of the people. You want to destroy any idea that you as a pastor are making personal profit from this enterprise or that you are personally handling the money which comes in. If you are thorough and reputable, God will bless your offerings from the beginning.

Now pray and thank God for the offering you are about to receive and for what He is going to do through the church's out-reach. When you say "Amen," the ushers should immediately turn and receive the offering together, beginning at the front and working their way to the back. Be sure the organist or pianist is prepared to play an offertory during this time while you remain on the platform.

Continue using this procedure for taking the offering in future services: 1) point out the financial need, 2) encourage everyone to take part--even the children, 3) give each person an offering en-velope (this encourages people to give by providing a confidential means of giving) and 4) remind them of the blessing of giving.

Have the congregation stand for another hymn. Following this song, you may want the people to continue standing while you read the Scripture and pray for God's blessing on the message. A special musical number is also appropriate here.

Your Bible message on this special occasion should be simple, salvation-oriented and brief--no more than thirty minutes long.

Prepare a vibrant, enthusiastic sermon that will present Christ and stir hearts without antagonizing people. Let them clearly see that this is going to be a Bible-preaching church. Give a clear invitation and then share with the congregation any decisions which are made. End on a note of optimism and joy in the Lord.

As you dismiss the service, invite everyone back to the evening service at 6:00 (or whatever time is best in your area). Sound excited at what is planned for the evening service but do not pres - sure the people. If you have given them something solid, Biblical and practical, a good number will return for more.

If you have done all that you can do and bathed the occasion in prayer, the new church should have a glorious first Sunday. Some people may be saved, and the whole group will go away with the assurance that God is behind this work.


## The Day After

On Monday spend time evaluating your first day's ministry and each step taken. Ask God to help you see your strengths and weaknesses. How can you improve next week's service by building on your strengths? Three things should be considered:


• Evaluate the spiritual response

Did it seem as if the Spirit of God was present and working? Were people saved, decisions made and believers helped in their lives? Were people later testifying of blessings from the service, music or message? If not, why not? Do some honest soul searching.


• Evaluate the financial response

Money is ministry and ministry is money. This is a good barometer of what is going on in people's lives spiritually. No church will go far without finances. In a new church there is nothing that commands their support except its leader. People will tend to support you before they will support the church. If you have convinced them you are worthy and reliable, they should respond by giving. Be sure you keep accurate records and analyze the giving each week.

• Evaluate the numerical response

Although it is true that numbers are not everything, it is also true that each number represents a person. We must be concerned about reaching and holding as many people as possible. Every church has its high and low days, but you should be concerned about your average attendance at each service. Good records are vital–be sure your ushers get an accurate count for each service.

If things are not happening in these three areas–spiritual, financial and numerical–then little is happening in the church planter's heart! This kind of self-evaluation is needed regularly in a new ministry to keep you from getting off track

At this point the die is cast and you have made either a good or a poor mold from which to work. Do not feel the work is done just because you had a good first day. Obviously it has only begun. You must continue doing the same meticulous job and organize this fledgling group into a proper New Testament church. What should you do after your first Sunday? More of the same!

## When to Begin Other Weekly Services

Your first Sunday should be limited to morning and evening services unless you have a committed core of Christians who are experienced Sunday-school teachers. If this is not the case, wait until the third, fourth or fifth week to begin Sunday School. This will give you time to see who is going to be faithful and to train them. You should personally recruit all teachers, explaining the standards and responsibilities of each. (See chapter eleven.)

Begin midweek services immediately. A prayer meeting/Bible study will help you conserve the fruit from the first service and will show who your committed people are. It can be a natural carry-over of the "get-acquainted" meetings you held on Tuesday evenings before beginning public services.

It can be held either in the regular meeting place or in the homes of your people. Consider holding the service on Tuesday or Thursday night rather than the traditional Wednesday evening. This allows members of other churches to visit without missing their own services. It also permits you to speak in sister churches on Wednesday to raise support.

Introduce other new activities to the church as the need arises, but only if an adequate job can be done without putting a strain on the other ministries. The introduction of new features gives the impression of progress. Hopefully you will have a full schedule of services within three or four months from your first service.

The foundation is the most tedious part of a structure to build. Although it is the least visible, it is that part of the structure upon which everything else rests. So it is with the building of a new church. The practical guidelines given in this manual may seem unimportant and you may be tempted to overlook them. But they are necessary for a healthy beginning. Do not take any shortcuts. Carefully map out a clear-cut strategy of how and when you are going to start. Then you will be able to proceed with confidence and will find that people are more willing to follow your leadership.

### Endnotes

[1] Fredrick A Shippey, *Church Work in the City.* (New York: Abingdon, Cokesberry Press, 1952), pp. 228-230.

[2] J.V. Thomas, *How To Plant a Church Seminar.* (Pasadena, CA: Charles E. Fuller Institute of Evangelism and Church Growth, n.d.), author's notes.

[3] Elmer Towns, *Getting A Church Started.* (Lynchburg, VA: Impact Books, 1975), p. 140.

## Guidelines for Ushers

1. View your job as a ministry, one to be done with dignity to the glory of God.
   a. Be present at least 15 minutes before the service begins.
   b. Be well groomed, with your hair combed, your teeth brushed and your shoes polished.
   c. It is preferable that ushers wear coats and ties.
   d. Avoid chewing gum and whispering among yourselves.
2. Make friends for the church by greeting people with a warm smile and friendly handshake.
3. Distribute whatever materials are appropriate as people arrive:
   a. Bulletins should be handed to each adult or couple. Do not leave bulletins lying on the table for people to pick up.
   b. First time guests should be encouraged to sign the guestbook or be given a visitor's card to fill out.
   c. Be sure the literature table is arranged neatly.
4. Help parents and children find the appropriate Sunday-school class or nursery facilities.
5. Assist people in finding good seating near the middle and front of the auditorium.
   a. Seats in the rear should be reserved for latecomers, those with small children and those who must leave early.
   b. Do not allow people to enter the auditorium during prayer, Bible reading, special music or the invitation.
   c. Put up additional chairs whenever necessary.
   d. Count the number of people present in the building for each service.
6. Check the building before and after each service.
   a. Make sure there are adequate song books available.
   b. Maintain proper ventilation and temperature.
   c. Check on the nursery to be sure they have adequate help before you sit down for the service.
   d. Be sure the restrooms are clean, fresh smelling and properly supplied.
7. Assist in receiving the tithes and offerings.
   a. Walk forward together in step with each other
   b. Avoid extreme attitudes of pomposity or levity
8. Keep children from running within the confines of the church.
9. Be alert for signals from the pastor
10. Notify the head usher if you cannot be in your place at the assigned time so he can arrange for a substitute.

# Section III..

**Chapter 8.**.....The Organization of the Local Church

        Develop the Paperwork
        Formally Organize the Church
        Call a Recognition Council
        Secure Legal Documents

**Chapter 9.**.....The Oversight of the Local Church

        Setting Goals
        Conducting Business Meetings
        Church Officers and Workers
        The Team Ministry

**Chapter 10.**....The Orientation of the Local Church Services

        The Morning Service
        The Evening Service
        The Prayer Meeting Service
        The Nursery
        The Children's ChurchSpecial Meetings
        The Youth Ministry
        The Music Program
        The OrdinancesThe Invitation

**Chapter 11.**....The Operation of the Local Church Sunday
           School

        The Purpose of the Sunday School
        The Organization of the Sunday School
        The Classroom Space in the Sunday
           School
        The Equipment in the Sunday School
        The Curriculum of the SundaySchool
        Choosing & Training Teachers for the
           Sunday School
        Sunday School Contests

The Openings and Closings in Sunday
    School
Audio-Visuals in the Sunday School

**Chapter 12**... The Outreach of the Local Church

The Place of the Pastor in the Missionary
    Program
Organizing a Missionary Program
Giving to Missions
The Missionary Closet
Visit the Mission Field

# Chapter 8

# The Organization
# of the Local Church

The church is both a living organism and a local organization. Organization is essential if the church is to function effectively. In New Testament times, the church found it necessary to develop a structure to care for the needs of its people. The calling of a pastor, the election of officers, the discipline of members and the day-by-day administration of the church require some form of organization.

Care must be exercised not to organize the church too soon. Haste in this area will bring heartache later on. There is a form-ative stage each church goes through while the core group is being developed. This is frequently accompanied by a turnover of peo-ple. A nucleus of eight to twelve adults should be gathered before attempting to organize the church formally. It is hoped that this can be done within three or four months after beginning public services.

The organization of the church should be preceded by compre-hensive teaching in the following areas:

1. Basic Bible doctrine or comprehensive study of each section of the Statement of Faith,
2. Baptist practice and polity, that which distinguishes a Bap-tist church from other organizations and churches,
3. A thorough study of the local church, its work, ministry and role in world missions,
4. A detailed study of the ordinances and their meaning,
5. The responsibilities and privileges of church membership.

There are four basic steps in organizing a church:

## Develop the Paperwork

Several documents need to be prepared before organizing the church. The church planter should develop them before begin-ning the work. This ensures that the new church will be of sound doctrine and of like faith with its sponsoring churches. It also avoids the disunity which can arise as a result of new believers from many different backgrounds trying to write documents they do not fully understand.

**The charter of the church.** This is a formal statement in which the group declares itself to be an autonomous church with authority from Christ to exercise all the rights and responsibilities of a New Testament assembly. The charter may be worded in such a way as to approve the adoption of other church documents or they may be adopted separately.

**The covenant of the church.** This is the agreement which binds the church together. It is a statement of purpose and desire attested to by each member as a part of the local Body of Christ. It is a summary of New Testament teaching of the privileges and responsibilities of church membership.

**The constitution of the church.** This is the document by which the church is governed. It sets forth the rules, regulations and requirements for membership and leadership. It describes the administrative procedures by which the church is to be conducted.

**The creed of the church.** This is the doctrinal statement of the church detailing its beliefs. It is an expanded version of the brief Statement of Faith that was distributed at the "get-acquainted" meetings. It should touch on all the major doctrines and clearly set forth the church's position.

**The church planting agreement.** Missionary church planters working with Baptist Mid-Missions need to acquire copies of the "Baptist Mid-Missions Church Planting Agreement for North America" from their mission agency. This is an agreement the mission and the church each sign. It establishes the terms for the services of a missionary pastor.

(Samples of each of the above documents may be found at the end of this chapter.)

Many mistakes and unforeseen difficulties can be avoided by listening to the counsel of godly men who are more experienced in these areas. Seek out their advice. Examine the official documents of other Baptist churches for help.


## Formally Organize the Church

The charter, covenant, constitution and creed should be carefully explained to the core group. Each document should be presented as a unit rather than paragraph by paragraph. This will avoid misunderstandings and hurt feelings. While some may not agree with everything they contain, changes should not be made which weaken or alter the position of the church. Only those in agreement with the documents should become part of the new church.

Next, choose a date for constituting and organizing the church. Be certain everyone knows the date, time and place for the meet- ing. On the appointed day, open the meeting with singing and prayer. Allow for a time of testimonies when the people can share their joy on this special occasion. Have another pastor or a mis- sion administrator moderate the meeting if possible. Otherwise, you as the church planter may do so.

The meeting should be called to order and a clerk appointed to record the proceedings for future reference in a ledger secured be- forehand for this purpose. Review the development of the group and explain the purpose of the meeting.

A chartering resolution should then be read and adopted. (See a sample resolution at end of this chapter.) "The adoption of this resolution forms the company of believers into a local church with all the rights and privileges of a New Testament church."[1] Those who vote in favor of the resolution should then sign the charter, having previously been examined to determine their eligibility for membership.

Once the constituting act has been approved, the church may administer the ordinances. Unbaptized members of the core group should be baptized and sign the charter, thus becoming part of the "charter membership." The church should vote to keep this "charter membership" open for two or three months to allow other believers to become part of the initial church family.

A vote should then be taken to call you (the church planter) as the pastor of the church. If you are a missionary, have the church approve the "Church-Planting Agreement" required by your mis- sion agency.

Now elect or appoint a church clerk and a treasurer. These should be spiritually mature people who attend regularly. The election of deacons should be postponed until the church has had time to adjust to its new status and to determine which men are qualified to serve in this important office. Too often, people have been put in the place of leadership when they were not spiritually qualified. Perhaps they held a similar position in another church or have been instrumental in helping to start the church. This can undermine the entire ministry at its inception. An interim advisory council may be appointed from which deacons can later be selected.

The church should next adopt a budget. This may be the one under which it has been functioning during its formative stage or a revised financial plan to carry it through until the end of the year. It should include funds for the pastor's salary, missions and a building program. Also vote to receive the financial records and bank accounts from the formative stage of the church.

The church is now officially organized and ready to begin functioning as a local congregation. The meeting should be adjourned in prayer with thanksgiving. Serving the Lord's Supper or a fellowship meal will make a delightful end to the proceedings. If the Lord's Table is served, stress the principle that believers must be baptized before they can partake.

## Call a Recognition Council

A recognition council is a group of pastors and representatives from other churches of like faith and practice who have been invited to examine the charter, covenant, constitution and creed of the newly formed church. This is not a necessary procedure for the group to become a church. It is already a church by virtue of its constituting act.

A recognition council encourages public support of the newly formed church by verifying that it is properly organized and biblically orientated. People will know that this is a genuine church and not a cult or non-Christian group. It gives other churches the opportunity to get to know the church and to determine their relationship to the new work. Some state and national fellowships and associations require a recognition council be held before they will accept a church into their group.

A recognition council should be called as soon as possible after the church is organized. Letters stating the date, time, place and purpose for the council should be sent to all churches of like faith and practice in surrounding areas. Copies of the charter, covenant, constitution and creed should also be enclosed. Usually the pastor and two messengers are invited from each church. (A sample letter may be found at the end of this chapter.)

A recognition council is conducted very much like an ordination council. The church planter should welcome the members of the council and read the letter calling for the council. A moderator and clerk are then chosen from the group to conduct the proceedings.

Normally, the church planter will serve as spokesman for the new church. He should explain how it came into existence and answer any questions the council may have. Copies of the church's charter, covenant, constitution and creed should be available for those council members who do not already have them. These will be examined carefully by the council and any questions they have will be addressed to the pastor.

When the council has completed its examination, it will either vote its approval or disapproval of the church. If the vote is favorable, a "certificate of recognition" is signed by council members. Later that evening or on a future date, a "recognition service" can be held at which time the church is recommended to the public as a duly organized and biblically sound Baptist church worthy of their support and fellowship. (A sample of each of the documents mentioned may be found at the end of this chapter.)

## Secure Legal Documents

It is recommended that every new church in the United States be incorporated as a non-profit organization. This is a separate step taken after organizing the church. While incorporation is not necessary for the church to exist and function, it does grant the church legal status, much protection and many privileges. By incorporating, the church can buy, sell and hold property in its own name. It will be able to borrow money, make contracts and in some states and provinces may qualify you for tax exemptions. Individual members will be protected from legal suits which may be brought against the church as well.

> "A Corporation is a legal entity created by law, with an identity distinct and separate from that of its members or organizers, and endowed with certain powers and franchises to be exercised in its designated corporate name. It is a fictitious person existing in contemplation of law."[2]

A simple incorporation form for a church can be secured at the court house or from the secretary of state. However, in light of current legal actions involving churches and because of changing state laws, you should consult with a competent lawyer for advice before filing your incorporation papers. (See a sample at the end of this chapter.) The laws in Canada regarding incorporation differ greatly from those in the United States and even between provinces. For information on the incorporation and registration of churches in British Columbia, Canada, contact:

The Office of the Registrar of Companies
Ministry of Consumer and Corporate Affairs
940 Blanshard Street
Victoria, B.C. V8W 3E6

The church will need to appoint trustees when it incorporates. They may be either the deacons of the church or a separate group responsible for the legal affairs of the church.

In the United States, every church qualifies for exemption from Federal income taxes and may receive tax deductible contributions under Section 501 (a) of the Internal Revenue Code as a "religious" organization described in Section 501 (c) (3) of the Code.

However, the tax-exempt status of some religious groups is being denied by the IRS. Two basic guidelines must be met to qualify as a tax-exempt religious group:

1. The religious beliefs of the organization must be truly and sincerely held, and
2. The practices and rituals associated with the organization's beliefs must not be illegal or contrary to clearly *defined public policy.*

To avoid having their tax-deductible status called in question, some churches are filing IRS Form 1023. This form in effect grants you IRS recognition as a tax-exempt religious organization and removes all doubt about your standing before the government. However, this raises the question of "state licensure" of the church. Each church should carefully evaluate this issue before filing for what might be interpreted as permission to function as a church.

Churches which are part of a fellowship, an association or a mission agency are usually covered by that group's tax-exempt status.

Every local church is required to have a nine-digit "Federal Employer Identification Number" (EIN). Even if the church has no employees (the pastor is self-employed), it still must obtain the EIN for use in all correspondence, forms and documents submitted to the federal government. This may be obtained by filing IRS Form SS-4, "Application for Employer Identification Number."

To be exempt from state sales taxes, the church must obtain a "certificate of exemption" from the State Department of Revenue.

This will save the church considerable money, especially when it is in a building program. A lawyer will help you file the proper forms.

The need to prepare carefully your charter, covenant, constitution and creed, and to file your incorporation papers and other legal documents cannot be stressed too strongly. Many heartaches and legal problems will be avoided if you properly care for these items at the beginning of your church-planting ministry.

## Endnotes

1 J. Irving Reese, *A Guide for Organizing and Conducting a Baptist Church.* (Elyria, OH: J. Irving Reese Publications, 1962), p. 24.

2 Richard F. Schmidt, *Legal Aspects of Church Management.* (Los Angeles, CA: Christian Ministries Management Association, 1984), p. 31.

# Charter

*of the*

(name of church)

(city, state)

On this        day of                    we the undersigned, having received Jesus Christ as our personal Savior and being baptized by immersion in obedience to His command, do hereby constitute ourselves to be an independent Baptist church patterned after the New Testament example.

Moreover, this church through the authority invested in it by Jesus Christ shall have the right to administer the ordinances of believer's baptism by immersion and the Lord's Supper and shall seek the salvation of the lost through the proclamation of the Gospel while encouraging one another in Christian love.

Furthermore, this church shall be governed by the will of God as revealed in the Holy Scriptures and in accordance with the covenant, constitution and articles of faith which we do hereby adopt by the affixing of our signatures to this document.

Sample # 1

## Church Covenant

Having been led by the Spirit of God to receive the Lord Jesus as my personal Savior, and having been immersed in obedience to His Word, I enter into covenant with the members of this local representation of the Body of Christ. I promise by the aid of the Holy Spirit to:

Honor Jesus Christ through my efforts to advance His cause; by seeking the salvation of my relatives and acquaintances; by having family and personal devotions; and by training my children according to the Word of God.

Help this church by promoting its spirituality, program and prosperity and by attending its services regularly.

Walk in Christian love by avoiding gossip, slander and anger; by praying for the members of this church and helping them in sickness or distress; by cultivating Christian empathy and courtesy; and by being sincere and without offense.

Walk wisely by being honest and exemplary in my conduct; by dressing modestly and appropriately; and by abstaining from anything that would be a detriment to my testimony for Christ. Furthermore, I promise to abstain from the use of alcoholic beverages and/or drugs for non-medicinal purposes.

If I move from this area, I will unite as soon as possible with another Bible-believing, fundamental Baptist church in which I can carry out the principles of the Word of God and the spirit of this covenant.

Sample # 2

## Membership Covenant

Having been brought together providentially by our common relationship to Jesus Christ as our Savior, and having a mutual desire to serve Him faithfully as our Lord, we do now both solemnly and joyfully enter into covenant with one another as a body of baptized believers comprising a New Testament local church.

WE PURPOSE THEREFORE to live daily by the strength and guidance of God's Holy Spirit; to search the Scriptures regularly and faithfully for direction in personal, family and church life; to seek the salvation of souls for whom Christ died; to strive heartily for the building up of this Body of Christ in faith, hope and love; and to function within the Body according to the gift(s) given each one for its benefit.

WE FURTHER PURPOSE to put away from us progressively the patterns of thought, word and deed of the "old life," putting in its place the patterns of the "Christ-life"; to do all things to the glory of God and in the name of the Lord Jesus; to exercise our Christian liberty in such a way as not to grieve, offend or cause our brother to stumble; and to recognize the Bible as the final Authority in all relationships with one another.

TO THESE ENDS WE PURPOSE to consider the local church an essential part of our lives; to pray for, encourage and submit to the rightful authority of its leadership; to attend its meetings when not providentially hindered; to support financially its ministry as God enables and directs; to guard its public testimony; and in any way possible to further its goals of reaching the lost and teaching the believer.

THIS COVENANT WE MAKE GLADLY, in humble dependence upon the Spirit of God for the power to carry out its provisions.

## Suggested Basic Constitution for Baptist Churches

### Article I - Name

The name of this church shall be _____ Baptist Church in (city) and the state of (state) and shall be so incorporated under the laws of this State.

### Article II - Purpose

The purpose of this church shall be:

1. To evangelize the lost through personal soul-winning, visitation and preaching of the Word of God;
2. To edify believers through the systematic teaching of the Bible;
3. To establish fundamental Baptist churches around the world through an energetic missionary program;
4. To carry out the scriptural responsibilities of an autono- mous Baptist church in accordance with the principles of God's Word;
5. To earnestly contend for the faith which was once delivered to the saints (Jude 3,4).

### Article III - Associations and Cooperation

**Section 1.**

This church shall be an independent, autonomous Baptist church subject only to Jesus Christ, its Head. It has the right to cooperate and associate with other biblical groups on a vol- untary basis.

**Section 2.**

This church shall not associate nor cooperate with any person or group which is a part of or approves of liberalism, neo-evangelicalism, the charismatic movement, secret soci- eties or cults (II Corinthians 6:14-17; Romans 6:17; I Timothy 6:3-5).

### Article IV - Articles of Faith

(Insert your articles of faith.)

### Article V - Membership

**Section 1. Reception of Members**

A. Membership in this church shall be open to all those who
   1. Profess to be born-again through faith in Jesus Christ;

2. Have been baptized by immersion following the profession of faith in Christ;
3. Seek to live a Christ-honoring life;
4. Are in agreement with the Covenant, Constitution and
Articles of Faith of this church.
Membership shall not be denied to any person on the
basis of race, color, sex or social status.

B. Candidates may be received into membership by majority
vote of the church in one of four ways:
1. Baptism by immersion following salvation;
2. A letter of recommendation from another church of like
faith;
3. Statement of Christian experience (when it is impossible
to secure a church letter), provided the candidate has
been saved and immersed;
4. Restoration to membership after having been dismissed
from membership.

C. All candidates for baptism and/or membership shall be
interviewed by the pastor and deacons. They shall give
satisfactory evidence of their conversion, Christian experience and acceptance of the covenant, constitution and
articles of faith of this church. The pastor and deacons shall
recommend qualified candidates to the church for
appropriate action.

**Section 2. Discipline of Members**

A. The purpose of church discipline shall be
1. To help errant members recognize and repent of their
sins so they may be restored to fellowship with the Lord
and this church (Galatians 6:1);
2. To maintain the purity of this church by removing those
who are unrepentant toward their sins (I Cor. 5:7,11);
3. To restrain others from committing sin (I Timothy 5:20).

B. Any unscriptural attitude, action or violation of the church
covenant may be deemed sufficient cause for discipline.
Situations which may require disciplinary action shall be
handled by the pastor and deacons confidentially. Discipline may include loss of office, placement on the inactive
list or dismissal from membership. Dismissal from
membership shall be by vote of the church.

C. Members who are absent from the services of this church for
a period of 90 days without due cause shall be placed on the
inactive membership list. Those on the inactive list may
not vote, hold office or serve in the church.

D.  Persons on the inactive list who desire to be restored to full membership shall meet with the pastor and deacons to give satisfactory evidence of a repentant attitude and renewed interest. The full privileges of membership may be restored to them by vote of the church upon the recommendation of the pastor and deacons.

E.  Persons whose names remain on the inactive list for nine months shall be removed from membership by vote of the church.

## Section 3.  Termination of Membership

A.  Members who unite with other churches shall be removed from membership. Letters of dismissal with a recommendation may be sent upon request to other churches of like faith for those members in good standing.

B.  Members who have been on the inactive list for nine months shall be removed from membership.

C.  Members who are disciplined by exclusion shall be removed from membership.

D.  Members who have died shall be removed from membership.

## Article VI - Ordinances

Ordinances are ceremonies established by the Lord Jesus Christ which He gave as symbolic reminders to the Church.

### Section 1. Baptism

Those professing faith in Jesus Christ as their personal Savior shall, upon authorization of the church, be immersed in water by the pastor or someone appointed by the church. Those who are baptized shall at the same time be received into the membership of this church. This church shall not baptize infants.

### Section 2. The Lord's Supper

The Lord's Supper shall be served at regular intervals to the assembled church by the pastor and deacons. Since it is the Lord's Supper, none who are born-again and baptized by immersion shall be barred. The pastor shall explain the meaning of the ordinance, encouraging those present to examine their own lives before participating. The elements shall be unleavened bread and grape juice.

## Article VII - Officers
### Section 1. Officers and Leaders

A. The elected officers of the church shall be pastor and deacons, clerk, treasurer and financial secretary.

B. No person shall be elected to office who has not been a member of this church for at least six months. All officers and leaders shall be spiritually mature, loyal to the Word of God, faithful in attendance and support of the regular services and business meetings of the church. Their moral conduct shall be beyond reproach and free of carnal indulgences, such as the use of intoxicating beverages, tobacco in all forms, narcotic drugs and other worldly practices.

C. All officers shall normally assume their duties at the conclusion of the annual business meeting. Any officer unable or unwilling to fulfill the duties of his office shall resign or the church may vote to declare the office vacant and shall elect another to fulfill the duties of that office.

### Section 2. Pastor

A. The pastor shall be a fundamental Baptist minister who meets the qualifications listed in I Timothy 3:1-7 and Titus 1:5-9. He shall be a spiritually mature man who evidences a burden for lost souls and who is in agreement with the covenant, constitution and articles of faith of this church. He shall be a man who has never been divorced nor married to a divorced woman.

B. A candidate for the pastorate shall be carefully examined by the pulpit committee as to his salvation, doctrine, Christian conduct and call to the ministry. If he has served in other churches, his ministry should be explored for evidence of the Lord's blessing. Pastoral candidates shall have opportunity to question and be questioned by the church membership.

C. A vote to call a candidate as pastor may be taken at a meeting of the church called for that purpose and announced from the pulpit for two Sundays immediately preceding the date of the meeting. Voting shall be by written ballot. Only one candidate shall be considered at any given meeting. A three-fourths majority of those present and voting shall be necessary for a call. The deacons shall inform the candidate of the church's decision as soon as possible. If favorable, a written notification shall also be sent to the prospective pastor giving details of the church-pastoral

relationship, including salary, housing and car allowances, insurance, vacations, etc.

D. The pastor shall serve for an indeterminate time, and shall
continue as pastor as long as it is mutually agreeable to
him and the church. The pastor may announce his resig-
nation at any time but shall not terminate his duties until
thirty days after his announcement or at a time mutually
agreeable to both him and the church.

E. The pastor may be dismissed by a two-thirds ballot vote at a
meeting called for that purpose and announced from the
pulpit on the two preceding Sundays. If dismissed, the pastor's duties shall end immediately. He shall receive sixty
days' salary and have sixty days' use of the parsonage.

F. The pastor, his wife and qualified children shall be
received into the membership of this church.

G. The pastor shall be the administrative overseer of the
church. He shall be responsible for co-ordinating the
church's programs and ministries. The pastor may call a
meeting of the church, deacons or committees at any time
and may moderate such meetings. He shall be an ex officio
member of all committees.

H. The pastor shall receive no less than two weeks of paid
vacation annually. He and his wife may be sent to two conferences per year approved by the deacons with all expenses
paid by the church. Time so spent shall not be considered as
vacation time.

## Section 3. Deacons/Trustees

A. The church shall elect from its membership at least two
qualified men to serve as deacons. They shall be spiritually
mature men who have been members of this church for at
least six months. They shall be actively engaged in seeking
to win the lost, have a good family testimony with neither
the husband nor his wife having been divorced and shall be
in hearty agreement with the policies and programs of this
church. They must meet the standards of Acts 6:3 and I
Timothy 3:8-13. One additional deacon shall be elected for
every fifty active members.

B. The term of office shall be two years, arranged so that one-
half of the deacons are elected each year. Men who have
served two consecutive terms shall be required to take one-
year recess before being eligible for re-election. If a deacon
is unable to complete his term of office, a special election

may be held to choose a replacement to complete the un-expired term.

C. The deacons shall assist the pastor in promoting the spirit-ual welfare of the church, serving as his helpers and coun-selors. They shall exercise prudent watchcare over the church membership, visiting the sick and examining candidates for baptism and membership. They shall assist at baptisms and with the preparation and distribution of the Lord's Supper.

D. The deacons shall serve as the trustees of this church for legal purposes. They shall have authority to acquire and dispose of church property up to the value of one thousand dollars. All transactions exceeding that amount shall first be approved by vote of the church except for routine budget matters. The deacons shall be responsible for the upkeep and maintenance of the church facilities, equipment and properties.

E. The deacons shall serve as the pulpit committee when a vacancy occurs in the office of pastor. They shall also serve as the nominating committee.

## Section 4. Staff Personnel

A. All staff personnel shall be approved by the pastor, work under his supervision and be in harmony with the program of this church.

B. Salaried staff personnel shall be called by majority vote of the church upon the recommendation of the pastor and deacons.

C. Non-salaried staff personnel may be appointed by the pastor with the approval of the deacons.

D. Staff personnel may be dismissed at any time by the pastor and deacons. Salaried personnel shall be paid thirty days' salary and shall have thirty days to vacate church-owned housing. Their duties shall terminate immediately or at the time set by the pastor and deacons.

## Section 5. Clerk

A. A church clerk shall be elected each year at the annual business meeting. The clerk shall record and maintain a printed record of the minutes of all business meetings of this church, receive and keep on file the quarterly and annual reports from all administrative committees, maintain a current record of membership, baptisms, receptions and dismissals of members.

B. The church clerk shall be responsible for all official correspondence requiring an official signature. The clerk shall certify annually to the bank the names of officers who are authorized to have access to the safety deposit boxes and to sign the checks for disbursement of funds.

C. The church clerk shall make available all records, files or documents upon request to the pastor, deacons or church. Upon retirement or removal from office, the clerk shall promptly deliver all records, files and papers belonging to the church to the newly elected clerk or to the deacons.

## Section 6. Treasurer

A. A treasurer shall be elected each year at the annual business meeting. He shall be responsible for keeping an accurate and permanent record of all financial transactions of church funds and shall make monthly, quarterly and annual reports to the pastor, deacons and church.

B. The treasurer shall be responsible for depositing all funds in appropriate accounts at an approved banking facility. He shall pay and record all bills and routine expenses approved by the pastor and deacons as well as disburse funds and salaries as directed by the church.

## Section 7. Financial Secretary

A. A financial secretary shall be elected to assist the treasurer. He, along with others so appointed, shall be responsible for receiving, counting and recording all offerings of the church. He shall promptly turn all monies over to the treasurer for deposit and shall give an accurate record thereof to the treasurer and pastor each week.

B. The financial secretary shall provide members of the congregation with offering envelopes and keep an accurate, confidential record of all individual contributions and shall issue annual statements of receipt to all donors.

## Article VIII - Finances

## Section 1. General Fund

A. This church and its ministries shall be financed through the tithes and offerings of God's people. No sales, suppers or other commercial means shall be used. All monies are to be placed in the General Fund under a unified budget. Additional monies may be borrowed when approved by vote of the church.

B. The salaries of the pastor and staff personnel shall be paid from the General Fund and shall be reviewed at least once a year with consideration being given to the rising cost of living.

C. All expenses for special meetings and speakers shall be paid from the General Fund with speakers being reimbursed for their travel expenses. They shall receive honorariums determined by the pastor and deacons.

## Section 2. Missions Fund

All missionary support shall be paid from the Missions Fund. Each month at least ten percent of the regular income of the church (or a higher amount approved by the church) shall be transferred from the General Fund to the Missions Fund. In addition, all special offerings received for missions shall be transferred to the Missions Fund. Monies will be received for and sent only to those missionaries who meet the requirements of Article X.

## Section 3. Building Fund

A Building Fund shall be maintained for the purpose of acquiring properties, constructing and maintaining the facilities of this church. Each month at least ten percent of the regular income of the church (or an amount approved by the church) shall be transferred from the General Fund to the Building Fund. In addition, all special offerings received for the Building Fund shall be transferred to the Building Fund.

## Section 4. The Budget Committee

The budget committee shall consist of the pastor, at least two deacons, the treasurer and the financial secretary. It shall be the duties of the committee to prepare the budget for the ensuing year for presentation to the church for its approval at the annual meeting. The committee shall function throughout the year to recommend budget revisions to the church as may be deemed necessary.

## Section 5. The Auditing Committee

The auditing committee shall consist of two members appointed by the budget committee. It shall audit all accounts of the church and its organizations and certify the same by written report at the annual business meeting. All financial records shall be made available upon request to the auditing committee. The committee may be assisted by a professional auditing firm if authorized to do so by vote of the church.

## Article IX - Business Meetings

### Section 1. Calling Business Meetings

A. The annual business meeting shall be held during the month of January on a day set by the pastor and deacons and shall be announced at least two weeks in advance.

B. Quarterly business meetings shall be held during the months of April, July and October on a day set by the pastor and deacons and shall be announced at least two weeks in advance.

C. Special business meetings may be called at any time by the pastor or deacons (with the pastor's knowledge) or upon written request to the pastor and deacons by ten unrelated, voting members.

D. The official church year shall coincide with the calendar year.

## Section 2. Procedures at Business Meetings

A. All items for church action shall first be submitted to the pastor and deacons for their consideration and recom- mendation. If an item is rejected by the pastor and deacons, it may be re-submitted with the signatures of ten unrelated voting members and shall be placed on the agenda of the next quarterly business meeting.

B. The pastor shall moderate all business meetings. If the office of pastor is vacant, the chairman of the deacons shall serve as the moderator.

C. Robert's Rules of Order shall be the final authority when disagreement arises in procedural matters, unless such matters are covered by this constitution.

## Section 3. Voting at Business Meetings

A. The presence of twenty-five percent of the voting members shall constitute a quorum. Active members eighteen years of age and older shall be eligible to vote.

B. All elections and matters of business shall be decided by majority vote of members voting unless otherwise stated in this constitution.

C. Election of deacons shall take place at the annual business meeting. Special elections to complete unexpired terms shall be held as the nominating committee recommends. Newly elected officers shall assume their responsibilities at the close of the business meeting during which they were elected.

## Section 4. Nominating Committee

A. This committee shall be composed of the pastor, two deacons and two members selected by the deacons from the church at large. No elected officer of the church whose term expires shall be appointed to the nominating committee.

B. All nominations shall be submitted in writing to the nominating committee for review. Unqualified names shall be dropped from consideration. The committee shall meet with each qualified nominee and secure consent to serve in harmony with the pastor and the constitution of the church, if elected.

C. Names of qualified nominees shall be made public two weeks prior to elections. If qualified candidates are available, two or more members shall be nominated for each office. No nominations shall be made from the floor.

D. The committee shall provide ballot forms for all elections.

## Section 5. Committees

A. Such committees as may be deemed necessary may be appointed by the pastor and deacons or established by vote of the church for the furtherance of this ministry.

B. Each committee chairman shall submit a written report of discussions, decisions and plans to the pastor and deacons and shall submit written quarterly and annual reports to the church.

C. Committees shall make available upon request all records and materials to the pastor, deacons or church. The pastor and deacons shall have the right to overrule any plans or decisions made by any committee.

D. No committee or subsidiary organization shall engage in any practice or conduct contrary to the position and policies of this church.

## Article X - Missions

### Section 1.

Missionaries, mission agencies and organizations desiring to speak in or be supported by this church shall be Baptist in name and practice. They shall be in agreement with the doc-trinal position of this church and shall be separated from all forms of apostasy and those who compromise therewith. Mis-sionaries shall be affiliated with a fundamental Baptist mission agency whose policies and practices are in agreement with those of this church.

### Section 2.

A. It shall be the policy of this church to support missionaries who are primarily engaged in evangelism, the training of national church leaders and the establishment of Baptist churches at home and abroad.

B. Missionaries supported by this church shall receive equal amounts of financial aid, unless they are members of this church, in which case the church may vote to grant a larger amount not to exceed sixty percent of their total support needs.

C. Missionary support levels shall be reviewed and determined at least once a year with consideration being given to the rising cost of living.
D. The mission agency of each missionary supported by this church shall receive an amount equal to ten percent of the missionary's monthly support to help with administrative expenses.

## Article XI - Property
**Section 1. Property**
A. This church shall have the right to own, buy and sell tangible properties, both real and personal, in its own name and through properly elected officials, when author- ized by vote of the church.
B. While this church has "mission" status with Baptist Mid- Missions, the above shall be subject to the property holding policy of the mission as agreed upon in the "Baptist Mid- Missions Church Planting Agreement."
C. No profit shall ever accrue to the benefit of any individual from the assets, holdings or other transactions in which this church may become involved.

**Section 2. Dissolution**
In the event of the dissolution of this church, all of its debts shall be paid in full. None of its remaining assets or holding shall be divided among the members or other individuals, but shall be irrevocably designated by corporate vote of this church prior to dissolution to non-profit fundamental Baptist organizations which are in agreement with the articles of faith adopted by this church and in conformity with the requirements of the United States Internal Revenue Service Code of 1954 (Section 501 C-3) and the laws of the State of (your state), and in consultation with Baptist Mid-Missions (as long as this church is under the "Baptist Mid-Missions Church Planting Agreement").

## Article XII - Amendments
This constitution may be amended, altered or revised by a three-fourths vote of the members voting at a business meeting of this church called for that purpose. The proposed amend- ment(s) shall be printed in the church bulletin for at least two weeks prior to said meeting.

The church may adopt from time to time such bylaws in amplification hereof as may be necessary or desirable, and shall provide therein for amendment of the same.

## A Sample Doctrinal Statement

1. We believe in the Scriptures of the Old and New Testaments as verbally inspired of God and inerrant in the original writing, and that they are of supreme and final authority in faith and life. (II Timothy 3:16,17; II Peter 1:19-21)
2. We believe in one God, eternally existing in three persons: Father, Son and Holy Spirit. (Exodus 20:2,3; Matthew 28:19; I Corinthians 8:6)
3. We believe in God's direct creation of the universe, without the use of pre-existent material, and apart from any process of evolution whatever, according to the Genesis account. (Genesis 1:1-31; Exodus 20:11; Colossians 1:16,17; Hebrews 11:3)
4. We believe that Jesus Christ was begotten by the Holy Spirit, and born of Mary, a virgin, and is true God and true man. (Isaiah 7:14; Luke 1:35; Galatians 4:4)
5. We believe that the Lord Jesus Christ died for our sins according to the Scriptures as a representative and sub-stitutionary sacrifice, and that all who believe in Him are justified on the ground of His shed blood. (Isaiah 53:4-11; Acts 13:38,39; Romans 3:24,25, 4:5, 5:1,8,9, 6:23; II Corinthians 5:19-21)
6. We believe in the resurrection of the crucified body of our Lord, in His ascension into heaven, and in His present life there as High Priest and Advocate. (Matthew 28:1-7; Acts 1:8-11; I Corinthians 15:4-9; Hebrews 4:14-16)
7. We believe that the Holy Spirit baptizes, seals, and indwells every believer at the moment of salvation and that the Holy Spirit empowers every believer for holy living. We believe that the Holy Spirit today bestows service gifts upon believers and that the sign gifts were restricted to the Apostolic period. (Ephesians 1:13, 4:11-12, 5:18; Romans 8:9, 12:6-8; I Corinthians 12:13; Hebrews 2:3,4; I Corinthians 13:8-13; Ephesians 2:20)
8. We believe that man was created in the image of God, that he sinned and thereby incurred not only physical death but also that spiritual death which is separation from God, that all human beings are born with a sinful nature and are sinners in thought, word and deed. (Genesis 1:26,27, 3:1-6; Romans 5:12, 19, 3:10-13; Titus 1:15,16)
9. We believe that all who receive by faith the Lord Jesus Christ are born again of the Holy Spirit and thereby become

children of God. (John 1:12,13, 3:3-16; Acts 16:31; Ephesians 2:8,9)

10. We believe in the "Eternal Security" of the believer, that it is impossible for one born into the family of God ever to be lost. (John 6:39,49, 10:28, 29; Romans 8:35-39; Jude 1)

11. We believe in "that blessed hope": the personal, premillennial, pretribulational and imminent return of our Lord and Savior Jesus Christ, when the Church will be "gathered together unto Him." (John 14:1-3; I Thessalonians 4:13-18; I Corinthians 15:51-58; II Thessalonians 2:1-13)

12. We believe in the literal fulfillment of the prophecies and promises of the Scriptures which foretell and assure the future regeneration and restoration of Israel as a nation. (Genesis 13:14-17; Jeremiah 16:14,15, 30:6-11; Romans 11)

13. We believe in the bodily resurrection of the just and the unjust, the everlasting blessedness of the saved, and the everlasting punishment of the lost. (Matthew 25:31-46; Luke 16:19-31; I Thessalonians 4:13-18; Revelation 21:1-8)

14. We believe that a local New Testament Baptist Church is an organized body of believers immersed upon a credible confession of faith in Jesus Christ, having two offices (pastors and deacon), congregational in polity, autonomous in nature, and banded together for work, worship, the observance of the ordinances and the worldwide proclamation of the gospel. We further believe in the church which is Christ's body, the spiritual organism consisting of all born-again believers of the New Testament dispensation. (Matthew 28:18-20; Acts 2:41,42; I Corinthians 12:13; Ephesians 1:22,23; I Timothy 3; I Peter 5:1-3)

15. We believe that the Scriptural ordinances of the church are Baptism and the Lord's Supper and are to be administered by the local church; that Baptism, by immersion, should be administered to believers only as a symbol of their belief in the death, burial and resurrection of our Lord and Savior Jesus Christ and as a testimony to the world of that belief and of their death, burial and resurrection with Him; and that the Lord's Supper should be partaken of by baptized believers to show forth His death, "till He come."(Matthew 28:18-20; Acts 2:41-47, 8:26-39; I Corinthians 11:23-28; Colossians 2:12)

## Baptist Mid-Missions
# Church Planting Agreement
### for North America

The following agreement is intended to establish a clear understanding between Baptist Mid-Missions and the newly constituted Baptist Fellowship/Mission Church for the purpose of church planting in obedience to the Great Commission.

Inasmuch as the _____
of _____has been led to this point by a Baptist Mid-Missions missionary or has requested the services of a Baptist Mid-Missions missionary to lead it in establishing a fundamental Baptist testimony, the following agreement is hereby entered into by the members of the Fellowship/Mission Church and by Baptist Mid-Missions.

1. Baptist Mid-Missions will assume the responsibility of providing the Mission Church with a missionary pastor, as the Lord provides, until the Church reaches maturity* (or it is agreed upon by both parties to disband according to the Church Constitution).

2. The Mission Church should not purchase property until the Church has been organized, recognized, and incorporated, thus permitting the acquisition and holding of property in its corporate name. Before any construction is initiated, the Mission Church is required to obtain builders risk insurance in adequate amounts to cover both salaried and volunteer workers. Adequate comprehensive and liability insurance must be in force before and during occupancy.

3. The Mission Church shall cooperate fully with the missionary pastor and the administration of Baptist Mid-Missions, praying that maturity* will be reached as soon as possible. This will include dedication on behalf of members in view of Ephesians 4:11-15, recognizing that the missionary pastor is "to equip the saints unto the work of the ministry," and periodic evaluation of the Mission Church progress.

4. The Mission Church shall, at all times, be responsible for its own finances. It is expected that it will maintain a sound financial policy governed by a carefully prepared budget for current operation as well as future goals.

From the time of its organization, the Mission Church shall provide some financial support for its missionary pastor. This salary shall be reviewed periodically and increased proportionately to the growth of the Church. This salary shall be sent monthly to the Baptist Mid-Missions office clearly designated as such for the ministry of _____(name of missionary pastor). When this salary, combined with that received by the missionary pastor as missionary support (most are not fully supported), exceeds his needs, the Mission Church will be counseled regarding the establishing of an escrow account for its future pastor, as well as the needs of the missionary pastor in relocation. (The account for the future pastor will be held by the Mission Church in its local bank).

The Mission Church shall also annually provide the Baptist Mid-Missions Home Office with the following information in dollar amounts:

   a. amount of housing allowance or rental value of parsonage provided by the Mission Church (annual)
   b. transportation allowances (annual)
   c. other benefits

5. By acceptance of this agreement, the Mission Church affirms its doctrinal position to be in complete agreement with that of Baptist Mid-Missions found at the close of this agreement.

*Maturity is indicated when the Mission Church manifests its ability to be:

   a. self-supporting financially–that time when a church is paying all its operating expenses, providing sufficient pastoral salary and housing or, in some circumstances, the pastor is able to augment his financial needs through part-time employment or other income source;
   b. self-propagating; and
   c. self-governing

The above conditions have been fully discussed by all members of the Fellowship/Mission Church and were agreed upon by at least three-quarters of the voting members present at a duly-called business meeting.

Date of Meeting:_____19__

Signature:_____
Chairman, Board of Deacons

Signature:_____
Church Clerk

Accepted and approved by Baptist Mid-Missions:

Signature:_____
President

Date _____    Signature:_____
Secretary

## The Articles of Faith
## of Baptist Mid-Missions

1. I believe in the Scriptures of the Old and New Testaments as verbally inspired of God, and inerrant in the original writing and bodily that they are of supreme and final authority in faith and life.
2. I believe in one God, eternally existing in three persons: Father, Son and Holy Spirit.
3. I believe that Jesus Christ was begotten by the Holy Spirit, and born of Mary, a virgin, and is true God and true man.
4. I believe that man was created in the image of God, that he sinned and thereby incurred not only physical death but also that spiritual death which is separation from God, that all human beings are born with a sinful nature, and are sinners in thought, word and deed.
5. I believe that the Lord Jesus Christ died for my sins according to the Scriptures as a representative and substitutionary sacrifice, and that all who believe in Him are justified on the ground of His shed blood.
6. I believe in the "Eternal Security" of the believer, that it is impossible for one born into the family of God ever to be lost.
7. I believe in the resurrection of the crucified body of our Lord, in His ascension into heaven, and in His present life there as High Priest and Advocate.
8. I believe in "that blessed hope"–the personal, premillennial, pretribulational and imminent return of our Lord and Savior Jesus Christ, when the Church will be "gathered together unto Him.
9. I believe in the literal fulfillment of the prophecies and promises of the Scriptures which foretell and assure the future regeneration and restoration of Israel as a nation.
10. I believe that all who receive by faith the Lord Jesus Christ are born again of the Holy Spirit and thereby become children of God.
11. I believe in the bodily resurrection of the just and the unjust, the everlasting blessedness of the saved, and the everlasting punishment of the lost.
12. I believe that the Scriptural ordinances of the church are Baptism and the Lord's Supper, and are to be administered by the local church; that Baptism, by immersion, should be administered to believers only as a symbol of their belief in the death, burial and resurrection of our Lord and Savior Jesus Christ and as a testimony to the world of that belief and of their death, burial and resurrection with Him; and that the Lord's Supper should be partaken of by believers only to show forth His death, "till He come."

148

## Sample Articles of Incorporation

### Articles of Incorporation
### of the
### (name) Baptist Church of (city), (state)

We, the undersigned, desiring to become incorporated under the laws of _____, as a religious, non-profit corporation, do hereby make, execute and adopt the following articles of incorporation, to wit:

First, the name of this corporation, and by which it shall be known in law, is _____ Baptist Church of _____, _____.

Second, The location of said church shall be in the (township, city or village) of _____, County of _____, and State of _____. The mailing address shall be
_____

Third, the time for which this corporation shall be created shall be perpetual.

Fourth, the members of said church shall worship and labor together according to the teachings of the New Testament, as set forth in the articles of faith adopted by this church.

Fifth, this church shall have the authority to conduct a Baptist church in accordance with the Word of God, the articles of faith, the covenant and the constitution of this church. It shall have the right to own, buy and sell tangible properties, both real and personal, in its own name and through properly elected officers, when authorized by vote of the church.

This church shall be independent and autonomous, not subject to any ecclesiastical control whatsoever from any convention, conference, association, council, group or individual outside of the local church; but it shall have the right to affiliate voluntarily with any association or council of Bible-believing churches separated from the apostasy, and the right to dissociate from any group with which it may have become affiliated.

The government of this church shall be vested in its membership. Voting privileges shall be extended to members in good and regular standing sixteen years of age and over, except that the minimum age shall be eighteen years for the transaction of all legal matters.

Sixth, no profit shall ever accrue to the benefit of any individual from the assets, holdings or other transactions in which this corporation may become involved.

In the event of the dissolution of this corporation, all of its debts shall be fully satisfied. None of its assets or holdings shall be divided among the members, or other individuals, but shall be irrevocably designated by corporate vote, prior to dissolution, to such other non-profit religious corporations as are in agreement with the letter and spirit of the articles of faith adopted by this church, and in conformity with the requirements of the United States Internal Revenue Service Code of 1954 (Section 501 C-3).

In witness whereof, we, the parties hereby associating for the purpose of giving legal effect to these articles, hereby sign our names and places of residence:

Done at the (township, city or village) of _____,County of _____, and State of _____, this _____ day of _____, 19___.

(signatures)                                  (residence)

_____      _____
_____      _____
_____      _____
_____      _____
_____      _____

State of _____
County of _____ SS

I, _____, a Notary Public, do hereby certify that on the _____ day of _____, 19___,

_____
_____
_____
_____

(names of incorporators)

personally appeared before me and in my presence signed the foregoing document in the respective capacities therein set forth and declared that the statements therein contained are true.

IN WITNESS WHEREOF, I have hereunto set my hand and seal on the day and year above written.

_____
(Notary Public)

(SEAL)

Sample 2

## Articles of Incorporation
## of the
## (name) Baptist Church of (city), (state)

### Article I

We the undersigned, a majority of whom are citizens of the United States, have associated and do hereby associate ourselves together for the purpose of forming a religious, non-profit corporation, in accordance with Chapter ____ of the State Statutes, and we do hereby adopt the following Articles of Incorporation:

### Article II

The name of this corporation, which is a congregation of believers, shall be known as (name of the church) and shall be located at (complete address).

The corporation is and shall be charitable in its nature. The objective of the corporation shall be to minister the Gospel of Jesus Christ for all purposes required in or consistent with the Bible, including but not limited to the purpose of

1. evangelizing the lost through personal soul-winning, visitation, and preaching of the Word of God;
2. edifying believers through the systematic teaching of the Bible;
3. establishing fundamental Baptist churches around the world through an energetic missionary program;
4. educating our adults and their children in a manner consistent with the requirements of the Holy Scriptures, both in Sunday and weekday schools of Christian education.

### Article III

This church shall be an independent, autonomous Baptist church subject only to Jesus Christ, its Head. It shall have the authority to conduct itself as a Baptist church in accordance with the Word of God as interpreted by the Covenant, Constitution and Articles of Faith adopted by this church.

This church has the right to cooperate and associate with other fundamental Baptist groups on a voluntary basis, but shall not be subject to any control by such groups. This church shall not associate nor cooperate with any person or group which is a part of, or cooperates with liberalism, neo-evangelicalism, the charismatic movement, secret societies or cults. It has the right to disassociate from any group with which it may have become affiliated.

## Article IV

The government of this church shall be vested in its membership. Membership in this church shall be open to all those who

1. profess to be born again through faith in Jesus Christ alone;
2. have been baptized by immersion following their profession of faith;
3. are in agreement with the Covenant, Constitution and Articles of Faith of this church.

Membership shall not be denied to any person on the basis of race, color, sex or social status.

The presence of twenty-five percent of the voting members shall constitute a quorum. Active members in good standing who are sixteen years of age and older shall be eligible to vote, except in those matters for which the law of this State requires the minimum age to be higher.

The pastor and deacons shall serve as the trustees (directors) of this corporation.

## Article V

This church shall have the right to own, buy or sell tangible properties, both real and personal, in its own name and through properly elected officers, when so authorized by vote of this church.

No part of the earnings of this corporation shall inure to the benefit of, or be distributable to any officers, trustee, or member of this corporation or to any other private person; provided however, that the corporation shall be authorized and empower-ed to pay reasonable compensation for services rendered and ex-penses incurred in furtherance of the purposes of the corporation.

Notwithstanding any other provision of these Articles, the corporation shall not carry on any other activities not permitted to be carried on by a corporation exempt from Federal income tax under Section 501 (c) (3) and 170 (c) (2) of the Internal Revenue Code of 1954 or corresponding sections of any prior or future Internal Revenue Code or federal, state or local government for exclusive public purpose.

## Article VI

In the event of the dissolution of this church, all of its debts shall be paid in full. None of its remaining assets or holdings shall be divided among the members or other individuals, but shall be irrevocably designated by corporate vote of this church prior to dissolution to non-profit fundamental Baptist organizations which are in agreement with the Articles of Faith adopted by this church and in conformity with the requirements of the United States Internal Revenue Service Code of 1954 (Section 501 C-3) and the laws of this state.

IN WITNESS WHEREOF, we, the undersigned subscribers, have hereunto set our hands and seals this _____ day of _____ 19_____.

(signatures)                               (residence)

_____        _____

_____        _____

_____        _____

State of _____
County of _____

BEFORE ME, the undersigned authority personally appeared (names of the above signatories) known to me to be the subscribers to the foregoing Articles of Incorporation of (name of the church) and they acknowledge to me that they intend in good faith to carry out the purposes and objects set forth in the foregoing Articles of Incorporation.

WITNESS, my hand and official seal at (address where signing occurs), this _____ day of _____. 19____.

_____
(signature of notary public)

My Commission Expires: _____

## Sample Letter Calling for a Recognition Council

Date of letter

First Baptist Church
Main Street
USA

Dear Brethren:

Being a company of immersed believers who have organized ourselves into a local independent Baptist church on (date of organizational meeting) and desiring to have fellowship with other churches of like faith and order, we invite you to send your pastor and two brethren to sit in council on (date of recognition meeting) at the (name and location where the meeting will be held)to consider the propriety of recognizing us as a duly organized Baptist church.

The council will convene at (time).

The following churches and individuals have been invited:
(List the names of churches,individuals & addresses.)

We are enclosing copies of our charter, covenant, constitution and articles of faith for you to examine prior to the meeting of the recognition council.

Done by order of and in behalf of the church.

(name of the church)
(address)

_____
(church clerk)

# Agenda for a Recognition Council

1. Congregational Song: "How Firm A Foundation"
2. Prayer
3. Reading of the letter calling for a recognition council
4. Motion to convene the recognition council
5. Election of a moderator
6. Election of a clerk
7. Roll call of churches and individuals invited
8. Motion to seat messengers and other visitors
9. History of the new church (pastor or representative of the new church)
10. Reading of the Church Covenant (questions & answers)
11. Reading of the Church Constitution (questions & answers)
12. Reading of the Church Creed (Articles of Faith) (questions & answers)
13. Council moves into executive session for discussion
14. Motion to approve or disapprove the recognition of the new church
15. Signing of the "recognition certificate" if approval is granted
16. Right hand of fellowship extended to the new church (if approved) or the announcement of a recognition service later in the day
17. Motion to adjourn and dissolve the council

**Recognition Certificate**
**for the**
**(name of the church)**
**(address)**


We the undersigned, being independent Baptist brethren in Christ, and meeting together in council on this _____ day of _____, 19____, have carefully examined the covenant, constitution and articles of faith of the_____ Baptist Church of _____.

We hereby declare that we find these documents to be in accor-dance with the principles of the Word of God and the policies of historic Baptist churches.

We therefore recognize and recommend said church as a duly organized independent Baptist church.

<table>
<tr><td>(name)</td><td>(church)</td></tr>
<tr><td>_____</td><td>_____</td></tr>
<tr><td>_____</td><td>_____</td></tr>
<tr><td>_____</td><td>_____</td></tr>
<tr><td>_____</td><td>_____</td></tr>
<tr><td>_____</td><td>_____</td></tr>
<tr><td>_____</td><td>_____</td></tr>
<tr><td>_____</td><td>_____</td></tr>
</table>

## Recognition Service

1. Congregational Song:  "How Firm A Foundation"
2. Opening Prayer
3. Report of Council Action by Moderator
4. Scripture Reading:   I Timothy 3:1-16
5. Charge to the Church
6. Prayer:  Commending the Church to God
7. Congregational Song:  "The Church's One Foundation"
8. Charge to Local Association of Churches
9. Congregational Song:  "Blest Be the Tie"
10. Message
11. Right Hand of Fellowship
12. Benediction

(Use visiting pastors or guest speakers
for the various responsibilities.)

DR-14

## STATE OF FLORIDA
# DEPARTMENT OF REVENUE
### SALES AND USE TAX DIVISION
#### CONSUMER'S CERTIFICATE OF EXEMPTION
Issued Pursuant to Sales and Use Tax Law
Chapter 212, Florida Statutes
This Certificate Is
Non-transferable

| DATE ISSUED | | |
|---|---|---|
| MO. | DAY | YR. |
| 12 | 06 | 82 |

| CERTIFICATE NUMBER |
|---|
| 05  02682  00  16 |

**TO BE RECORDED ON DEALER'S RECORDS AT TIME OF SALE**

**THIS CERTIFIES THAT**

Bethlehem Baptist Church of Broward
County, Inc.
7102-04 Southgate Boulevard
N. Lauderdale, Florida

is hereby exempt from the payment of sales or use tax for the reason indicated opposite.

Executive Director

| | | |
|---|---|---|
| 1. | ☐ | Federal |
| 2. | ☐ | State |
| 3. | ☐ | County |
| 4. | ☐ | City |
| 5. | ☒ | Religious |
| 6. | ☐ | Charitable |
| 7. | ☐ | Educational |
| C1. | ☐ | Federal Credit Unions |
| C2. | ☐ | State Credit Unions |

## EXEMPT INSTITUTIONS ARE:

1.—UNITED STATES GOVERNMENT; 2.—STATE OF FLORIDA; 3.—ANY COUNTY UNIT OR AGENCY; 4.—ANY CITY UNIT OR AGENCY; 5.—CHURCHES OR ELIGIBLE RELIGIOUS ORGANIZATIONS; 6.—NON-PROFIT CHARITABLE INSTITUTIONS AND 7.—EDUCATIONAL INSTITUTIONS MEETING LEGAL REQUIREMENTS.
If your organization operates a shop, store or restaurant you are required to be registered as a vender with the Sales Tax Bureau and file monthly reports for the tax collected with the exception of churches.
This Certificate is issued to the above indicated institution with the understanding that it is to be used solely by the institution in purchasing tangible personal property that will be used directly in the course of their institutional activities and will not be used to personal benefit of any individual or officer of such institution. Misuse of this certificate will necessitate its revocation.

Department of the Treasury
**Internal Revenue Service**

07214110 L

Date of This Notice

If you inquire about
your account, please
refer to this
number or attach a
copy of this notice

12-22-82
Employer Identification Number
59-2237236

BETHLEHEM BAPTIST CHURCH OF BROWARD
COUNTY FLORIDA
7305 NW 80TH ST
TAMARAC          FL  33319

575 B 045555555W
55555555

### NOTICE OF NEW EMPLOYER IDENTIFICATION NUMBER ASSIGNED

Thank you for your application for an employer identification number. The number above has been assigned to you. We will use it to identify your business tax returns and any other related documents, even if you have no employees.

Please keep this number in your permanent records. Use the number and your name, exactly as shown above, on all Federal tax forms that require this information, and refer to the number in all tax payments and in tax-related correspondence or documents. You may wish to make a record of the number for reference in case this notice is lost or destroyed.

Note that the assignment of this number does not grant tax-exempt status to nonprofit organizations. For details on how to apply for this exemption, see IRS Publication 557, Tax-Exempt Status for Your Organization, available at most IRS offices.

We appreciate your cooperation.

# Chapter 9

# The Oversight
# of the Local Church

## Importance of Pastoral Leadership

The importance of pastoral leadership cannot be underestimated. To a large degree the pastor's ability to lead will determine the success or failure of his efforts. The work will go no further than he is able to lead it.

Since the pastor has been given the "oversight" of the flock by God, he is the chief administrator and leader of the church (Acts 20:28; I Timothy 3:4,5; 5:17; Hebrews 13:7,17; I Peter 5:1-3). People look to him for leadership. He must provide that leadership if he hopes to establish a new church.

A good leader is able to plan, organize, delegate and coordinate the work of the church. He knows he must gain the confidence and cooperation of his people if he is to achieve his goals in the ministry.

## Setting Goals

As a church planter, you must set goals. Without them, you will become hopelessly lost in a sea of frustration. Goals enable you to determine your priorities, measure your progress and achieve greater results than would be otherwise possible. Goal setting will help you determine where you are, where you are going and how you are going to get there.

Write them down so as to crystallize them in your mind. Good goals are realistic, flexible, and measurable. By realistic we mean obtainable. Goals should not be impossible to achieve. If they are, they become self-defeating. Set your goals high enough to challenge the people, but low enough that they can reach them.

Goals may need to be adjusted as you go along. Sometimes unforeseen circumstances will require you to alter your goals. Perhaps a major contributor dies or several new families are added to the church. If the goal is too high, lower it. If it has been achieved, raise it.

Set specific times when goals are to be reached. This enables you to measure your progress. Break down annual goals into quarterly segments. For example, a Sunday-school teacher may set the goal of having all the children in her class memorize the books of the New Testament in the first quarter and the books of the Old Testament in the second quarter. These are measurable goals.

Have the church adopt goals in its annual meeting. Include such things as income, attendance, souls saved, new members, property and anything else that is appropriate. Make the goals specific. For example: you might determine to increase your income by $100 per week or to add twelve new families to the church during the coming year.

Set goals for yourself as well as for the church. What do you expect to achieve in your family life? How many books do you plan to read? What new skills do you want to acquire? If it is important to set goals in your ministry, it is equally important to have them in your personal life.

Establish short-term, intermediate and long-range goals. A five-year plan will enable you to get the big picture of where you are going. Intermediate goals will help you know what must be accomplished in the next two years to reach the overall goal. Six-month and one-year goals enable you to concentrate on what must be done right now to achieve the ultimate goal. Failure to plan, to set goals, is planning for failure.

Each year, the church planter should plan an annual calendar. It will help him to organize his schedule, plan the program of the church and achieve the goals which he has set for the coming year. He should include all special meetings, banquets, contests, camp and youth activities. He may even want to list specific messages he plans to preach during the year.

Once goals have been established, review them frequently. What has been accomplished? What still needs to be done? Why didn't you reach your goal? What adjustments need to be made? Honest, periodic evaluations will help you develop goals that are workable and that will enable you to plant a church successfully.

Report on the progress being made toward your goals. This is in order at any time, but especially at the quarterly and annual business meetings. Prepare a report that shows where you were at the beginning of the year, what has been accomplished and where you are going. People will readily support a ministry that demonstrates God's hand of blessing upon it.

## Conducting Business Meetings

A properly organized Baptist church will conduct business meetings on a regular schedule. Most churches hold quarterly and annual meetings when progress reports are made, elections are held and major decisions are agreed upon. Monthly and special meetings may be called as often as the need arises.

Business meetings need not be boring nor a source of contention. Rather they should be a blessing and challenge. A properly conducted business meeting will produce rejoicing and unity among God's people.

Begin preparing the people from the start to have proper attitudes toward the business session. Let them know that you value their opinions and need their help in making major decisions. Instruct them in proper parliamentary procedures. Teach them to respect and follow those who rule over them.

Adequate preparation is important if you expect your business meeting to function smoothly and be a blessing. Meet with the deacons or advisory council several days prior to the business session. Discuss and agree upon all items of business which are to be brought before the church. Seldom should a matter be presented to the church unless you have the complete backing of these leaders. Without it, the item in question will become a source of contention, may be defeated and will surely undermine your leadership position. It is far wiser to respect their opinions. They may know something you do not or have a better suggestion as to what to do. Learn to respect their counsel.

Print and distribute all reports prior to the business meeting if possible. Ask the people to read them before they come to the meeting. This will help them be better prepared and more informed. During the business session, do not read the reports which have been distributed. Simply mention each one and allow for any questions the people may have. This will save considerable time and help the meeting move along smoothly.

Who should moderate the business meeting? The pastor/church planter is the administrative as well as spiritual leader of the church. As such, he should conduct all the business sessions of the church. No business meeting should ever be held without the pastor's knowledge. If the church does not have a pastor, then the head deacon or someone chosen by the church may serve as the moderator.

It is recommended that the church planter be acquainted with *The New Directory of Baptist Churches* by Edward Hiscox and Robert's *Rules of Order*. These will provide valuable guidance in conducting the business meeting and should serve as the final court of appeal when procedural problems arise.

The proper order for a church business meeting is as follows:

> Open the session with prayer
> Call the meeting to order
> Reading of the minutes
>     (if not distributed already)
> Presentation of reports
> Unfinished business
> New business
> Adjournment

The minutes from previous meetings are not normally read at special business meetings unless they pertain to the subject under consideration. Be sure you have the required number present to constitute a quorum. (25% of the membership is recommended.)

It is not necessary to bring every minor item to the church for its consideration. Churches using the congregational form of government follow the democratic-republican procedure. They delegate certain responsibilities to elected leaders. These elected officials then carry out their duties in accordance with the constitution and the decisions previously made by the church. Only those matters not covered by the constitution and previous decisions need to be presented to the church for its consideration.

A well planned, carefully thought-out agenda that has the backing of your leaders will usually produce a cooperative spirit among your people. Do your homework well, and the church business meeting will become the source of blessing it should be.

## The Role of Deacons

Deacons are valuable workers who fulfill a vital role in the local church. They are men who have been selected for their spiritual maturity and willingness to serve or help others. They must have a servant's heart, for service is the very essence of their ministry.

Great care should be exercised to ensure that only spiritually qualified men are chosen to fulfill the position of deacon. They are to be Spirit-filled men who are separated from the world, agree with the doctrines, practices and convictions of the church, faithful to the services, soul winners and loyal to the pastor.[1] Deacons must also have exemplary wives, marriages and children. It is better to be without deacons than to have unqualified ones who will hinder the work.

The primary function of deacons is to render assistance to others. They are not to lead or direct the church. That is the pastor's God-given responsibility. There are three areas in which this assistance may be rendered. First of all, they are to assist their pastor by working under his supervision to relieve him of the things which would distract him from his primary ministry of praying and preaching (Acts 6:2,3). This might include personal work at the altar, serving the Lord's Supper and helping with baptisms. They are to support and sustain him, both publicly and privately just as Aaron and Hur supported Moses (Exodus 17:10-13). They may also assist him by serving as his advisors. A wise pastor will seek the advice and support of his deacons in planning and carrying out the work God has given him to do. Monthly deacon meetings will go a long way toward gaining the help and cooperation necessary for a successful ministry.

Deacons are also to assist the people in the church. They should care for the physical needs of the church family, visiting the sick, encouraging the downhearted and seeking ways to help those in need. They can listen to the concerns and complaints of the people and communicate them to the pastor. At the same time they can explain and encourage support for the issue in question.

Finally, deacons can assist with the physical plant of the church. They often serve as trustees who are responsible for the upkeep and care of the building and grounds.

Godly deacons are the greatest blessing a pastor can have. Working together they form a team which can result in wonderful blessings and substantial growth for the church (Acts 6:7).

## Church Workers

Every church planter needs help developing the church. He cannot possibly do everything himself. Scripture teaches us that God places gifted people in the church to meet the needs of the local Body of Christ. The church planter must seek out these people to assist him. They will serve as deacons, teachers, musicians, ushers, bus captains, trustees and in many other valuable ways.

Care must be exercised in choosing and appointing those who will serve in a leadership position in the church. The wrong person in the wrong position can create enormous problems. The Bible cautions: "Lay hands suddenly on no man" (I Timothy 5:22).

Determine from the beginning what qualifications and standards must be met by officers and workers. It is easier to establish them before you start, than to implement them later. It is better to leave a position empty than to have an unqualified person in it. Qualified personnel can be developed if you patiently train those the Lord has given you.

Establish leadership standards. They will provide incentive for those who want to be involved in a quality program. They will also improve efficiency and give you a valuable evaluation tool. Leadership standards should include items pertaining to the attitudes, dress, behavior and loyalty of those involved. They may be incorporated in a leadership covenant similar to the one at the end of this chapter.

Recruit workers rather than asking for volunteers. Look for people who are teachable, cooperative, faithful and growing spiritually. When you ask for volunteers, unqualified people sometimes present themselves, creating a delicate situation for the pastor to work around. Moreover, qualified people who are shy or new in the church may be reluctant to offer help.

It is far better for the church planter to seek the Lord's direction in choosing the right person. Ask for the advice of other church leaders. Approach prospective workers individually and privately. Explain the nature of the job involved and tell them that you feel they are qualified for the position. Give them an accurate job description so they know what will be expected of them. Ask them to consider prayerfully taking the responsibility and to let you know of their decision by a specific date.

Workers should be appointed by the pastor and deacons rather than elected by the church. You may want to have those appointed to major positions approved by congregational action. This helps to maintain clear lines of communication and authority. It also makes it easier to remove those who fail to fulfill their roles. Each worker should be taught that he is part of a team effort and that they must work together under the direction of the pastor to achieve the greatest results. Individualists who "do their own thing" will contribute little to the overall ministry of the church.

It has been said that people do not do what is expected, only what is inspected. Explain to each worker before you appoint him that his work will be inspected periodically. This can be done individually or as a group. It may be in the form of a written report, a personal interview or simple observation. There are several reasons for such an evaluation: it helps the worker be more efficient, it ensures that the work is being done properly, it reveals areas that need improvement and shows when a worker needs help.

There will be times when people do not do their jobs well. Meet with them individually and privately to discuss the situation and see if there is a reason for their poor performance. Perhaps they need training or encouragement. Perhaps changes need to be made in the program. Find out the reason they have not kept their commitment and try to rectify it. Encourage them and give them another chance to improve. If this does not help, they must be replaced. This should always be done privately. Never embarrass people in front of others or you will find it difficult to recruit volunteers.

Maintain open lines of communication with those who work in the church. Meet with them regularly. Inform them of plans and progress. Encourage them to share their problems and views. Let them know their opinions are welcome. Schedule regular group and individual conferences for this purpose. Good communication will help you avoid many problems and result in happier and more productive laborers.

## The Team Ministry

A team ministry can be one of the most effective means for developing local churches. The Lord Jesus used it when he sent his disciples two by two (Luke 9:2-6; 10:1-12). The book of Acts indicates that team ministries were a vital part of the missionary outreach of the early church. We read of Barnabas and Saul (13:2), Barnabas and John Mark (15:39), Paul and Silas (15:40), Silas and Timothy (17:4) and Timothy and Erastus (19:22).

There are a number of advantages to a team ministry. It provides more workers, greater resources, and more talents to draw upon when starting a church. What one lacks, the other can supply. Two working together will normally be more effective than when they work alone (Ecclesiastes 4:9). They speak with greater authority when witnessing or administrating the church (II Corinthians 13:1). They can encourage and pray for one another during the difficult stages of the work. Solomon, the wisest of men, recognized the advantages of a partnership when he said, "Two are better than one; because they have a good reward for their labor" (Ecclesiastes 4:9).

A team ministry is not for every one. Before entering into such an arrangement, sit down with your potential partner and honestly discuss such things as: Are our abilities, personalities, backgrounds and attitudes compatible? Do we agree on doctrine and standards of separation and policy? Ask yourself: Am I willing to take second place, if necessary? Can I do things "his" way? Am I willing to expose my life, with all its weaknesses and failures, to my partner? Can we pray together, even when we differ on details of the ministry? Are our wives similarly compatible?

There must be open, honest communication in a team ministry. Differences of opinion must be discussed and resolved in a mature fashion. There is always the possibility of jealousy arising when one partner receives more attention or acclaim than the other. Resentment may develop when one member of the team is perceived as not carrying his or her "fair share" of the load. As with Paul and Barnabas, there may be disagreement over procedures (Acts 15:36-40). A team ministry does not require uniformity, but it must have unity.

The success and compatibility of a team ministry can be enhanced if the team members will observe the following principles:

1. Develop a written agreement which delineates the responsibilities of each team member. Who will do what? Recognize each other's spiritual gifts. One may do most of the public preaching while the other concentrates on private evangelism and discipling of converts. One may administer the Sunday School while the other heads the youth or music ministry of the church. Allow your partner to minister where he or she feels comfortable and can be the most effective. At the same time there must be a willingness to help out in areas where your help is needed.

2. Determine how much time and money will be contributed by each member of the team. This may differ since responsibilities, income and physical capabilities vary. A minimum should be agreed upon, however, to avoid resentment or misunderstandings. If you can do more, great!

3. Decide who is going to be the leader. Usually one will have greater administrative abilities. This does not mean he will "run the show." Both must recognize that neither is boss. But for the sake of the work, a chain of command must be established.

4. Establish a regular time for planning, praying, reporting, evaluating, setting of goals and problem solving each week. Discuss problems and differences as soon as they arise. Do not ignore them or hope they will go away. If genuine areas of disagreement exist, use the Word of God as the final authority. Include your wives in this planning and praying as much as possible.

5. Determine to build up your partner. Never criticize him or her to the members of the congregation. Never question your partner's teaching or actions publicly. Discuss them with him or her privately at a later time.

6. If a single lady is part of the team, be careful not to abuse her gifts, demand too much of her or expect her to provide you with free babysitting. She needs time to herself just as the other members of the team do. Allow her to exercise her gifts fully within biblical parameters.

7. Record the entire agreement in writing so there will not be misunderstandings later. Too often people forget what was promised or remember things differently at a later date.

Recognize that a team ministry is often temporary in nature. They usually dissolve when they have achieved their purpose or when they cease to function effectively (Acts 15). Once the work becomes established and laymen are trained to fulfill the responsibilities carried by the team, or when irreconcilable differences arise, it is time for the team to disband. Do so in a Christ-honoring way. Part as friends. You may want to review the partnership ministry each year.

The way in which the team ministry is administered will determine to a large degree the success or failure of your administration in the church as a whole. So set a good example for them to follow.

### Endnote

[1] Roy L. Thomas, *Planting and Growing A Fundamental Church.* (Nashville: Randall House Publications, 1979), p. 150.

## A Leadership Covenant

Having received Jesus Christ as my personal Savior and being an active member in good standing of this church, I recognize the privilege that is mine to serve in a leadership position. I realize that it is my duty to be "an example to believers, in word, in conversation, in charity, in spirit, in faith, in purity." Therefore, I promise that with the aid of the Holy Spirit I will strive to fulfill my leadership responsibilities and to abide by the following covenant:

1. I readily subscribe to the doctrinal position, the policies and program of my church and will support them both publicly and privately.

2. I will faithfully attend the regular services of my church including Sunday School, Sunday Morning and Evening Services and Prayer Meeting and all other meetings that may be expected of me as a leader in this church.

3. I will support the ministry of our church through my prayers, presence and finances.

4. I will be loyal to my pastor. I will cooperate with him, pray for him and seek to encourage him as we labor together.

5. I will be exemplary in my conduct, not using tobacco, alcohol or illicit drugs and will dress appropriately for all services.

6. I will seek to fulfill my responsibilities on time and in accordance with the instructions I am given.

7. If for some reason I cannot fulfill my obligations, I will notify the appropriate leaders and will cooperate fully in seeking a replacement.

Name  _____

Date  _____

# Chapter 10

# The Orientation
# of the Local Church Services

Henry Vedder, the Baptist historian, points out that from the earliest days of its existence the local church came together for regular times of worship and fellowship. "By the year A.D. 55, this first-day meeting of Christians seemed to have become a recognized custom" (Acts 20:7; I Corinthians 16:2).[1]

In his definition of the local church, Dr. Paul Jackson described the purpose of its services when he wrote that the church was "... banded together for work, worship, the observance of the ordinances and the worldwide proclamation of the gospel."[2] Others are reminded of the purposes of the local church by the acrostic "WIFE": worship, instruction, fellowship and evangelism.

As a church planter, you will have to plan and direct the services of the new church until leaders are trained to do so. Stress the privilege and responsibility of Christians to set aside the first day of the week for worshipping God (Hebrews 10:25). This is a necessary part of their relationship with God. "Worship is an active response to God whereby we declare His worth. Worship is not passive, but it is participative. Worship is not simply a mood; it is a response. Worship is not just a feeling; it is a declaration."[3]

Worship reveals the attitude of our heart toward God. Every aspect of the service: music, tithes and offering, prayer, and sermon should all be for the honor and glory of God. Seek to make the services a time of genuine devotion to the Lord. Otherwise, they will become empty rituals devoid of meaning, a response condemned by the Lord Jesus (Matthew 15:8,9).

Involve your people in the services of the church as much as possible. Allow them to participate through music, testimonies, giving, Scripture reading, prayer and speaking. Train people to handle different parts of the service. One can read Scripture, another can lead the song service, still others can minister through special music. Use the young people as ushers in the evening and Wednesday-night services. People must feel a part of the service if you expect them to attend faithfully.

## The Morning Service

The morning service should be designed as a worship service. It should seek to lift the hearts of the people to God in praise and worship. This does not mean that it should be formal and dry, but orderly and respectful. It will also be the most evangelistic service of the week since this is the time when most unsaved people attend church. In the past, this was true of the evening service, but that is no longer the case. Take advantage of the opportunity to present the gospel, to call attention to Jesus Christ and His finished work at Calvary. What better way to exalt our Lord and Savior than to point men to Him and provide the opportunity for them to be saved?

Plan the morning service around the sermon you will be preaching. Choose songs that reinforce the theme of the message. A typical order of service might look like this:

> Hymn
> Opening Prayer
> Hymn
> Scripture Reading
> Pastoral Prayer
> Announcements
> Tithes and Offering
> Hymn
> Special Music
> Sermon
> Invitational Hymn

Keep the announcement time brief and to the point. You do not need to mention everything in the bulletin, only those items that require special emphasis.

Prepare a weekly bulletin. Make it as attractive as possible by using a good quality typewriter and mimeograph. A dry copier would be even better. Proofread the material before you print it to avoid errors. Throw away any copies that are smudged or not printed clearly. The quality of your bulletin reflects the quality of your church. A professional bulletin service (such as Baptist Bulletin Service, Cathedral Press, Long Prairie, MN. 56347) will provide you with bulletin covers and helps at a very reasonable cost.

## The Evening Service

The evening service should be used to disciple your people. It is a time for grounding your people in the Word. It will be a little more relaxed than the morning service and provides an excellent opportunity for people to participate in the service. Encourage some of the men to bring short devotionals, develop singing groups, and use a variety of teaching methods. Use the chalk-board, overhead projector, dramas, skits and quizzes to teach new truths. Remember, your people are learners, disciples who need opportunities for response.

## The Prayer Meeting Service

Wednesday is the day most commonly accepted by fundamental Baptist churches for prayer and Bible study, although any day can be selected. Make the prayer meeting a "prayer" meeting. Keep the Bible study brief, no more than twenty to twenty-five minutes. This service is a time for sharing the burdens, heartaches and desires of the people with each other and God. Allow ample time for people to share their burdens. Provide a printed prayer sheet on which requests can be recorded.

Divide the church into various groups. One week the men can pray in one group and the ladies in another. The next week you can divide the people into small cells of two or three. Another time mix the groups. No one should be required to pray. This can be mentioned from the pulpit or by the leader of each prayer group. Some people are shy and feel embarrassed to pray out loud. If you force them to do so, they are unlikely to return. Be patient, don't force them, and in time you will find they will gain the confidence to pray audibly. You may want to set aside one Wednesday night each month for reading missionary letters and praying specifically for the requests contained therein. End each prayer meeting on a high note with a "testimony time" when people can share blessings of the past week and answers to their prayers.

## The Nursery

The nursery is an important part of any church's ministry. If well run, it will help to attract and hold young couples with small children. The nursery enables them and those around them to enjoy the services without the distractions which often accompany small children.

Set aside a room for this purpose and arrange to have nursery workers available for all public services. The nursery should be well equipped. The floor should be carpeted for the safety of the children and to deaden sound. There should be cribs, a rocking chair and a changing table. You will also need a supply of moist towelettes, diapers and plastic bags for dirty diapers. The room should be well lit with cheerful pictures on the wall. Have soft, quiet toys which cannot be swallowed available for the toddlers.

Only children under 36 months of age should be allowed in the nursery. If space permits, divide the nursery into "sleepers" (0 - 12 months) and "creepers" (13 - 36 months).

Choose a responsible lady to serve as the nursery director. She should arrange to have one worker in the nursery for every three children present. Usually ladies, couples and teenagers are willing to serve in this way. At least one adult should be present at all times. It is best if workers can be present at least fifteen minutes before services begin to receive the children as they arrive. People not working in the nursery should not be allowed to congregate there since this distracts the children and disrupts the work.

Keep a record of each child's name, parents' name, address, phone number and other pertinent information. Do not feed children anything unless it is provided by the parents. Children should be kept as quiet as possible; they should not be be allowed to run, jump, climb, scream or throw things. Encourage them to sit and play quietly, or to listen to stories read by one of the workers. Empty the waste baskets and change the crib sheets after each service. Toys should be washed regularly. All toys and equipment should be picked up and put in their places before leaving. (See the "Guidelines for Nursery Leaders and Workers" at the end of this chapter.)

Remind your nursery workers that this is a ministry, not a babysitting job. It is to be done joyfully unto the Lord with a lot of tender loving care shown to the children. If viewed in this way, the nursery can become a source of great blessing to the parents, children, workers and church involved.

## Children's Church

If personnel and space permit, a "children's church" can be a great blessing. This not only eliminates disruptions during the pastor's message, but it allows the children to be taught on their own level.

You will have to decide whether the children's church will be held at the same time as the adult church or if the children will attend the adult service with their parents until they are dismissed prior to the pastor's message. Many parents prefer to attend part of the regular church service as a family. If dismissed from the adult service, the children should be taught to leave as quietly as possible.

The children's church should not be an extension of the Sunday-school hour. It should be exactly what the name implies, a church service for children. Use children's songs, have the children take up the offering and provide special music. In doing so, you are training them for service in the adult church when they are too old for the children's church.

Remember that children's attention span is shorter than adults; therefore you will have to keep the program moving, changing from one thing to another frequently. Action choruses can be interspersed with the Bible lesson, prayer time, and story time.

Everything should be kept on the children's level. When telling the Bible story, try dramatizing it. Children love the suspense and excitement involved. Never, never read the lesson to the children. Their little minds will soon wander, and you will have lost them for the rest of the hour.

The children's-church program must be somewhat flexible. It must last as long as the adult service. Under no circumstances should it end earlier. Use crafts, Bible memorization or review to keep the children occupied until their parents come for them.

## Special Meetings

In addition to the regular services of the church, schedule special meetings throughout the year to meet the needs of your people. Missionaries, Bible teachers and special-emphasis speakers can be invited to speak on a Sunday at various times throughout the year. In addition, when planning your annual calendar, schedule two or three major conferences. These can be for a three-day weekend or the entire week. Include an annual missionary conference, revival or evangelistic meetings, and perhaps a soul-winning conference, a Bible conference or a Christian-workers seminar. These are not intended to replace the regular pulpit ministry of the pastor, but should supplement, support and extend his effort to lead his people into conformity with God's purpose for the New Testament church.

Line up the speakers and plan every detail well in advance. Do not leave things to the last moment. Publicize the meetings from the pulpit, in the church bulletin, in local newspapers and on radio. Make each meeting a highlight in the church program. Emphasize the importance of being present. Finally, bathe the meetings in prayer. Set up special prayer groups and specific prayer times. Lead your people to expect God to work in their midst during the special meetings. If you do your part, God will do His.

## The Youth Ministry

An effective youth program is essential to church planting. The young people of the church are its future leaders. They must be reached and trained if the church is to continue. Many of the standard youth programs are designed for larger churches. Church planters often lack the finances, facilities and families to use them. How then can we attract and hold teens in a new church situation?

Young people enjoy three things: fun, food and fellowship. They like to get together with kids of their own age, especially when there is food involved. In his book on church planting, Grant Rice describes an excellent youth program for new churches which incorporates the above features.

The program is divided into three segments. During the *first hour* the young people are allowed to play table games donated by families in the church. They can change as often as they want. The *second hour* is given to singing choruses, Bible study and Scripture memorization. Emphasize things of importance to teens and allow them to express their views. Have them learn at least one verse each night. Memorize the books of the Bible. Use "Sword drills." Make it interesting. Serve refreshments during the *last hour*. Have church families donate cookies, cakes, pizza and soft drinks. Check to see if the local bakery will contribute day-old goods to the church.

Baptist Mid-Missions has developed two excellent youth programs for new churches. BIBLE SEEKERS is designed for junior-age children; BIBLE TEENS is aimed at junior and senior high schoolers. Many churches use the AWANA program, but this does require more space, money and personnel. Additional information can be obtained by contacting these organizations directly. Their addresses are located at the end of this chapter.

As your youth ministry grows, seek to involve the young people in visitation, open-air meetings, nursing-home services, music, Christian sports activities, camping programs, vacation Bible school, or Baptist Mid-Missions' STAMP program (Senior Teens Apprentice Missionary Program). Consider having a young people's representative named as a member of the Missions Committee. This provides not only an opportunity for growth in that individual's life, but also a liaison between the Missions Committee and youth department. Their input is not only valuable, but necessary.

## Music

Music has always played a very important part in the ministry and worship of the local church. Paul wrote:

> "Let the word of Christ dwell in you richly in all wisdom; teaching and admonishing one another in psalms and hymns and spiritual songs, singing with grace in your hearts to the Lord" (Colossians 3:16).

Music encourages and comforts us when we are in distress. Paul and Silas "sang praises unto God" while they were in prison at Philippi (Acts 16:25). It can stir our emotions, lift our spirits and prepare our hearts to worship God if properly done. It will be necessary to teach discernment regarding music.

Much of what is heard in churches today reflects the world's music and does not glorify God. Jackson wrote:

> "The music that is borrowed from the world should be banished from the church. Many songs and choruses in common usage today have within them the beat of the jungle and the dance floor. They stimulate the flesh, not the spiritual life. Words of many songs and choruses are light, frivolous, meaningless–utterly unscriptural and unworthy of a place in a Christian service."[4]

The music program in your church should be clearly defined. Establish standards for the music to be used. Go through the song book and mark the songs which may be sung. You may want to appoint a music coordinator to oversee the music program. (See a job description at the end of this chapter.) All special music should be approved in advance by him or the pastor.

You may have to lead the music in the beginning, but start training someone to take over this important task as soon as possible. Have a pianist or organist available for every service. Select the hymns in advance and not as people arrive. The musicians should be given a list of the music early enough to allow for rehearsal. Have them commence playing five to ten minutes before the service begins to set the tone for the meeting.

Be sure that those who will have part in the special music have been informed and are ready. Nothing is quite so embarrassing as a poorly rehearsed song. You have the responsibility for leading your people into a closer walk with God. The music you use will either help or hinder your efforts.


## The Ordinances

Paul Jackson defines ordinances this way:

"Ordinances are established rights or ceremonies. Baptists believe that the Lord has given two to His church–baptism and the Lord`s supper....He knew the practical value of such repeated enactments of truth. Each time we witness a baptism we are reminded tangibly of our union with Christ as we are identified with Him in His death, burial, and resurrection. Each time we participate in the Lord's supper we are reminded of our communion with Him....The Lord did not suggest these ceremonies. He commanded them. He said: '...This do...' (I Corinthians 11:24); "Go...teach...baptizing...' (Matthew 38:19). These ordinances are His orders and we should observe them as sacred, God-given responsibilities."[5]

When should the church planter implement the ordinances? Just as soon as the new church is officially organized. Since both baptism and the Lord's Supper are church ordinances, they should not be practiced by the group prior to the organizational meeting.

**Baptism**: Baptism is the first step of obedience for a new believer. It is a public declaration of his identification with Jesus Christ. It is a testimony to the world that he has accepted as his personal Savior Jesus Christ and all that He did on Calvary. It gives witness to the fact that the Holy Spirit has accomplished the work of regeneration in his heart.

When should the new believer be baptized? In his excellent book, *The Pastor-His Life and Work*, Dr. Charles Wagner points out:

> "Some believe there should be a long waiting period before a person is baptized. Others feel that it should be immediate, even the same day the person is converted.... I have no objection to the person being baptized the same day if he is not forced into it, and as long as there is sufficient instruction for him to understand the meaning of it. However, there is a benefit to a short waiting period."[6]

Teach new believers the importance and significance of baptism as soon as they trust Christ. This should not be an extensive course for new believers (that comes later), but a simple explanation of the purpose and picture it represents.

Arrange to baptize new believers as soon as possible after they are saved. This could be the same day, the following Sunday, or at the next regularly scheduled baptismal service. If baptism is clearly explained at the time of salvation, many, if not most of those accepting Christ will submit to it. (Additional teaching may be necessary before baptism in cases where people are reluctant to be baptized or when they have been involved in false teaching on the subject.)

If you do not yet have a building of your own, you can arrange to use the facilities of another church, a swimming pool or near-by lake, river or stream. Dr. Wagner's book gives very practical helps for baptism. He covers such areas as

Instructing the candidate in preparation for baptism,
Presenting the candidate to the church,
Baptizing the candidate,
Personnel needed in preparing for baptismal service,
Post-baptism activities,
Helpful hints on installing a baptistry in the church.

Baptism is a local-church ordinance and therefore is to be administered only by direction of the local church and only to those who are coming into its membership. Para-church organizations have no scriptural authority to baptize.

**The Lord's Supper:** The early church "continued steadfastly in the apostles' doctrine and fellowship and in breaking of bread and in prayers" (Acts 2:42). The "breaking of bread" or the Lord's Table is the second ordinance commanded by Christ to be observed by the New Testament church. Christ did not specify a frequency, but rather simply stated: "This do ye, as oft as ye drink it, in remembrance of me" (I Corinthians 11:25).

Make the Communion service very special. It is a time of intimate fellowship with the Lord and fellow believers. Make it a precious time for remembrance, repentance and rededication. Seek to focus the attention of your people on the person and work of the Savior.

The church planter as pastor will normally preside at the Lord's Table. In the beginning you may have to serve the elements yourself. But as soon as possible, choose spiritually qualified men to assist you in this ministry until deacons can be chosen to help. Should the church be without a pastor, it may still observe the ordinance by designating one or two spiritually qualified men to oversee the service.

Fermented wine is not to be used for the Lord's Table. To do so would be to present a distorted picture of the shed blood of the Lord Jesus Christ. The Passover feast, from which the wine was taken when the Lord's Table was instituted, was to be totally free of leaven or fermenting agents since they were figures of sin. The Bible clearly teaches that priests of God (and Christians are priests) should abstain from the use of alcoholic beverages (Leviticus 10:1-11; Proverbs 23:29-32; Ephesians 5:18). Again, we highly recommend Wagner's book, *The Pastor-His Life and Work*, as a source for description of the ordinance of the Lord's table. You will find this most helpful.

## The Invitation

Jesus Christ set the example for evangelists, pastors and church planters. He never hesitated to invite sinners to trust in Him. In His discussion with the Samaritan woman (John 4), He offered her the "Water of Life." This woman was thirsty. She accepted Him as Messiah and immediately went back to her village to announce that the Messiah had come. He also gave a public invitation to hundreds of lost Jews in the temple at Jeru-salem. Standing in the temple area, He cried saying, "If any man thirst, let him come unto me and drink" (John 7:37).

Paul certainly gave a public invitation when he wrote: "God hath committed unto us the word of reconciliation...we are ambassadors for Christ; we pray you in Christ's stead, be ye reconciled to God" (II Corinthians 5:19,20). Even the closing appeal of the Bible (Revelation 22:17) is an invitation for the unbeliever to accept Christ. Charles Hadden Spurgeon in his *Lectures to My Students* warned his disciples:

> "Brethren, we must plead. Entreaties and beseechings must blend with our instructions...In our Master's name we must give the invitation, crying, "Whosoever will, let him take the water of life freely.' "[7]

Learn to use every opportunity to invite men to come to Christ. You do not have to resort to gimmicks or pressure to induce people to accept Christ. The preaching of the gospel combined with a well planned invitation will result in genuine conversions.

The invitation should be well planned. This is the most important time in the service. Your entire message should move toward making a decision. Plan to end your sermon on a high note and move directly into the invitation. Avoid reaching an obvious "ending" that says, "It's time to go home." The invitation should be a planned part of your message, not an afterthought tacked onto the end of the service.

Be earnest and sincere when giving the invitation. This may be the most important decision of people's lives. Emphasize the urgency of responding to the Holy Spirit's pleading. It might be their last opportunity for all we know. Do not pressure people into a decision for which they are not ready, but do not let them slip away without having made a definite decision one way or the other.

Move directly into the invitation. Do not ask people to open song books or to stand until later, for this breaks the impact of the message. Simply ask them to bow their heads while they are still thinking about what you just said.

Be specific when giving the invitation. Tell them exactly what you want to know and what you want them to do. Tell them when to bow their heads, when to raise their hands, when to come forward. Do not assume people know what to do. Give them detailed instructions. Ask specific questions. Do they want to accept Christ as their Savior? Be baptized? Join the church? Do they have a problem they need help with? Ask a series of questions and wait for a response to each, rather than giving a general invitation. Be careful with your wording. If you say, "Just slip up your hand and say 'pray for me,' " it suggests that they must speak aloud. It is better to say, "Just slip up your hand to indicate you want me to pray for you."

Be positive when you give the invitation. Expect someone to respond. Never imply that people might not come. Say, "As you come," rather than, "Will you come." Or, "As I leave the platform, you come and meet me here at the altar." Do not create roadblocks which people must climb over to come to Christ. Make it easy for them to respond to the invitation.

Have trained counselors waiting to deal with those who respond to the invitation. Do not allow people to come forward without getting the help they are seeking. Have someone talk with them and pray with each one. This will go a long way toward avoiding the false professions of "easy believism" so prevalant in our day. This counseling can be done at the altar or in the privacy of a side room. Have appropriate literature and decision cards prepared for those who come forward.

There may be individuals who desire to profess Christ, but for one reason or another do not respond publicly to the invitation. They should not be pressured into doing so. Provide an opportunity for them to indicate their need for counseling or for assistance. An upraised hand or a brief word to you at the close of the service can let you know of their desire for help. Many individuals, after hearing the gospel, but not responding to the invitation, receive Christ in the pastor's study or at home. The important thing is that the individual clearly understand and be given an opportunity to respond to God's free offer of salvation.

## Guidelines for the Nursery Leader

1. Make up a list of nursery workers for each service. Post this
   schedule in the nursery on the last Sunday of the month and
   give a copy to your supervisor.
   a. Try to maintain a ratio of *one worker* for every *three
      children.*
   b. Nursery helpers should be at least 12 years old.
   c. Contact nursery workers to remind  them when they are
      scheduled to be in the nursery.
2. Meet with nursery workers once each quarter.
   a. Impress upon your workers that the nursery is a ministry,
      both to the parents and to the young children. It is not just
      a baby-sitting job.
   b. Encourage workers to teach Bible truths to toddlers rather
      than simply letting them play all the time.
   c. Discuss any problems, equipment needs or supplies.
   d. Keep your supervisor advised of problems and progress.
3. Check on the nursery each Sunday to be sure it is functioning
   properly.
   a. Only nursery workers should be allowed in the nursery.
      Teens, children and parents are not to be in the nursery
      unless bringing or picking up children.
   b. Only children 0 - 36 months should be in the nursery.
4. Be sure all teaching materials are in agreement with the
   policy and position of the church.
5. Remove broken toys and worn-out books. Keep equipment in
   good repair. Keep the cabinets neat and well organized.
6. Empty the waste basket and dispose of dirty diapers after each
   service.
   a. Sheets should be washed every week, toys every other week
      and the cribs at least once a month.
   b. Do not leave food in the nursery.
   c. Maintain a supply of fresh water, moist towelettes and
      plastic bags (for diapers) at all times.
7. Inform your workers that the nursery will be open 15 minutes
   before and after the services to encourage fellowship among
   parents and to alleviate possible pressure on any parents who
   may wish to respond to the invitation.

# Guidelines for the Nursery Worker

1. Consider the nursery a ministry to the Lord and to parents with small children. Your willingness to serve here makes it possible for many others to enjoy the worship service without disruption.
   a. Children should be kept as quiet as possible.
   b. Encourage activities that will not excite the children (story telling, reading, coloring, playing quietly).
   c. To protect small children and babies, no running, jumping, climbing, wrestling or throwing of toys is to be allowed.
2. Only children under <u>36 months</u> of age should be permitted in the nursery.
   a. Teens, children and parents should not be allowed in the nursery unless bringing or picking up children.
   b. Discourage people from entering or leaving the church through the nursery. (This disrupts the nursery and is a health hazard.)
3. Be in the nursery 15 minutes before the beginning of the service and remain until the last child has been picked up by his or her parents.
   a. A "nursery registration" card should be filled out for each child the first time he or she is placed in the nursery.
   b. Ask for help whenever the ratio of *one worker* for every *three children* is exceeded.
   c. Remain in the nursery until all children have been picked up by their parents. DO NOT ALLOW THE CHILDREN TO LEAVE BY THEMSELVES WHEN THE SERVICE IS OVER.
   d. Leave the nursery neat and clean. Pick up all toys, paper and books. Replace things taken from the cabinets. Put diapers in plastic bags and dispose of them.
4. Do not feed the children anything without the parent's permission. NO FOOD SHOULD BE LEFT IN THE NURSERY.
5. Remove books and coloring items from the cabinets for the children and replace them neatly on the shelves when finished. Do not allow the children to open cabinets or to throw things back into them.
6. Report to your nursery leader any problems you have.
   a. If you cannot be in the nursery on your assigned Sunday, inform the nursery leader as far in advance as possible.
   b. Please do not arrange for your own substitute.

## Sample Nursery Registration Card

### All About Me

My name is: _____

My address is: _____

_____

My parents are: _____

I was born on: _____(date)

I like to sleep on my
( ) back
( ) stomach
( ) side

When I take my bottle, please
( ) hold me in your arms
( ) place me in bed with bottle
( ) _____

Mother says I may
( ) be held & rocked
( ) creep on the floor
( ) play in the playpen
( ) eat crackers

Special care and allergies:

_____

_____

BIBLE SEEKERS and BIBLE TEENS materials may be ordered from:

Baptist Mid-Missions
4205 Chester Avenue
Cleveland, Ohio 44103
phone: (216) 432-2200

AWANA materials may be ordered from

AWANA Youth Association
3201 Tollview Drive
Rolling Meadows, IL 60008
phone: (312) 394-5150

AWANA Youth Association
178 Highway 20W
Fonthill, ON
Canada LOS 1E0
phone: (416) 892-8204

Children's Church materials may be ordered from:

Faith Venture Visuals
510 East Main Street
Lititz, PA 17543
phone: (717) 626-8503

Bible Visuals, Inc.
Box 4842
Lancaster, PA 17604
phone: (717) 569-7800

## Job Description for the Music Coordinator

The music program in your church should be clearly defined. You may want to consider this definition as part of your church constitution.

"A music coordinator shall be appointed annually by the pastor and approved by the board of deacons. This office may be filled by a lay member, a staff member, or by several sharing in the responsibilities. The duties shall be to

1. Supervise the total music program of the church. He shall work in close harmony with the pastor as to music, personnel, and selection.
2. Select with the approval of the pastor and Christian Education Committee, the choir leaders and assistants, pianists, organists, and other personnel needed in the music program of the church.
3. Prepare a written music schedule for those who are to participate in special music."

(Taken from the constitution of the First Baptist Church in Elkhart, Indiana)

## Endnotes

[1] Henry C. Vedder, *A Short History of the Baptists*. (Valley Forge, PA: Judson Press, 1907), p. 33.

[2] Paul R. Jackson, *The Doctrine and Administration of the Church*. (Des Plaines, IL: Regular Baptist Press, 1968), p. 27.

[3] Ronald Allen and Gordon Borror, *Worship—Rediscovering the Missing Jewel*. (Portland, OR: Multnomah Press, 1982), p. 16.

[4] Jackson, *op. cit.*, p. 92.

[5] *Ibid.* pp. 61 - 62.

[6] Charles U. Wagner, *The Pastor-His Life and Work*. (Schaumburg, IL: Regular Baptist Press, 1976), pp. 178-9.

[7] C.H. Spurgeon, *Lectures To My Students*. (Grand Rapids: Zondervan, 1954).

# Chapter 11

# The Operation of the Local
# Church Sunday School

## Purpose

The Sunday School is an essential part of the church-planting process. You cannot build a strong church without a strong Sunday-school program. It is the evangelistic and educational arm of the church. The Sunday School attracts, wins and trains more people for Christ than any other activity of the church.

It is basically through the Sunday School that we carry out the second half of our Lord's command in the Great Commission to teach "them to observe all things whatsoever I have commanded you" (Matthew 28:20).

J. Edward Hakes lists seven specific purposes for the Sunday School. They are

1. bringing the student to Christ for salvation,
2. building up the student in his Christian life,
3. teaching the student how to live with other people,
4. helping the student to understand God's gracious and glorious purpose for His children,
5. developing proper attitudes toward God in worship and daily "spiritual exercise",
6. teaching God's plan for His children (John 14:2),
7. preparing those who are saved to be effective witnesses for Christ.[1]

A well organized Sunday School will minister to the needs of the entire family, children, teens and adults. In addition, new believers will be nurtured and brought to spiritual maturity through the opportunities for growth in the grace and knowledge of Jesus Christ.

## Organization

An unorganized Sunday School is like a football team with no game plan, no coach and no player knowing his position. You can imagine the confusion on the field during the game. It is important to organize and administrate the Sunday School carefully. "Ninety percent of failure is lack of organization."[2] In the beginning, keep the organizational structure simple. It should be based on three factors:

1. the number of people attending the Sunday School,
2. the available space and equipment,
3. the number of qualified leaders and teachers.

Unless you have a number of experienced Sunday-school teachers, it is best to wait three or four weeks after the first public service before holding Sunday-school classes. This will allow you time to recruit and train teachers from among the core group.

As soon as possible, divide the Sunday School into five classes: pre-schoolers, primaries, juniors, youth and adults. Helpers need not be fully trained, but they should meet spiritual qualifications and have some teaching ability. Help them improve their skills by providing teacher-training classes for them.

As the church grows and God provides capable leaders, depart-mentalize the Sunday School. This can be done step by step as need requires, but you should eventually have nine groups:

1. cradle roll–birth to 2 years,
2. nursery–2 to 4 years,
3. beginners–4 years through kindergarten,
4. primary–1st through 3rd grades (6-8 years),
5. junior–4th through 6th grades (9-11years),
6. junior high school–7th through 9th grades (12-14 years),
7. senior high school–10th through 12th grades (15-18 years),
8. young adults–college & career (18-24 years),
9. adults–(25 years old and up).

Ideally, classes should have no more than six to eight children. Teens and adults, however, generally fit into any size class with little difficulty.

## Classroom Space

It is amazing what can be done with limited space. A large room can be subdivided to accommodate more than one class. Simple moveable partitions can be built at minimal cost. Make the partitions of light-weight, sound-absorbing materials. Allow twelve square feet per student. A class of six to eight students should have a room measuring no less than ten by ten in size.

## Equipment

Equipment should fit the students, especially tables and chairs. Avoid putting children on chairs too large for their feet to touch the floor. Provide tables for the younger children. Kidney-shaped tables are best. They allow the teacher to be closer to the students. Because small children are overwhelmed by adults towering over them, have the teacher sit at the table with the children during the class time.

An overhead projector is an excellent teaching tool, especially for high-school students and adults. Chalkboards, bulletin boards and flannelgraph boards are also extremely useful.(See the section in this chapter on audio-visuals for more inform-ation.)

## Curriculum

A well-planned curriculum is vital if you are going to have a well-organized Sunday School. The curriculum is like a race course: "it is the path traversed by the pupil and teacher in reach-ing a desired objective."[3] It is composed of all that is needed to reach the stated objectives of the Sunday School. It includes not only teaching materials but plans for using them.

Curriculum materials should be carefully chosen after much planning and study. The materials should be

1. biblically sound,
2. attractive to teachers and students alike,
3. encouraging of Bible study by the students,
4. equipped with adequate helps for the teacher.

In addition, be sure that the curriculum materials you use are produced by a Baptist publisher which takes the same position as the church on doctrine and separation. Use graded materials which are produced by the same publisher for every class . Don't mix publishers or you will not have a properly balanced curricu-lum for all age groups. Be sure special emphasis is given in the materials to

1. Baptist distinctives,
2. stewardship,
3. missions,
4. Scripture memorization,
5. believer's baptism and church membership.

(See the end of this chapter for a list of publishers from whom you can order dependable Sunday-school materials.)

## Choosing and Training Teachers

The selection of teachers is extremely important. Rather than asking for volunteers, a situation which sometimes results in unqualified individuals volunteering, hand out a "service questionnaire" similar to the one at the end of this chapter. Ask the congregation to check those areas where they have had experience and also to note the areas of ministry in which they would be willing to serve. Go over the questionnaires and select qualified personnel to be teachers. You may start them out as assistant teachers, observing and learning from a more experienced teacher. It is essential that you provide training for your teachers.

Anyone operating a sophisticated piece of equipment must be trained for the job. If he is a conscientious worker, he will be committed to doing the very best job possible. He will seek to sharpen his skills. It is even more important for a Sunday-school teacher to be trained. "A local Christian-education program will be no stronger than its leaders. Its over-all success is determined largely by the quality of the teachers who teach the Word of God."[4]

Sunday-school teachers will feel more comfortable and confident if they know what is expected of them. Develop standards or guidelines which set forth the qualifications and responsibilities of teachers. These standards should be in effect from the very first class that is held. Do not use people who fail to meet the requirements. It is better to combine classes than to allow unqualified people to serve in the classroom. Every teacher should:

1. be saved and baptized,
2. be a member of the church in good standing,
3. support the total ministry of the church,
4. faithfully attend the regular services of the church,

5. be a student of the Word of God,
6. love people,
7 be willing to cooperate with those in charge.

The above may be included in a Sunday-school worker's covenant similar to the one at the end of this chapter.

Meet with your workers every month. You may need to "sell" them on the value of such a meeting. You must motivate your people to improve their skills. This can be done by making the monthly meeting  both inspirational and instructional. Share your goals and dreams for the Sunday School; inform the workers of impending contests and plans; provide useful ideas for improving their classes and discuss problems that have arisen since the last meeting. Use part of the time to cover one or more of the standards for teachers. A list of topics to cover might include

1.  pre-session planning,
2.  reclaiming absentees,
3.  leading pupils to Christ,
4.  pupil participation,
5.  laws of effective teaching,
6.  lesson preparation,
7.  using visual aids,
8.  Scripture memorization,
9.  keeping and using records,
10.  making home visits,
11.  teaching methods,
12  personal devotional life,
13.  promoting missions in class,
14.  solving discipline problems.

Conduct a teacher-training program at least once a year. Teacher training is a long-range solution to the Sunday-school teachers' need. An on-going training program will prepare individuals who will be more receptive when asked to teach. Many people do not respond to a request for teachers because they feel unqualified. Teacher training removes this obstacle.

The Evangelical Teacher Training Association (Box 327, Wheaton, Illinois 60187) provides a workable program for training teachers. Their preliminary courses "provide a good foundation for Sunday School teachers. Individuals who have completed the preliminary course are excellent candidates for teachers. Enlist as many individuals in the training course as possible. Often the course will be taken and completed by those who have no intention of teaching. The challenge and desire will come later."[5]

Other teacher-training materials are available from publish-ers of Sunday-school materials, Christian college libraries and Christian bookstores. You can also use a book like John Gregory's *The Seven Laws Of Teaching* (Grand Rapids, MI: Baker Book House, 1972) for your training sessions. Include in the church budget provisions for purchasing resource materials for the church's Christian-education department. Store teaching materials in a well organized file cabinet (with lock) for repeated use. Begin a bookshelf library of basic reference works for teachers.

## Sunday School Contests

Growing Sunday Schools result in growing churches. But how do you get the Sunday School to grow? How do you overcome the lack of interest and enthusiasm which is evident in so many schools? Contests and special days can help eliminate these problems. They will result in new people enrolling in the classes and more members enlisting to help. You must build enthusiasm before you can have expansion and you must have evangelism before you can have enlistment.

Dr. Fred Barlow points out that a contest will do five things for the Sunday School:

1. it enlarges the vision of the workers,
2. it emphasizes special days on the calendar,
3. it enlists new workers,
4. it evangelizes the unreached in the community,
5. it enrolls more people in the Sunday School.[6]

A good contest or special day requires three things: planning, promotion and perspiration. No contest will bring the desired results without these.

First, plan the contest or special day thoroughly. Build these special events into the regular church calendar. Make them part of the overall program of the church. You should plan to have at least one major attendance contest, either in the Fall or Spring. Additional special days can be built around holidays and special occasions on the secular calendar like the Fourth of July, Thanksgiving, Flag Day, Mother's Day or Father's Day. It would not hurt to have a special day once a month or at least once a quarter.

Your contest can be self-contained within your own church. You might pit the men against the women, the children and youth against the adults or divide the church into various teams. Or you may choose to enter a contest against another church or group of churches. If this is the case, be sure the churches are of the same approximate size or work out a percentage of growth formula to determine who wins.

Special days are by nature only one day long. Contests can run from four to ten weeks in length. If they are too long, people will lose interest and the contest will be a failure.

You must promote the contest or special day if you expect it to succeed. Inform your leaders and those who will have special part in the contest several weeks in advance. Put up posters and flyers, begin announcing the contest two to three weeks before it begins. Offer rewards to those who participate or excel. This can be done on a weekly basis or at the end of the contest. Appropriate Christian books are gifts which both reward and edify. Have a skit or humorous dialogue to promote the contest. There is no limit to what you can do if you use your imagination.

A special event requires special effort. In addition to planning and promoting your contest or special day, you will need to do more work. There are posters to be made, letters to be printed, flyers to be distributed, people to be enlisted and rewards purchased. You can purchase books from many Sunday-school publishers which will give you detailed helps. Excellent materials are also available from Bethesda Baptist Church, 7950 N., 650 E., Brownsburg, Indiana 46112.

## Sunday School Openings and Closings

Many Sunday Schools have opening and closing exercises or assemblies. However, these detract greatly from the effectiveness of the Sunday School. The main purpose seems to be to allow latecomers to arrive before classes begin. We would suggest that students go directly to their classes upon arrival and that classes begin at the time Sunday School begins. This will give teachers more time to do the job they have been assigned. It also follows the pattern children are accustomed to in school. The opening and closing assemblies greatly reduce the teaching time available for teaching the Word to the students. If Sunday School is only

45-50 minutes long to begin with, you do not want to further reduce that time by holding opening or closing exercises.

## Audio-Visuals (Multi Media)

There is an old proverb that goes: "A picture is worth a thousand words. "Studies have shown that we retain far more of what we see than what we hear. Educational researchers tell us that eighty-five percent of what we remember is gained through visual stimuli."[7]

The media invest millions of dollars in sophisticated technology to get their message across. They have successfully used audio-visual communications (especially television) to change the world during the past two decades. The average high-school graduate spends 12,000 hours in classroom study and 22,000 hours viewing TV.

Audio-visuals are an effective tool for communicating the message of Christ. You do not have to invest thousands of dollars in electronic equipment if you use your resources wisely. Flannelgraph materials still captivate young audiences. Chalkboards or erasable dry felt pens can be used to diagram your teaching.

An overhead projector is a valuable investment. You can use it for teaching gospel choruses, memory verses, illustrations, sermon notes and various graphics. Map overlays and lesson helps are available from major publishers, such as Regular Baptist Press and Moody Press. Faith Venture Visuals is an excellent source of materials for the pastor desirous of using the overhead projector. Overhead transparencies are easily made by preparing your copy and then using acetate film in a Xerox machine. The 3M Thermofax machine also has transparency kits that are relatively inexpensive. Color can be added to the transparency by the use of overhead marking pencils available both in permanent and water-soluble colors. Be sure you purchase a large, good-quality screen to allow people in the rear of the room to see the pictures easily.

Other valuable projectors available include the Kodak carrousel 35mm projector, with automatic focus and zoom lens, film-strip projectors and 16mm movie projectors. All are valuable teaching tools. There are many slide programs, film strips and films available for teaching and training purposes. If you can afford any of these pieces of equipment, choose a good quality machine that will stand up over the years. Keep a spare bulb and heavy-duty extension cord on hand as well.

Puppets are effective communicators made popular by the "Muppet Show." Who in our society today, young or old, does not know who Kermit the Frog is? Try using puppets in your church; you will see that they really work in reaching not only children but adults as well. These lovable creatures are available from various sources including Christian bookstores. There is plenty of resource material available to help you create and use your own puppets in telling Bible stories.

Display boards and bulletin boards are an inexpensive form of audio-visuals. Assign the responsibility for bulletin and display boards to a talented church member. Idea books can be obtained at a teacher's supply store. Contact your local elementary or junior high school and ask them about resource materials for their bulletin boards. The public library or school library also would have this information on hand. An attractive Sunday school classroom can be a real help in encouraging students to study. Change the theme of the classroom to emphasize the sub-ject of your study each quarter.

Carefully plan and budget the equipment you purchase. Choose good-quality equipment even though it is more expensive. It will last longer, serve you better and be less costly in the long run. Whatever audio-visuals you use, learn how to use them properly, then use them frequently.

## Endnotes

[1] J. Edward Hakes, *An Introduction to Evangelical Christian Education.* (Chicago: Moody Press, 1967), p. 60.

[2] Henrietta Mears, quoted in *Ways to Plan & Organize Your Sunday School.* (Glendale, CA: International Center for Learning, 1971), p. 107.

[3] Kenneth L. Cover, *Shaping the Church's Educational Ministry* . (Valley Forge, PA: Judson Press, 1971), p. 27.

[4] Hakes, *op. cit.,* p. 96.

[5] James F. Dersham, *Enlisting Teachers. (Regular Teacher,* a publication of Regular Baptist Press, vol. 6, No. 2, Winter, 1981), p. 1.

[6] Fred M. Barlow, *Special Days in the Sunday School.* (Des Plaines, IL: Regular Baptist Press, 1971), pp. 9-14.

[7] Ron Wilson, *Multimedia Handbook for the Church.* (Elgin, IL: David C. Cook Publishing Co., 1975), p. 13.

## Sunday School Worker's Covenant

Having received Jesus Christ as my personal Savior, and being a baptized member of this church, I acknowledge that I have been afforded a special privilege in teaching the Word of God. In view of my appointment as a Sunday School worker, and relying on the help and guidance of the Holy Spirit, I promise to fulfill my responsibilities and to abide by the following covenant:

1. I readily subscribe to the doctrinal statement of my church and will teach nothing that is in conflict with its position.
2. I will cooperate fully with the educational program of this church, use the materials provided, attend the teachers' meetings and accept the supervision, advice and training offered by those in charge.
3. I will set aside time daily for communion with my Lord in prayer and Bible reading.
4. I will faithfully attend and promote the services of my church (Sunday School, Morning Service, Evening Service and Prayer Meeting) and will support this church through my tithes, offerings and prayers.
5. I will be exemplary in my conduct, not using tobacco, alcohol nor illicit drugs and will dress appropriately for all services
6. I will earnestly pray for the conversion of unsaved class members and for the spiritual growth of those who are Christians.
7. I will faithfully prepare each lesson, not waiting until Saturday to begin and will be in my classroom fifteen minutes before Sunday School is to begin. In class I will teach from the Bible and not from a lesson book.
8. I will contact all visitors and absentees before the following Sunday and will visit in the home of each pupil in my class at least once this year.
9. If for some reason I must be absent or cannot fulfill my responsibilities, I will notify the chairman of the education committee immediately and will cooperate fully in seeking a replacement rather than seeking my own substitute.

Name _____

Date _____

## A Service Questionnaire for Christian Workers

Please check the areas in which you have had experience:

[ ] S. S. Teacher      [ ] Sunday School Supt.
[ ] Pri. or Jr. Church      [ ] Youth Leader

[ ] Choir      [ ] Visitation
[ ] Song Leader      [ ] Usher
[ ] Special Music      [ ] Bus Ministry
[ ] Piano/Organ      [ ] Bookkeeping
[ ] Nursery      [ ] Electrical Work
[ ] Deacon      [ ] Custodian
[ ] Artistic Work      [ ] Painting
[ ] Secretarial Work      [ ] Carpentry
[ ] Missionary Leader      [ ] Other_____

Please check the areas of ministry in which you are willing to serve:

[ ] S. S .Teacher      [ ] Sunday School Supt.
[ ] Pri. or Jr.Church      [ ] Youth Leader
[ ] Choir      [ ] Visitation
[ ] Song Leader      [ ] Usher
[ ] Special Music      [ ] Bus Ministry
[ ] Piano/Organ      [ ] Bookkeeping
[ ] Nursery      [ ] Electrical Work
[ ] Deacon      [ ] Custodian
[ ] Artistic Work      [ ] Painting
[ ] Secretarial Work      [ ] Carpentry
[ ] Miss. Leader      [ ] Other_____

Sound, biblical Sunday School materials may be ordered from

Regular Baptist Press
P.O. Box 95500
Schaumburg, IL 60195
phone: (312) 843-1600

Missionary church planters can get free Sunday School materials from

Gospel Literature Services
1300 N. Meacham Road
P.O. Box 95500
Schaumburg, IL 60195
phone: (312) 843-1600

Excellent children's materials are available from

Bible Visuals, Inc.
650 Main Street
Box Z
Akron, PA 17501-0153
phone: (717) 859-1131

Teacher Training materials are available from

Evangelical Teacher Training Association
Wheaton, IL 60187
phone: (312) 668-6400

Advertising banners of all sizes are available from

Superior Banner Service
P.O. Box 135
Bellevue, NE 68005
phone: (402) 291-2575

# Chapter 12

# The Outreach
# of the Local Church

Missions is a vital part of the church-planting ministry. Begin teaching your people to pray for and support missionaries from the very first Sunday you start holding meetings. Set aside ten percent of your offerings for missionary support and schedule a missionary speaker during the first three months of your existence.

Someone will ask: "But should a newly planted church or a mission church support missionaries when it cannot support its own pastor?" The answer is an emphatic, "YES"! If you want your people to be concerned about winning souls and to support the work at home, give them a vision of the fields abroad. But keep a balance. If you limit your missionary giving to ten percent and follow the salary schedule outlined in this book, neither the pastor nor missions will be neglected.

The responsibility of a newly planted church is no different from that of other churches which have been in existence longer. "The church is responsible to present world missions as God's priority in every area of church life, so that those who should be foreign missionaries will be exposed, challenged and encouraged to go overseas, and those God calls to stay at home will have a correct view of the foreign mission field and the significance of their participation from the homeland." [1] "World missions is not a *part* of the church program; it is the program of the church." [2]

According to Acts 13:1-4, the task of the local church is to produce missionaries, and to send them to the field. If you wait until the church is fully developed and can afford a missionary program, you will never have a missionary program. Begin now and let the vision of your people grow with the church.

## The Place of the Pastor

As pastor, you must provide leadership in developing the missionary program of the church. "As the pastor goes, so goes the missions program of the church. The church rises no higher than its pastor. If the pastor is weak on missions, the church will be weak on missions....The key to any effective program of a church, including the missions program, is the pastor."[3]

Be informed in the area of missions. Study the missionary program found in the Scriptures. Take time to read mission periodicals and journals. Peruse books on the strategy and history of missions. Become familiar with the stories of great missionaries. Share missionary letters with your people. Encourage them to pray for the needs mentioned in the letters. Include missionaries in your public and private prayer times. You hold the key to raising and maintaining the missionary consciousness of your people.

## Organizing a Missionary Program

The old cliche, "There is no time like the present," holds true for missions in the local church. The Scripture teaches the urgency of preaching the gospel to every creature NOW. Do not wait until you have seen a substantial growth in the church. Begin organizing your missionary program right now.

Begin by appointing a missionary committee. Ask two or three interested people to help you develop the missionary program of the church. This number can be increased as the church grows and need requires.

Work with your missionary committee to set forth the church's missionary policy. Be specific. Put it in writing. (See the sample at the end of this chapter.) Only those missionaries and mission agencies which are in agreement with the church's Statement of Faith and practices should be invited to speak or be considered for support. Certainly, in this case it should be "Baptist money for Baptist work."

Not only should missionaries be in agreement with the doctrines and position of the church, but they should also be associated with a mission agency which follows sound financial policies. Does your gift go entirely to the missionary, or does the home office keep a percentage? Are they willing to give you a yearly, audited financial statement?

As part of the church's mission policy, have every missionary meet with the missions committee when he or she comes to your church. Use the time to hear a detailed report of his/her ministry on the field and plans for the future. The committee should question missionaries concerning their stand on current issues and any possible changes in their doctrinal position. This is not a time of inquisition, but of honest sharing of views to be sure the missionary still holds the same position and beliefs as the church.

Plan to hold a missionary conference within the first year and annually thereafter. Make it a highlight on the church calendar. You can begin with a three-day conference (Friday through Sunday) with just two speakers. Later this can be expanded to a Sunday through Wednesday conference. Include a banquet, posters, special music from other churches, a display table supplied by the missionaries and slides. Begin planning well in advance, bathing the entire process in prayer. If you need help, Baptist Mid-Missions and other mission agencies have the expertise and personnel to assist you in planning a successful missionary conference.

Advertise the conference; use your local newspaper. Most papers have a religious section in which you can announce the conference free of cost. Let the Sunday-school classes compete in preparing posters for the conference, based on the theme of the conference. These should be placed in various places in the church two weeks before the conference. Awards can be presented on the first night of the conference to winners of the poster-drawing contest. Plenty of missionary literature should be made available. Have well prepared special music that highlights the missionary theme.

There are a number of ways to keep missions before your people. Preach on missions or invite missionaries to speak at least once a quarter. Another time, read a prayer letter and have your people pray for that missionary. Arrange for a brief taped message from the missionary to be played for the congregation, or show a few slides of that missionary's ministry on the field.

## Missionary Maps and Bulletin Boards

The missionary committee should put up a missions map in a highly visible place in the church. Along with the map put up a special bulletin board just for missions. The map would indicate places where your missionaries are working. Place pictures of the missionaries on the map along with information about them: their names, mission, field of service and type of work. A more sophisticated map with lights which indicate the location of each missionary is very impressive.

Use the bulletin board to post letters from your missionaries. Put up short articles and other items with a missions emphasis.

Have someone on the missions committee responsible for changing the bulletin board periodically. Be sure it is kept up to date.

## Giving to Missions

There are three different plans for giving to missions:

1. the budget plan,
2. the percentage plan,
3. the faith promise plan.

In the budget plan, a fixed amount is included in the overall budget of the church. That amount is sent to the missionaries each month.

The percentage plan calls for a certain percentage of the total offerings received each month to be set aside for missions. The amount fluctuates every month depending on income.

The faith promise plan encourages a person to give an amount to missions over and above his regular tithes and offerings. He makes a commitment to contribute whatever amount he believes God would have him give. Then he trusts God to provide exactly that amount in the coming year. The church also gives a committed amount or proportion of its general receipts.

Don't put all your eggs in one basket when it comes to missionary support. It is better to support two or three missionaries rather than one or several rather than a few. This will give you a more balanced view and burden for the world. Be sure to include home missionaries in your budget. Keep a rough balance between the missionaries, giving each one approximately the same amount unless they are associated with the church in some way.

The number of missionaries you help will depend on the funds available and the amount of support given. A mission church might start with at least $25 per month. Larger churches should start at $50 or even $100 per month. The missionary committee should review the missionaries' support needs each year before the annual budget meeting. They can then recommend that missionaries' support be increased to keep pace with the inflation rate in the country where they work. Otherwise, the missionaries will experience a very real loss of purchasing power on the field. Include in the church's mission program the policy of continuing to support your missionary in his retirement years at a certain percentage of what you were giving during his active years of service.

## The Missionary Closet

A missionary closet, if properly operated, can be a real blessing to missionaries and the church. It is the responsibility of the missions committee to set down clear guidelines concerning what will be placed in the closet and by what method the items will be given to missionaries who visit the church. Only new items should be included. Don't give missionaries "hand-me-downs" or out-of-style clothing that no one wants.

At the end of this chapter you will find a list of things which can be included in your missionary closet. Reproduce the list and make it available to your people every time the supply of goods begins to run low. Keep the closet well stocked at all times. Assign each item one point for every twenty-five cents of value. Then allow each missionary couple to take fifty, seventy-five or one hundred points from the closet. This method avoids embarrassment for both the missionary and the church.

## Visit the Mission Field

A trip to the mission field can be one of the greatest experiences of your life. It will give you a far greater understanding and burden for missions. "Impossible! My little church could never send me to the mission field," you say? Have you ever considered visiting one of the mission fields in your own backyard? Why not arrange to visit a missionary on the North American field?

You'll find all the varied cultures, languages and color of the foreign field right here at home. There are missionaries planting churches in the numerous Spanish, French and Portuguese speaking communities across this country. Visit missionaries on the university campuses, in the Indian villages of the Southwest or the Northeast. Go to those living on the frozen tundra of Alaska and Canada or the golden sands of Hawaii. You can see what is being done to reach the largest Jewish population in the world or visit missionaries laboring among the Mormons of Utah. Can't go to the mission field? Why, it is right at your doorstep.

If the Lord should make it possible for you to visit a mission field, spend time with the missionary. Get to know him. What are the special problems involved in his work? What needs does he have? How can churches in America help? When you go to the the mission field, plan to minister to the missionary, his family and his people. Perhaps you can preach a revival meeting for him. Some churches take their young people and run vacation Bible schools for the missionary. Does he need help with visitation or building? Then take your men on a mission trip for a few days to help meet that need. You don't have to wait until you have a big church to go to the mission field. It's all around you. Take advantage of the opportunity to visit soon. You'll never be the same.

## Endnotes

[1] Dick Pearson, *Missionary Education Helps for the Local Church.*(Palo Alto, CA: Overseas Crusades, Inc., 1966), p. 2.

[2] *Ibid.*, p. 2.

[3] Kenneth N. Steward, *Strategy for an Effective Church Missionary Program.* (Grand Rapids: Grand Rapids Baptist Seminary, 1973), p. 4.

# A Suggested List of Items for the Missionary Closet

Linens:                  Pillow cases, sheets, quilts, blankets, bath
                         towels, washcloths, bedspreads, table-
                         cloths, dish towels, aprons, doilies, dresser
                         scarfs, yard goods for curtains and drapes,
                         crochet or braided rugs, pot holders
Toiletries:              Toothpaste, Kleenex, deodorants, sham-
                         poos, combs, toothbrushes, soap, toilet
                         paper, powders, hair tonic, razor blades,
                         aftershave lotion
Tupperware:              Any type of plastic covered dishes or con-
                         tainers
Paper items:             Cups, plates, napkins, wax paper, alumi-
                         num foil, Saran wrap, paper towels, handi-
                         wipes, typing paper, stationery, greeting
                         cards, thank you notes, envelopes
Teaching Aids:           Crayons, glue, scotch tape, masking tape,
                         pens, pencils, marking pens, correction
                         tape for typing, paper punches, stapler and
                         staples, hi-liters, rubber bands, construc-
                         tion paper, carbon paper, stencils, flash-
                         card stories, illustrated songs, easels,
                         flannelgraph stories
Sewing supplies:         Yard goods, tape measures, thread, needles,
                         pins, snaps, hooks, pincushions, scissors,
                         sewing patterns
Tools:                   Hammers, pliers, wrenches, assorted nuts
                         and bolts, screwdrivers, tape measures,
                         high-speed drill bits, electric drill, sand-
                         paper, wood glue, clamps, heavy-duty ex-
                         tension cords, paint brushes, hacksaws,
                         hand saws, squares, chisels, batteries,
                         flashlights, stud finders, files

** All items placed in the missionary closet should be new and
unused.
** Please leave the price tag on your items so the proper point
value can be placed on it (one point for each 25 cents). The
price tag will be removed when the point value is placed on it.
** Look for sale items to s-t-r-e-t-c-h your missionary dollar.

# A Suggested Missionary Policy

(The following missionary policy can be adopted by the church at the recommendation of your missionary committee.)

I. Missions Philosophy

A. **The Missionary and his work:**
The missionary is a Spirit-called individual used in the fulfillment of the Great Commission. The local church is the agent God uses to commission or send the missionary to the mission field. The mission agency is that organization directed by God for the purpose of assisting the local church in the administration of the missionary's ministry.

B. **Extension of the local church:**
A local church, by nature, is in a permanent location. Any missionary supported by the church is considered to be an extension of our ministry. The missionary will be requested to subscribe to our Statement of Faith and attest to his agreement with the stand of the church.

C. **Church planting/evangelism extension:**
Believing that the winning of souls is not the complete fulfillment of the Great Commission, the missionary should also view as important the establishment of local indigenous churches, based on the Word of God.

II. Missions Committee

The primary function of the missions committee will be to carry out the missions policy of the local church, including responsibility for the annual missionary conference. Its overall objective is to encourage all church members to become more actively involved in missions.

III. Missions Program

A. **Balance:**
Missions is a worldwide responsibility of this church and should be balanced in regard to

1. General and special
Since there is no Biblical substantiation for specialization in the missionary endeavor, a missionary supported by this church shall be primarily involved in general missionary outreach.

2 Home and foreign

Believing that the witness is to be borne in "Jerusalem, Judea, Samaria, and unto the uttermost part of the world," home missions is to be deemed necessary and of equal importance with foreign missions.

B. **Mission Agencies:**

This church will support only missionaries serving with a Baptist agency whose doctrine is in conformity to the Statement of Faith of our church.

C. **Candidates:**

Candidates for support shall be interviewed by the missions committee. They should be willing to answer questions that the committee considers essential to their ministry.

1. Frequency

Candidates will not exceed four in number during the course of a year, preferably one a quarter (including the missionary conference).

2. Selection for recommendation to the church

Candidates will be interviewed by the missions committee before recommendation to the church for support.

3. Members of the church

Members of this church appointed by approved mission agencies shall be supported (_____) level: amount or proportion).

D. **Finances:**

Missions calls for faith in the provision of God for the needs of those who have been called to minister the gospel. The fact that missionaries need support does not indicate a lack of faith on their behalf, but is in keeping with the faith principle.

1. Honorariums

Special offerings will be taken for missionaries who present their work or report to the congregation. Honorariums should be at least $50.00 plus expenses, with cash being given to the missionary if there is a present need.

2. Support levels, minimums

No missionary will be supported for more than 60% of his or her total support. The minimum support will be ($25.00, $50.00, or $100.00) per month.

3. Retirement, support for retirees
Missionaries will be urged to include in their support planning an amount that will be designated as retirement fund. The committee suggests $35.00 per month minimum for this purpose. The missions committee will interview each retiree to determine his or her retirement needs. If a need is in evidence, then the committee will recommend continued support up to 50% of that which had been received during the active ministry.

E. **Prayer**:

Prayer is the church's intercessory ministry for the missionary on the field. The missionary as well should be encouraged to remember the supporting church in prayer.

1. Monthly bulletin
Each missionary letter received will be excerpted and given to each member of the church in a monthly prayer-request bulletin. This should be distributed as soon as possible after the first Sunday of the month.

2. Emergency requests
As information is received concerning emergencies, the committee should notify the entire church. Any monetary needs should be handled by the church as quickly as possible.

F. **Women's Missionary Fellowship**:

Women's Missionary Fellowship will be an adjunct of the total missions program of the church. It will not support any missionaries in its own name. Women's Missionary Fellowship will continue to supply such work and needs as set forth in the constitution. It will be responsible to maintain a missionary cupboard which will help meet the needs of the missionaries. The entire church should be advised of needs for the missionary cupboard and be encouraged to participate in this ministry.

G. **Missions and Satellite Churches**:

In the event a satellite church is started or a local mission is established, the missions committee would encourage members of the church to become personally involved in them, even to joining these works in the formative years.

IV. Missionary Personnel
A. **Communication**:

It shall be the responsibility of missionaries to keep the church informed (at least quarterly) as to the progress of their work, including special items, both for prayer and praise. Should there be any proposed change of ministry, i.e. country, organization, etc., the church is to be notified by the missionary as soon as possible.

B. **Interview and evaluation of ministry:**

Prior to the missionary's return to the field, he or she should meet with the committee to reaffirm his or her commitment to the church's Statement of Faith. The missionary shall also provide a personal testimony and answer any questions which the committee may have.

C. **Withdrawal of support and reinstatement**:

The decision to recommend support withdrawal of a missionary rests with the missions committee. Reinstatement will follow the same policy as for new missionaries.

D. **Furlough responsibilities:**

Each missionary shall write to the church a year prior to furlough so that the scheduling of meetings can be arranged as far in advance as possible. This will permit them to participate in VBS and missionary conferences.

## Section IV..

**Chapter 13**....The Finances of the Local Church

    The Financial Principles of Church Planting
    A Financial Program for Church Planting


**Chapter 14**....The Fund Raising Program of the Local Church

    Developing a Stewardship Program


**Chapter 15**....The Facilities of the Local Church

    Choosing a Building Site
    Developing the Building Funds
    The Building Program


**Chapter 16**....The Fallacies in the Local Church

    Discouragement
    Burnout
    Laziness
    Quiet Time
    Family Problems
    Church Problems
    Success in the Ministry
    Communicating with Supporters


**Chapter 17**....The Finished Job–A Local Church

    How to Determine Maturity for Graduation
    Calling a Pastor

# Chapter 13

# The Finances
# of the Local Church

Church planting is an expensive proposition. Many thousands of dollars will be required for the purchase of land, construction of a building and regular ministry expenses. It is therefore important that a man understand the basic financial principles involved in developing a new church. He must know how to prepare a budget, raise funds and manage the church's finances.

People must have confidence in the new church if they are to support it financially. The pastor is the key to developing that confidence. This is done not only through his preaching on the subject, but also by his personal integrity. He must demonstrate that he can properly manage his own financial affairs. If he cannot live within his personal budget, or incurs debts he cannot pay on time, or has a bad credit record, he will not be able to persuade people to support the new church. He must be a good steward of what God has given him, if he is to be a good steward of what people give the church.

## Financial Principles of Church Planting

There are four financial principles that the church planter must keep in mind:

• It takes money to plant a church.

This is true wherever you go. Costs, however, will vary greatly from area to area. Rural and small towns are generally less expensive than suburban and metropolitan areas. What costs one hundred dollars in one place may cost over one hundred thousand dollars somewhere else. The church planter must evaluate realistically the financial costs involved in starting a new church.

• God has a financial plan for the church.

The plan is called "tithing" or "proportionate giving." Throughout the Scriptures, God's people have been taught to give at least ten percent of their income and resources to God. It commenced with Abraham, was continued by Jacob, commanded by Moses, commended by Jesus and communicated by Paul. Tithing is God's program for meeting the financial needs of His house (Malachi 3:10).

The church planter must set the example for his people by tithing regularly to the new church. If he doesn't tithe, the people will not tithe either. He should preach on the subject periodically, teaching his people that the church is not financed through bake sales, raffles and bingo parties, but through their giving to God.


• The local church is to be supported by the local church

While the church planter may receive some outside assistance and special gifts may be given to help the new church get started, care must be taken that the people do not become dependent on that outside assistance. A "welfare mentality" can develop when financial help is extended over a long period of time. It is easy for the people to let someone else meet their financial needs rather than to assume that responsibility themselves.

From the very beginning, the church should be taught to carry its own financial responsibility. While it may not be able to support its pastor fully, it should contribute as much as possible. This amount can then be increased on a regular basis as the church grows. Encourage the church to set a goal of being self-supporting in five years or less.


• The laborer is worthy of his hire.

Teach the people to support their pastor from the beginning. This should be their number-one financial priority. They can begin by giving him one hundred dollars a month and then increasing it twenty-five dollars each month. Even a larger increase may be given if finances permit. If this schedule is followed, the church can become self-supporting in three to five years. (See the schedule at the end of this chapter.)

The man who does not teach the church to support him is defeating his purposes. He will find he is the one making the sacrifices while his people show little concern for the work. On the other hand, the people will be more faithful and will give sacrificially if they are encouraged to be self-reliant. People appreciate what they pay for.

In the case of missionary church planters, the pastor's salary should take priority over the building fund. This enables the church to call a full-time pastor sooner. He in turn can lead the church in its building program, freeing the church planter to start more churches. This is especially preferable in high-cost areas where it may take years to accumulate the funds for property and buildings.

## A Financial Program for Church Planting

The church planter is responsible for developing the financial program of the new church. He must put the program together and then train people to perform each responsibility. From the very beginning, he should choose at least two people whom he can train to count, record and deposit the money. The church planter should avoid personally handling, keeping or depositing church funds.

There are four things you must develop in order to have a good financial system: a balanced program, a workable budget, a good bookkeeping system and a stewardship program.

● Develop a balanced program.

A good financial program provides money for the needs of the pastor, the facilities, missions and the local ministry. Too often, the mistake is made of putting most of the money in the building fund while skimping on other areas. This is shortsighted and self-defeating.

A more balanced approach would be to give ten percent of the income to missions, another ten percent to the building fund and the rest would go for the pastor's salary and the local ministry. In this way all areas of the work develop together as the church grows. Even though the church may be a "mission church," it needs to develop its missionary program and vision.

It is important for the church to assuume responsibility for its pastor. In addition to a salary, the church should be taught to contribute to a retirement fund such as an "Individual Retirement Account" (IRA) or to help with his social security taxes (his are twice as high as those of his members because he is self-employed). While the new church may not be able to assume all these responsibilities in the beginning, they should assume some of them. Start out small and increase the amount as the church grows.

- Develop a budget.

A budget puts God's work on a business basis. It enables you to be a better steward of the resources God has given you by using systematic planning and cost-control methods. It will help you manage money and reach your goals. A budget helps people understand why their money is needed and how it will be used. It builds confidence among the members. A budget is a tool, a guideline, a servant that will make you more effective in the work God has called you to do.

Develop a weekly survival budget before starting the church. (A weekly budget is better than a monthly budget because the lower figures seem more attainable to the people.) This will help you calculate what you need to get started. These preliminary figures will vary from area to area. One excellent method is to figure what you need for a month, then multiply that amount by 12 and divide by 52. This will give you an accurate weekly figure that compensates for those months with five Sundays.[8]

Start with the pastor's salary. Begin with twenty-five dollars per week and increase it each month in accordance with the salary schedule listed at the end of this chapter. Rent and utilities for a meeting place will be a major consideration. A minimum of fifty dollars should be budgeted for this. (Some areas will require much more.) Office supplies, paper, postage and telephone may require twenty dollars. Advertising and promotional materials might be allotted another twenty dollars. The same is true of supplies for local evangelism, such as tracts, films and literature. Do not skimp on these items needed to reach people. Too often this money is placed in the building fund. If you do not reach people, you will not need a building fund!

Set aside twenty dollars for both the missions and the building funds. Plan to spend ten dollars a week for the Sunday School while allowing fifteen dollars for unexpected expenses that are sure to arise.

Print the weekly budget and distribute it at the "get-acquainted" meetings. Also make it available at all public services during the first six months. Your weekly survival budget might look like this:

| | |
|---|---|
| Pastor's Salary | 25.00 |
| Rent & Utilties | 50.00 |
| Office Supplies | 20.00 |
| Advertising | 20.00 |
| Local Evangelism | 20.00 |
| Building Fund | 20.00 |
| Missions Fund | 20.00 |
| Sunday School | 20.00 |
| total | $200.00 |

Remember that a budget is your servant, not your master. It is flexible and can be adjusted as need arises. If income exceeds the expected level, more money can be used for any item or new items can be added. If some expenses are not as great as expected, the extra money can be shifted to more needy areas.

After six months of use, you will have a good idea of what your income and expense levels are. You will also see where adjustments need to be made. Begin working on an annual budget. Make your budget year coincide with the calendar year, beginning in January and ending in December.

In preparing the annual budget, plan so your income will meet your budget needs, even if your largest contributor dies or leaves the church. Many churches have become financially strapped, unable to meet their obligations because they were counting on the income from someone who did not remain with the church throughout the year. A good rule of thumb is to budget ten percent below last year's total income. If the previous year's income exceeded the budget, you will be able to expand this year's budget with reasonable assurance of meeting your obligations. If last year's income was less than the budget, the reduction in this year's budget will be realistic enough to put you back on a sound financial basis.

Review the previous year's expenses. Project utility increases. Larger Sunday-school enrollment may require additional expenditures. Budget increases should be based on need and the projected financial growth of the church.

The annual budget may be divided into four general categories:

**Personnel expenses** should include the pastor's housing, utilities, car allowance, insurances and salary (including IRA or Social Security payments).

**Building expenses** include rent, maintenance, insurance, utilities, equipment repairs and legal fees.

**Ministry expenses** include anything that has to do with the local ministry of the church such as Sunday School, advertising, office supplies, local evangelism, special speakers, banquets and miscellaneous items.

**Missionary expenses** cover regular monthly support, missionary speakers, the annual missionary conference and projects for missionaries.

Arrange the budget in five columns like the one at the end of this chapter. The first column shows the previous year's budget. The second column displays the actual expenditures for each category during the past year. The third column represents the proposed budget for the coming year. The fourth column shows the monthly breakdown of each item while the fifth column does the same on a weekly basis. This arrangement makes it easy for your people to compare what has been achieved and where you are going financially.

If you did not have a budget the previous year, simply list the actual expenses under each category. This will represent last year's budget. Then proceed to prepare a budget based on those expenditures.

Initially the church planter may have to prepare the budget himself. But as soon as he has deacons, a treasurer or spiritually mature men, involve them in the budget planning process. By doing so, he will be training leaders in this vital area of church administration.

Once the budget has been prepared, it should be presented to the church for adoption. Present it as a statement of faith in God who provides all the needs of His church. The budget should be voted upon as a unit rather than item by item. This will avoid much hassle and disagreement among the people. It also ensures a balanced financial program.

It is wise to conduct a budget analysis every three months. This simply requires you to list each of the budget items along with the amount of money budgeted for the period of time that has passed (three, six, nine or twelve months). A second column shows the amount of money actually spent during that time. A third column shows the difference between what was budgeted and what was spent. A minus sign (-) indicates you spent less than you budgeted, a plus sign (+) indicates you spent more than you planned. A budget analysis enables you to shift money from one area to another without exceeding your total budget. It also tells you if you can spend more than you planned or if you need to cut back on expenses. Watch for periodic expenses with annual or quarterly peaks. (See the sample at the end of this chapter.)

**Develop a good bookkeeping system.** An accurate recording and reporting system is essential to building confidence among your people. If they suspect their money is being mishandled, they will not give. But if you keep good records and make regular financial reports, they will give willingly.

Choose a treasurer carefully. The church planter should begin training someone to handle the church money from the beginning. It is important that you pick the right person. After the pastor, the treasurer is often the most influential man in the church. His voice of approval or disapproval can easily influence the outcome of major financial decisions.

He should be a man who is faithful to all the services of the church since he is responsible for handling the offerings. He must be able to keep privileged information confidential, not revealing the giving of individual donors. He should be able to handle figures accurately. But most of all, he should be spiritually mature. He should share his pastor's vision and be a man who will step out in faith even when the money is not on hand. Some churches have found it wise to bond the treasurer, thus ensuring the return of any funds that are lost or stolen.

Offering envelopes should be made available to the people. These may be distributed at each service or a box of envelopes can be given to the members at the beginning of the year. The offering should be received by ushers who are well groomed and appropriately dressed. Teach them to take the offering together, going to the same row on opposite sides of the aisle at the same time. This will add dignity to the service.

The offering should be counted immediately after each service in a private, secure location. At least two people (including the financial secretary) should count the offering at all times. This not only ensures accuracy, but protects those doing the counting from charges of dishonesty.

Be sure the contents of each envelope are recorded accurately on the outside of the envelope. Checks should be examined to be sure they are properly filled out. The money should be counted individually and then recorded on the "tally sheet." There is a separate line for each denomination and a separate column for each service. The number of items for each denomination is placed in the parentheses ( ) and the total of each denomination in the spaces. For example: there may be four bills of five dollars each. The number"4" would be placed in parentheses and the amount "$25.00" written on the line. Now total each column at the bottom and record it on the "Weekly Attendance and Financial Record" form. This form should be filled out in duplicate, one going to the pastor and the other to the treasurer at the end of the day.

The offering should be recorded by the financial secretary at the end of the day. The amount given by each individual should be recorded in a "Record of Individual Contributions" books (available at most Christian bookstores). This will enable him to send letters to individual contributors at the end of the year, showing how much they gave during the year.

Next, the money should be given to the treasurer who will record the offering total in a cash receipts journal or a financial ledger under the heading, "Income." There may be separate columns for different kinds of offerings such as Regular, Building and Missions.

The money is then recorded on a bank deposit slip and put in a bank bag which can be locked and placed in the night depository at the bank. If this cannot be done, it should be taken to the bank for deposit early Monday morning. Do not leave the money in a "safe place" at home, nor use any of it to pay bills. Deposit everything that is received. Your deposit slip should show the same amount as the "Weekly Attendance and Financial Record."

Set up a cash disbursement ledger to record all expenditures. The ledger should have enough columns to cover each major catagory in the budget. If you have fifteen catagories, you need fifteen expense columns in your disbursement ledger. Whenever a purchase or expense is incurred, enter the item in the ledger showing the date, check number and amount under the appropriate column.

All expenses and purchases should be paid by check, and not with cash except for the petty cash fund. The church should have three people authorized to sign checks. The signatures of two of them should be required on all checks. Do not pre-sign the checks however. When a check is written, fill in the check stub with the date, check number, amount and account to be charged. All purchases should be approved in advance, either by the pastor or financial director. This will prevent people from making purchases which are not authorized or which exceed the budget.

Written financial reports should be made available to the church on a monthly, quarterly and annual basis. In some churches, the pastor and deacons receive monthly reports while the members receive quarterly and annual reports.

The financial report should be kept simple so people can understand it. It should reflect the income, expenses and balances of each fund the church maintains. The expense items should be listed under the same categories as were used in the budget.

The financial report at the end of the chapter is divided into three sections: the general fund, the building fund and the missions fund. The general fund shows the income from all sources. Expenses are listed in itemized fashion. Since all monies are funneled through the general fund, there is a transfer section showing how much money went to each of the other funds for distribution. The balance or deficit is then listed at the bottom.

The building fund receives ten percent of the general income (as long as there is not a deficit in the general fund), plus any interest income. Any equipment, repairs, construction or maintenance expense is paid from this fund. The missions fund is used to support missionaries and missionary projects only. No local expenses are paid from the missions fund.

The report also shows the total balance of all funds. A comparison of the total balance of all funds with the total amount in the bank accounts should be in agreement. The average weekly budget, the weekly income and the weekly expenses are listed at the bottom of the page.

The financial program of the church must be built around honesty and openness. Monies should always be used for the purpose given. Never conceal anything from your people. If you are aboveboard with them, they will respect and support your ministry.


### Endnotes

[1] Grant G. Rice, *Church Planting Primer*. (Louisville, KY:   Tabernacle Press, 1985), p. 41.

## Graduated Salary Schedules for Church Planters

|  | 6 years ($25) | 3 years ($50) | 2 years ($75) |
|---|---|---|---|
| **First Year** | | | |
| January | 100.00 | 100.00 | 100.00 |
| February | 125.00 | 150.00 | 175.00 |
| March | 150.00 | 200.00 | 250.00 |
| April | 175.00 | 250.00 | 325.00 |
| May | 200.00 | 300.00 | 400.00 |
| June | 225.00 | 350.00 | 475.00 |
| July | 250.00 | 400.00 | 550.00 |
| August | 275.00 | 450.00 | 625.00 |
| September | 300.00 | 500.00 | 700.00 |
| October | 325.00 | 550.00 | 775.00 |
| November | 350.00 | 600.00 | 850.00 |
| December | 375.00 | 650.00 | 925.00 |
| **Second Year** | | | |
| January | 400.00 | 700.00 | 1,000.00 |
| February | 425.00 | 500.00 | 1,075.00 |
| March | 450.00 | 800.00 | 1,150.00 |
| April | 475.00 | 850.00 | 1,225.00 |
| May | 500.00 | 900.00 | 1,300.00 |
| June | 525.00 | 950.00 | 1,375.00 |
| July | 550.00 | 1,000.00 | 1,450.00 |
| August | 575.00 | 1,050.00 | 1,525.00 |
| September | 600.00 | 1,100.00 | 1,600.00 |
| October | 625.00 | 1,150.00 | 1,675.00 |
| November | 650.00 | 1,200.00 | 1,750.00 |
| December | 675.00 | 1,250.00 | 1,825.00 |
| **Third Year** | | | |
| January | 700.00 | 1,300.00 | |
| February | 725.00 | 1,350.00 | |
| March | 750.00 | 1,400.00 | |
| April | 775.00 | 1,450.00 | |
| May | 800.00 | 1,500.00 | |
| June | 825.00 | 1,550.00 | |
| July | 850.00 | 1,600.00 | |
| August | 875.00 | 1,650.00 | |
| September | 900.00 | 1,700.00 | |
| October | 925.00 | 1,750.00 | |
| November | 950.00 | 1,800.00 | |
| December | 975.00 | 1,850.00 | |

## Fourth Year

| | |
|---|---|
| January | 1,000.00 |
| February | 1,025.00 |
| March | 1,050.00 |
| April | 1,075.00 |
| May | 1,100.00 |
| June | 1,125.00 |
| July | 1,150.00 |
| August | 1,175.00 |
| September | 1,200.00 |
| October | 1,225.00 |
| November | 1,250.00 |
| December | 1,275.00 |

## FifthYear

| | |
|---|---|
| January | 1,300.00 |
| February | 1,325.00 |
| March | 1,350.00 |
| April | 1,375.00 |
| May | 1,400.00 |
| June | 1,425.00 |
| July | 1,450.00 |
| August | 1,475.00 |
| September | 1,500.00 |
| October | 1,525.00 |
| November | 1,550.00 |
| December | 1,575.00 |

## Sixth Year

| | |
|---|---|
| January | 1,600.00 |
| February | 1,625.00 |
| March | 1,650.00 |
| April | 1,675.00 |
| May | 1,700.00 |
| June | 1,725.00 |
| July | 1,750.00 |
| August | 1,775.00 |
| September | 1,800.00 |
| October | 1,825.00 |
| November | 1,850.00 |
| December | 1,875.00 |

It will take six years to support a pastor fully if his salary is increased $25 per month, three years at $50 per month and only two years at $75 per month.

## Sample Annual Budget

| Building Expenses: | '83 annual budget | '83 actual expenses | '84 annual budget | '84 monthly budget | '84 weekly budget |
|---|---|---|---|---|---|
| Rent | 2,100.00 | 2,100.00 | 2,400.00 | 200.00 | 46.15 |
| Maintenance | 500.00 | 727.72 | 900.00 | 75.00 | 17.31 |
| Insurance | 161.00 | 161.00 | 180.00 | 15.00 | 3.46 |
| Utilities | 1,600.00 | 1,882.24 | 2,100.00 | 175.00 | 40.38 |
| Equip/Repairs | 600.00 | 476.25 | 900.00 | 75.00 | 17.31 |
| Legal Fees | 100.00 | 72.65 | 96.00 | 8.00 | 1.85 |
| subtotals | 5,061.00 | 5,419.86 | 6,576.00 | 548.00 | 126.46 |
| **Personnel Expenses:** | | | | | |
| Salary (housing) | 2,850.00 | 2,850.00 | 6,450.00 | 537.50 | 124.04 |
| IRA | 1,200.00 | 1,200.00 | 1,200.00 | 100.00 | 23.04 |
| Car Allowance | 780.00 | 780.00 | 780.00 | 65.00 | 15.00 |
| Health/Life Insurance | 177.00 | 177.00 | 120.00 | 15.00 | 3.58 |
| Education/Conference | 120.00 | 65.00 | 120.00 | 10.00 | 2.31 |
| subtotals | 5,127.00 | 5,972.00 | 8,736.00 | 728.00 | 168.01 |
| **Ministry Expenses:** | | | | | |
| Sunday School | 200.00 | 200.00 | 300.00 | 25.00 | 5.77 |
| Advertising | 1,200.00 | 1,200.00 | 1,200.00 | 100.00 | 23.08 |
| Office Supplies | 250.00 | 258.00 | 300.00 | 25.00 | 5.77 |
| Local Evangelism | 600.00 | 800.00 | 1,200.00 | 100.00 | 23.08 |
| Special Speakers | 300.00 | 425.00 | 600.00 | 50.00 | 11.54 |
| Banquet/Entertain | 75.00 | 150.00 | 240.00 | 20.00 | 4.62 |
| Miscellaneous | 125.00 | 89.00 | 180.00 | 15.00 | 3.46 |
| subtotals | 2,750.00 | 3,149.00 | 4,020.00 | 335.00 | 77.32 |
| **Missionary Expenses:** | | | | | |
| Missionary Support | 1,480.00 | 1,480.00 | 2100.00 | 175.00 | 40.38 |
| Missionary Speakers | 200.00 | 226.00 | 300.00 | 25.00 | 5.76 |
| Missionary Conference | 150.00 | 165.82 | 240.00 | 20.00 | 4.61 |
| subtotals | 1,830.00 | 1,872.32 | 2,640.00 | 220.00 | 50.75 |
| Total Budget | 14,768.00 | 15,513.18 | 21,972.00 | 1,831.00 | 422.54 |

The pastor's salary begins at $400 per month and increases $25 per month.

## Sample Budget Analysis
## 1st Quarter, 1984

| Building Expenses: | 1stQuarter budget | 1st Quarter expenses | + over - under |
|---|---|---|---|
| Rent | 600.00 | 600.00 | --.-- |
| Maintenance | 225.00 | 186.50 | - 38.50 |
| Insurance | 45.00 | 180.00 | + 135.00 |
| Utilities | 525.00 | 495.00 | - 30.00 |
| Equipment/Repairs | 225.00 | 60.00 | - 165.00 |
| Legal Fees | 24.00 | ---.-- | - 24.00 |
| subtotals | (1,644.00) | (1,521.50) | (- 122.50) |

**Personnel Expenses:**

| | | | |
|---|---|---|---|
| Salary | 1,275.00 | 1,275.00 | --.-- |
| IRA | 300.00 | 300.00 | --.-- |
| Gas Allowance | 195.00 | 195.00 | --.-- |
| Insurance | 46.50 | ---.-- | - 46.50 |
| Education/Conferences | 30.00 | 75.00 | + 45.00 |
| subtotals | (1,846.50) | (1,845.00) | (- 1.50) |

**Ministry Expenses:**

| | | | |
|---|---|---|---|
| Sunday School | 75.00 | 85.00 | + 10.00 |
| Advertising | 300.00 | 289.00 | - 11.00 |
| Office Supplies | 75.00 | 238.00 | + 163.00 |
| Local Evangelism | 300.00 | 198.00 | - 101.50 |
| Special Speakers | 150.00 | 75.00 | - 75.00 |
| Banquets | 60.00 | ---.-- | - 60.00 |
| Miscellaneous | 45.00 | 85.00 | ± 40.00 |
| subtotals | (1,005.00) | (970.00) | (- 35.00) |

**Missionary Expenses:**

| | | | |
|---|---|---|---|
| Missionary Support | 525.00 | 525.00 | -------- |
| Missionary Speakers | 75.00 | 238.00 | + 163.00 |
| Missionary Conference | 60.00 | ---.---- | - 60.00 |
| subtotals | (660.00) | (763.00) | (+ 103.00) |
| Total Budget | 5,155.50 | 5,099.50 | - 56.00 |

This church spent $56.00 less in the first quarter than budgeted.

# Sample Monthly Financial Report
### May '84

## General Fund

Balance on hand April 30, 1984        +  866.87

### Income:

| | | |
|---|---|---|
| May 6 | 398.41 | |
| May 13 | 330.60 | |
| May 20 | 528.50 | |
| May 27 | 222.09 | |
| total | | + 1,479.60 |

| | |
|---|---|
| Bank interest | +  138.76 |
| Love Gift (missions) | +   75.76 |
| Building Fund | +   70.00 |
| VBS | +   63.18 |

### Expenses:

| | | |
|---|---|---|
| Rent | 200.00 | |
| Utilities | 61.69 | |
| Salary | 350.00 | |
| IRA | 100.00 | |
| Gas Allowance | 65.00 | |
| Local Evangelism | 29.65 | |
| Advertising | 56.00 | |
| Sunday School | 15.03 | |
| Office Supplies | 8.07 | |
| Miscellaneous | 9.50 | |
| total | | -  894.94 |

### Transfers:

Missions Fund
| | |
|---|---|
| 10% of offerings | 147.96 |
| love gift | 75.48 |

Building Fund
| | |
|---|---|
| 10% of offerings | 147.96 |
| bank interest | 138.76 |
| designated | 70.00 |
| total | - 579.68 |

Balance on hand May 31, 1984        +  1,219.55

**Building Fund:**

| | | |
|---|---|---|
| Balance on hand April 30, 1984 | + 9,151.78 | |
|   Transfer from General Fund | + 356.72 | |
|   Cement for sidewalk | - 131.00 | |
|   Paint | - 23.09 | |
| Balance on hand May 31, 1984 | | + 9,354.41 |

**Missions Fund:**

| | | |
|---|---|---|
| Balance on hand April 30, 1984 | + 178.46 | |
|   Transfer from General Fund | + 223.44 | |
|   Missionary Support | - 198.00 | |
|   Love Gift | - 75.48 | |
|   Banner for conference | - 11.00 | |
| Balance on hand May 30, 1984 | | + 117.42 |

Total Balance on hand May 30, 1984      + 10,691.38

| | |
|---|---|
| Money Market Account (savings) | + 8,834.05 |
| NOW Account (checking) | + 1,857.33 |
| | +10,691.38 |

| Weekly Budget | Weekly Income | Weekly Expenses |
|---|---|---|
| 288.46 | 456.76 | 333.38 |

●   ●   ●   ●   ●

| Average Attendance | Sunday School | Morning Service | Evening Service | Prayer Meeting |
|---|---|---|---|---|
| | 37 | 45 | 26 | 19 |

** (The Total Balance on hand and the total of the savings and checking accounts will be the same if the books have been kept accurately.)

226

TALLY SHEET

Date: _____

|  | S.S. | M.S. | E.S. | P.M. | Special |
|---|---|---|---|---|---|
| Checks: | ( )_____ | ( )_____ | ( )_____ | ( )_____ | ( )_____ |
| Bills: | | | | | |
| 100s | ( )_____ | ( )_____ | ( )_____ | ( )_____ | ( )_____ |
| 50s | ( )_____ | ( )_____ | ( )_____ | ( )_____ | ( )_____ |
| 20s | ( )_____ | ( )_____ | ( )_____ | ( )_____ | ( )_____ |
| 10s | ( )_____ | ( )_____ | ( )_____ | ( )_____ | ( )_____ |
| 5s | ( )_____ | ( )_____ | ( )_____ | ( )_____ | ( )_____ |
| 1s | ( )_____ | ( )_____ | ( )_____ | ( )_____ | ( )_____ |
| Coins: | | | | | |
| .50s | ( )_____ | ( )_____ | ( )_____ | ( )_____ | ( )_____ |
| .25s | ( )_____ | ( )_____ | ( )_____ | ( )_____ | ( )_____ |
| .10s | ( )_____ | ( )_____ | ( )_____ | ( )_____ | ( )_____ |
| .05s | ( )_____ | ( )_____ | ( )_____ | ( )_____ | ( )_____ |
| .01s | ( )_____ | ( )_____ | ( )_____ | ( )_____ | ( )_____ |
| Total: | _____ | _____ | _____ | _____ | _____ |

\* Place the number of bills or coins of each denomination in the parentheses ( )
\*\* Place the total of each denomination in the spaces _____

**WEEKLY
ATTENDANCE AND FINANCIAL
RECORD**

For: _____ 19____

| | OFFERINGS | ATTENDANCE |
|---|---|---|
| Sunday School | | |
| Morning Service | | |
| Evening Service | | |
| Special Offerings | | |
| Total | | |

Notations: _____

_____

_____

_____     _____
Treasurer              Deacon

(To be completed in duplicate: 1 copy to Pastor and 1 copy to treasurer)

Baptist Mid-Missions CPD Form No. 101

## RECORD OF INDIVIDUAL CONTRIBUTIONS

NAME _____

ENVELOPE
NUMBER _____

ADDRESS _____ PHONE _____

_____

PLEDGED TO CHURCH BUDGET $_____     PLEDGE TO BUILDING FUND $_____

| MONTH | DATE | REGULAR | SPECIAL | BUILDING FUND | MONTH | DATE | REGULAR | SPECIAL | BUILDING FUND |
|---|---|---|---|---|---|---|---|---|---|
| JAN. | | | | | JULY | | | | |
| | | | | | | | | | |
| | | | | | | | | | |
| | | | | | | | | | |
| | | | | | | | | | |
| FEB. | | | | | AUG. | | | | |
| | | | | | | | | | |
| | | | | | | | | | |
| | | | | | | | | | |
| MAR. | | | | | SEPT. | | | | |
| | | | | | | | | | |
| | | | | | | | | | |
| | | | | | | | | | |
| APR. | | | | | OCT. | | | | |
| | | | | | | | | | |
| | | | | | | | | | |
| | | | | | | | | | |
| MAY | | | | | NOV. | | | | |
| | | | | | | | | | |
| | | | | | | | | | |
| | | | | | | | | | |
| JUNE | | | | | DEC. | | | | |
| | | | | | | | | | |
| | | | | | | | | | |
| | | | | | | | | | |
| SIX MONTH TOTALS | | | | | SIX MONTH TOTALS | | | | |
| | | | | | ANNUAL TOTALS | | | | |

SAMPLE LEDGER PAGE

| check | item | OFFERINGS | | | EXPENSES | | | | | | | | | |
|---|---|---|---|---|---|---|---|---|---|---|---|---|---|---|
| | | Regular | Special | Building | Rent | Maint. | Utilities | Supplies | Advert. | Equip. | S.S. | Salary | Evangel. | Mission | Misc. |
| 1 | Offering | 455.01 | | | | | | | | | | | | |
| 2 | Bank Interest | | | | | | | | | | | | | |
| 3 | Telephone | | 115.09 | | | | | | | | | | | |
| 4 | S.S. Material | | | | | | | 28.96 | | | | | | |
| 5 | Pastor Salary | | | | | | | | | 15.00 | 370.00 | | | |
| 6 | | | | | | | | | | | 10.00 | | | |
| 7 | IRA | | | | | | | | | | | | | |
| 8 | Offering | 346.08 | | | | | | | | | | | | |
| 9 | Blann - Brown | | | | | | | | | | | 45.00 | | |
| 10 | C.R.A. - Fund | | | | | | | | | | | 45.00 | | |
| 11 | Beautiful Page | | | 300.00 | | | | | | | | 45.00 | | |
| 12 | Rent + Ins. | | | | 40.38 | | | | | | | | | |
| 13 | B. Brown | | | | | 29.65 | | | | | | | | |
| 14 | Offering | 378.41 | | | | | | | | | | | | |
| 15 | Pastor Self-evangelist | | | | | | | | | | | | | |
| 16 | Bell Meeting | | 128.52 | | | | | | | | | | 128.52 | |
| 17 | Newspaper Ad | | | | | | | 63.63 | | | | | | |
| 18 | Rent | | | | | | 19.99 | | | | | 28.14 | | |
| 19 | Expiration Offer | | | | | | | | 51.70 | | | | | |
| 20 | Rent to banquet | | | | | | | | | | | | 36.67 | |
| 21 | Offering | 528.50 | | | | | | | 68.95 | | | | | |
| 22 | Christ.Lit. | | | | | | | | | | | | | |
| 23 | Love gift - evangelist | | | | | | | | | | | 128.52 | | |
| 24 | | | | | | | | | | | | | | |
| 25 | | | | | | | | | | | | | | |
| 26 | | | | | | | | | | | | | | |
| 27 | | | | | | | | | | | | | | |
| 28 | | | | | | | | | | | | | | |
| 29 | | | | | | | | | | | | | | |
| 30 | | | | | | | | | | | | | | |

# Chapter 14

# The Fund Raising Program
# of the Local Church

Financial support is an essential part of carrying out God's plan in the local church.[1] Without adequate funds, the church planter will be frustrated in his efforts to lead the church in acquiring property, erecting a building and fully supporting their pastor.

Most pastors underestimate the giving potential of the church they pastor and at the same time complain of some peculiar circumstance that excuses their people for their laxness.[2] Too often the pastor ends up making frequent appeals for money from the pulpit or simply resigns himself to accepting far less than God has for him.

People do not fail to give because they are too poor, but because they have never been properly taught the biblical principles of stewardship. God's plan for financing the local church does not involve soup suppers, garage sales, bingo or the selling of raffle tickets. Rather He intended His work to be supported by the systematic giving of His people through their tithes and offerings (Malachi 3:10). It is your responsibility as pastor to teach that plan to your people.

A good stewardship program coupled with sound financial practices will eliminate the frequent appeals for money, provide adequate funds for the ministry and reduce the heavy load of indebtedness carried by many church families. Moreover, your people will mature spiritually as they learn biblical concepts of money management.

Before attempting to introduce a stewardship program to the church, you must be convinced of its value. If you are not sold on it, you will not be able to sell it to your people. Begin by doing a thorough study of the biblical concept of stewardship and finances. Then read everything you can find on the subject. Talk to pastors who have successful stewardship programs. Contact some of the companies which specialize in this area. (See the list at the end of this chapter.)

Do not try to implement a stewardship program until you are committed to carrying it out on an annual basis. As with any new program, there will be some resistance at first. Your confident leadership will overcome the resistance and ensure the success of the effort. You will find it will grow year by year as the people see the blessings involved.

There are five basic steps involved in developing a good stewardship program:

*First,* plan the stewardship campaign well in advance. Begin meeting with your deacons, treasurer and financial committee (if you have one) in early October. Their understanding and backing are essential. Determine the dates, theme, goals and program for the campaign. January seems to be the best time for a stewardship emphasis. Begin working on the annual budget, the materials and speakers that will be needed. A detailed schedule of events leading up to and including the closing program should be developed.

*Next* publish a stewardship brochure. It should give a review of your numerical, spiritual and financial victories for the past several years. Income and attendance graphs can be used to illustrate recent progress. A pie chart showing what percentage of income goes for each expense will help people understand what is needed and how it will be spent to further the Lord's work. Include goals and a detailed budget for the coming year.

Prepare the brochure carefully. A great deal of thought and care should be given to its preparation. You must make it attractive if you want people to read it. After all, if you do not care enough to make it attractive and informative, your people will also think it is unimportant and will not take time to read it. Seek professional advice on the layout and have it professionally printed. Good printing is good stewardship of the Lord's money. The cost involved is not an expense, but an investment that will be paid back many times over through the increased giving of your people.[3]

Ideally, all plans should be completed by the middle of November and all printed materials should be ready for distribution by December 15.

The *third* step to a successful stewardship campaign is to promote the program aggressively. Enlist the support of your lay leadership during November and December. Tell them you need their enthusiastic support. Instruct your Sunday-school teachers that they will be teaching a three or four week series on "giving" during the month of January. You can either write the lessons yourself, use those at the end of this chapter or secure one of David Jeremiah's excellent books on stewardship (available through the Cedarville College Bookstore, Box 601, Cedarville, OH 45314). Be sure they have the teaching materials well in advance.

Begin announcing the stewardship campaign in December. Use bulletin boards, posters, inserts and announcements to build enthusiasm. During the month of January, send three or four letters to each church family and regular attenders. (An array of promotional materials is available from Arthur Davenport Associates, P.O. Box 18545, Oklahoma City, OK 73154.) Have laymen give enthusiastic testimonies of God's blessing on their lives and various aspects of the church's ministry. You may want to use a missionary speaker in an evening service. You want your people to gain an overall view of what God is doing in the church.

*Fourth*, preach on stewardship each Sunday morning. Emphasize the various aspects of stewardship. God is not only interested in our money, but our time and talents as well. Provide helpful information on family and personal finances. Tell them how to get out of debt, how to establish credit, how to handle credit cards. At least one message should be on tithing. Do not apologize or be timid. Present the biblical method of stewardship lovingly, positively and frankly. Emphasize the blessings which come with obedience to the Lord in this area of their lives. Recommend that they read books written on finances from a biblical perspective such as "What Husbands Wish Their Wives Knew About Money" by Larry Burkett.

*Last of all*, prepare a stewardship banquet. This should be the highlight of the campaign. Hold it in a good restaurant on the last Friday of the month. Have families arrange for babysitters for smaller children. Use reservation cards or a sign-up sheet to determine how many meals to order.

The banquet should be informative, inspirational and fun to attend. Use teens for putting on a skit. Provide good music and a special speaker who supports the stewardship concept.

Tell your people in advance that they will be asked to make a financial commitment at the banquet. Explain that this is not a pledge to the church, but a promise to the Lord. You may want to mail the commitment card with the last letter you send, to give them time to consider prayerfully what the Lord would have them give. You will need extra cards at the banquet for those who forgot or lost their cards.

Give each person a commitment card and ask them to record the amount of tithe and offering they believe God would have them give. This should be computed on a weekly basis. They are not to sign the cards. This way no one from the church will know what they put on the card and no one will  contact them if they are unable to keep their commitment.

Now collect and total the cards, announcing the amount to the group. On Sunday morning, tell how much was received at the banquet and distribute cards to those who were unable to be present. Ask them to make the same commitment, recording what they believe God would have them give. Collect the cards and announce the grand total in the evening service. The amount will often exceed the budget. This should be a time of rejoicing for your people as they see what can be done if everyone cooperates.

Set aside the first Sunday of February as "ALL TITHE" Sunday. This is the day they begin keeping their promise to God. Announce the total offering and compare it with the average offering from the previous year. People will be able to see how God is already blessing through the stewardship program.

Use weekly dated offering envelopes, keep careful records and give quarterly reports of progress being made. Keep financial appeals to a minimum during the year as this will undermine the entire program.

Each year there will be less resistance and the people will be more responsive as they see God's blessing upon their church through the systematic giving of the stewardship program.

## Endnotes

[1] Dollar, Truman E., *How to Carry Out God's Stewardship Plan.* (Nashville, TN: Thomas Nelson, Inc.), p. 11.

[2] Dollar, *op. cit.*, p. 28.

[3] Dollar, *op. cit.*, p. 104.

[4] Dollar, *op. cit.*, p. 116-120.

## Stewardship Campaign  Schedule

### October

7.  Meet with deacons and finance committee
    Begin to plan the stewardship campaign
    Choose the dates, theme, goals, speakers and
       develop the schedule

15. Meet with various department heads
    Plan the advertising, promotional aids and  banquet  outline

### November

1.  Meet with the deacons and finance committee
    Begin working on the annual budget

15. Finalize campaign plans

21. Complete the budget and brochure

30. Take all materials to the printer

### December

1.  Begin announcing the stewardship campaign
    Put up the first promotional materials, signs,
       bulletin boards, etc.

14. Be sure all printed materials and literature are
       ready for distribution

15. Meet with the Sunday-school teachers and give
       them the lessons they will teach in January

30. First stewardship letter is mailed to all members
       and friends

### January

1.  Missionary speaker supported by the church

6.  Second stewardship letter is sent

8.  Stewardship message by pastor

13. Third stewardship letter is sent

15. Special speaker

20. Fourth stewardship letter is sent

22. Message on tithing by pastor

27. BANQUET and commitment cards

29. Commitment Sunday

### February

5.  All Tithe Sunday

## Stewardship letter # 1

December 30, 19___

Dear Friends in Christ,

Our hearts are filled with thanksgiving and joy as we come to the close of another year. God has been good to us and our church. We are looking forward to His continued blessing in the coming year.

Each year, January is set aside as "Stewardship Month." It is a time of reviewing what God has done in our church and what we can do to ensure His continued blessing. During the next four weeks we will be sharing stewardship principles from the Word of God.

This year our theme is "_____." You'll not want to miss the special speakers and the reports that will be given during the various services this month.

The enclosed brochure gives a detailed account of our fiscal progress last year and the budget for the coming year. Please read it carefully. Pray and ask God what He would have you do as a good steward of His resources.

Our annual Stewardship Banquet will be held Friday, January 27, at the Sweden House Restaurant. Dr._____ will be our guest speaker. Pray much for God's blessings in these exciting days.

Your Servant,

Pastor_____

## Stewardship letter # 2

January 6, 19____

Dear Friends in Christ,

As you know, January is "Stewardship Month" in our church and we are excited about what God is doing among us. We are looking forward to His blessings during this special time of year.

Our theme, " _____," expresses our desire to be better stewards of the time, talents and treasure God has given to us. I trust that by now you have read the brochure and reviewed the budget for the coming year that was sent to you last week.

The details of our financial program will be presented at our annual "Stewardship Banquet" on January 27. The banquet will be held at the Sweden House Restaurant on Federal Highway. There will be skits, special music, a slide presentation of the past year's highlights and a stirring message by our guest speaker, Dr._____. There is no cost to those attending.

You will have the opportunity to make a stewardship commitment to the Lord's work at the banquet. Please plan to be present. The future of our church is dependent on your faith-fulness as a good steward of God.

Sincerely in Christ,

Pastor _____

## Stewardship letter # 3

January 13, 19___

Dear Friends of BBC:

The annual Stewardship Banquet is one of the highlights of our ministry here at Bethlehem Baptist Church. This special time of fun, food and fellowship is enjoyed by all who attend. The banquet this year will be held on Friday night, January 27, at the Sweden House Restaurant on Federal Highway. We will begin serving at 6:00 o'clock. I hope you can share this blessed time with us.

I assure you the banquet will be something you will long remember. The skits, music, slides and message will give you a greater appreciation of what God is doing in our church. Dr. _____will be our special speaker.

At the close of the banquet, you will be asked to make a commitment to the Lord concerning what you will give Him during the coming year. This is not a pledge to the church, but a promise to God. You will not be asked to sign anything, no one but you and God will know the amount of your giving. We only ask that you prayerfully consider what God would have you do to further His work.

The banquet is free; however, you need to make reservations. We must tell the restaurant manager how many we expect to attend. We are required to pay for that number of meals. Please indicate on the enclosed reservation card the number from your family who will be present. Those attending must be at least twelve years of age. Return the card to us this week if possible.

We are looking forward to having you with us for this special occasion.

In Christian love,


Pastor_____

## Stewardship letter # 4

January 20, 19____

Dear Friends,

I trust you have been sharing in the blessings we have received during our stewardship campaign this month. Isn't it exciting to see what God is doing?

Next Friday night, January 27, is our stewardship banquet. We have reserved a place for you at the banquet. If for any reason you are unable to attend, please call our office immediately. We must pay for the number we promised the restaurant to be present.

This is a "dress-up" occasion. Ladies, you can wear your finest and enjoy an evening with your husband when the kids aren't along. Those attending must be at least twelve years of age.

Come expecting a blessing and a good time of fellowship. The banquet will be held at the Sweden House Restaurant on Federal Highway. We will be serving at 6:00 o'clock.

Commitment cards will be distributed at the banquet so you can indicate your gift to the Lord for the coming year.

Dr. _____, our guest speaker, and I are looking forward to seeing you at the banquet.

Until then,

Pastor_____

238

(The following Stewardship Lessons were adapted from Dr. Truman Dollar's book, *How To Carry Out God's Stewardship Plan.*)[4]

**Lesson One**

### Giving is a Spiritual Decision

Basic Principle: Your control of financial matters is a direct indication of your control in spiritual matters (Luke 16:11).

Our Goal: Complete freedom from financial pressures, and to provide a testimony of God's power and love in His provision for us.

I. Finances are a Part of our Spiritual Life (Luke 16:11, 13;Matthew 6:24).
   A. Many people have a closed mind to seeing the spiritual effects of biblical financial principles and miss great blessings.
   B. Abiding by biblical principles of finance brings a promise of blessing (Malachi 3:10; Proverbs 3:9,10; Matthew 6:33; Proverbs 11:24,25).

II. Problems of Controlling our own Finances Instead of Making God our Financial Manager
   A. Debt often results.
      1. Debt destroys testimonies–yours and God's.
      2. Debt produces bondage to men instead of God. Proverbs 22:7; II Timothy 2:4).
      3. Debt limits flexible response to God's will and leading (Matthew 6:24).
      4. Debt presumes upon the future.(James 4:13-15; Matthew 6:34).
   B. Financial pressure dulls spiritual perception and hampers effectiveness in God's service.(Matthew 6:34).
   C. A door is left open for temptations to be unethical (Proverbs 28:22).

III. "How to Fail in Business Without Really Trying" or "Get Poor Quickly"

A. The strategy of debt
   1. Credit card mania
   2. Borrow heavily for depreciable items so that you can commit God's money to paying interest on items that are already worn out.
   3. Abandon spiritual discernment and spend carelessly for frivolous things so that when you really must have something, you have to go into debt to get it.
B. Solomon's six slippery steps to the slums

   1. Be stingy. (Proverbs 11:24)
   2. Get rich quick. (Proverbs 28:22)
   3. Be stubborn. (Proverbs 13:18)
   4. Cultivate laziness. (Proverbs 20:13)
   5. Feed the flesh.(Proverbs 23:21)
   6. Be crafty. (Proverbs 28:19,20)

IV. Why God Wants to Control your Finances (Proverbs 23:4).
   A. Things belong to God. (Acts 14:15; 17:24)
   B. God is a better financial manager and knows our needs far better than we do.
   C. God wants to demonstrate his love and power. (Matthew 6:26, 30, 33; Ephesians 3:20).
   D. God wants to protect both our testimony and His, too.
   E. God wants to unite Christians (II Corinthians 8:1-9, 14)
   F. God wants to use finances to guide us.
      1. Protect us from harmful things
      2. Strengthen our faith
      3. Change our direction

**Lesson Two**

### Steps to Financial Freedom

Principle: God promises freedom from financial pressure and worry, not riches.

Warning: These principles apply to the saved. They are designed as an aid to your spiritual growth and will be effective only if the heart attitude is one of surrender to God. You will not find financial freedom by these principles unless you are willing to make Christ Lord of all of your life. You do not make "deals" with God.

I. God Promises to Provide for the Needs of His Children
   A. Material needs (Matthew 6:24 - 34).
      1. food
      2. clothing
   B. Clear promises (Philippians 4:19; Psalms 37:25).
   C. This is a matter of priority. Which do we seek first? God or money?

II. Our Responsibility to Allow God to Bring About Financial Freedom
   A. We are to have a content state of mind (I Timothy 6:8).
      1. The principle (Matthew 6:30,33,34).
      2. The example (Philippians 4:11,12).
      3. The reason.(Proverbs 30:7-9).
   B. The work ethic (Romans 12:11; Ephesians 6:5-9; Proverbs 13:11).
   C. Exercising godly wisdom (James 1:5).
      1. In borrowing. Watch for interest rates that are deceiving, borrowing for depreciable items that are worn out before you finish paying for them, borrowing for more than your available assets.
      2. In co-signing (Proverbs 6:1,2; 11:15; 17:18;20:16)Six warnings are given in Proverbs 22:26: 27:13.
      3. In being resourceful
         a. Looking for best buys
         b. Learning how to perform simple tasks yourself or to make or repair simple things yourself. Example: virtuous woman in Proverbs 31.
      4. In building sales resistance.
      5. By allowing God to supply a need in His own way before jumping in and supplying in the power of the flesh.
   D. Watch for God's guidance by withholding or supplying funds.
   E. Follow God's established principles of giving.

III. Commitments you Need to Make to Experience Financial Freedom.
   A. Completely surrender your financial life to God.
   B. Purpose to make a personal Bible study of God's financial principles and His plan of giving.
   C. Purpose to pray about how to spend the money you receive. One hundred percent is God's, not just ten percent.

**Lesson Three**

## Biblical Principles of Giving

REVIEW: Our ability to handle spiritual matters is directly related to our ability to handle financial matters. God promises freedom from financial pressure and worry but does not promise riches. God is a better manager of our finances than we are.

I. The Purpose of Christian Giving
   A. To finance the spread of the Gospel(I Timothy 5:17,18). Paul gives five reasons in I Corinthians 9.
      1. Common sense (verses 7,8)
      2. Old Testament Law (verses 9-11)
      3. New Testament tradition (verse 12)
      4. Old Testament example (verse 13)
      5. Command of Christ (verse 14)
   B. To provide for the needs of Christians
      1. Obviously the church which is financed by the giving of God's people provides for the spiritual needs of Christians.
      2. Physical needs (I Corinthians 8:14; 9:12).
   C. To develop the character of Christ in us
      1. Giving is a grace (I Corinthians 8:14; 9:12).
      2. Giving is a measure of our devotion and spiritual discernment (I Corinthians 8:8,12).
      3. Giving is a means to strengthen our faith and discipline.

II. The Difference Between Tithing and Giving
   A. The tithe is an eternal principle (Genesis 14:17-18; Hebrews 7:9).
   B. We tithe today not because we are under law to do so, but out of a heart of love.
   C. The tithe is the minimum. God has established that of what He gives to us ten per cent returns to Him.
   D. An offering then is above the tithe.

III. The Storehouse Principle of Tithing.
   A. God finances his church by his people bringing their tithes into the "storehouse" from which they are fed. (Mal. 3:810).

B. The problems involved when the tithe is placed other than
in the church
1. De-emphasizes the doctrine of the local church for
which Christ died (Ephesians 5:25).
2. Old Testament example. God designated the place to
give. Not left to the discretion of the giver.
3. Encourages pride on the part of the giver.
a. Presumes you know more about the distribution of
God's money than does the local church.
b. The rich have an unfair advantage over the poor.
c. Missionaries become answerable to an individual
and not to the church which sent them.
4. The giver is easily deceived by false claims.
5. The basis of giving becomes friendship, emotions or
intellectual appeal rather than scriptural motivations.
6. The man who does not tithe through the local church
places an unfair burden on others (II Cor. 8:13-15).
a. Burden is on the poor
b. Limits the outreach of the church
C. The power of God's plan of storehouse tithing
1. Checks and balances system. Pastor and leaders must
give an accounting to the church.
2. Provides a fair way for each member to share in God's
work regardless of income.
3. Allows the church a balanced outreach. Church can
much better support missionaries and organizations
than individuals.
4. Money is translated into programs.


**Lesson Four**

## Discipleship Through Biblical Stewardship

REVIEW: 1) The ability to handle financial matters is directly
related to the ability to handle spiritual matters. 2)
Money is one of life's greatest factors of motivation and
control. To fail to look to God's Word for guidance in
this area would be foolish. 3) God provides a way to
freedom from contemporary financial pressure and
worry.

PRINCIPLE: The same principles that allow individual financial
freedom can and must be applied to the body as a

whole if the church is to experience true freedom and power in proclaiming the gospel to the world.

I. The Biblical Pattern
A. The call is to disciple men (Matthew 28:18-20).
B. The tithe is God's eternal principle of financing His work.
C. The offering is above the tithe as God prospers, and as a man purposes in his heart (II Corinthians 9:7; 16:2).
D. Christians have always assembled on the first day and there set aside their tithes and offerings (I Corinthians 16:2).
E. God's work is to be financed by God's people giving not by law but cheerfully out of a heart of love (II Corinthians 9:7).
F. The faith-trust principle is to be followed. Faith-trust is simply trusting God for the amount you should give to the gospel over and above the tithe (II Corinthians 9:7).

II. Total Committment to Abide by God's Financial Principles Allows Freedom to Develop Maturity as a Church
A. Allows God to guide a church.
B. Allows God to strengthen faith as a church, to supply financial needs.
C. Common goals and direction provide a strong unifying factor (II Corinthians 8:1-7).

III. In Return God Gives us the Freedom and Power to Spread the Gospel Effectively
A. Corporate discernment in the disbursing of God's money
B. The power of a balanced ministry has worldwide effect
C. Freedom from accusation by a system of checks and balances
D. Individuals provided with a proven channel of giving
E. Money becomes translated into programs

## Sources of Stewardship Materials

Arthur Davenport Associates, Inc.
P.O. Box 18545
Oklahoma City, OK 73154
(800) 654-8431

Neibauer Press
20 Industrial Drive
Ivyland, PA 18974

Virgil W. Hensley, Inc.
3739 East 31st Street
Tulsa, OK 74135

Stewardship Enrichment
11325 Pegasus, E157
Dallas, TX 75238
(800) 527-1354

Dr. David Jeremiah's books on Stewardship Campaigns may
be ordered from

Cedarville Bookstore
Cedarville College
Box 601
Cedarville, OH 45314

Offering envelopes may be ordered from

Duplex Envelope Company
P.O. Box 5445
Richmond, VA 23220

## PERSONAL STEWARDSHIP COMMITMENT CARD

Recognizing that everything I possess belongs to God and believing that He will supply my needs during this coming year, I joyfully covenant as His steward to give regularly to the work of Christ through His church.

### Approximate Weekly Amount

_____

This card represents a promise to the Lord and not a pledge to the church. It is clearly understood that I will not be contacted personally or by mail should I be unable to fulfill this commitment.

*"Bring ye all the tithes into the storehouse...*
*I will pour you out a blessing."*

---

**KANSAS CITY BAPTIST TEMPLE**

1973                                                                 1973

I understand that this card is a promise to the Lord, not a pledge to the church. It is clearly understood that I will not be contacted personally or by mail should I not meet this commitment.

DEPARTMENT _____

We do not presently tithe; but desiring to be obedient will trust God to help us do so in the coming year.

Approximate Tithe: Weekly _____

We presently tithe and believing it to be a clear command of the Lord will continue to do so in the coming year.

Approximate Tithe: Weekly _____

We will trust God to help us give a weekly Faith Trust Offering.
Approximate Faith
Trust Offering Weekly _____

TOTAL WEEKLY BUDGET GIVING _____

---

**TEACH ME TO GIVE...
MY TIME AND TALENT**

☐ Pastor Davis' messages this month have been a challenge to my life. I have a burden to serve in the following areas

_ Sunday School _Choir

_Bus Ministry _Visitation

_Youth          _Other _____

☐ I want Christ to be the Lord of my home. I commit myself to regular family (or personal) devotions

Name _____

## PERSONAL STEWARDSHIP COMMITMENT CARD

### TEACH ME TO GIVE...MY TREASURE

☐ Believing the tithe to be a command of God and the beginning place of Christian giving...I will be obedient to God's basic requirement for a steward and will give weekly:
$_____

☐ This is my first year to tithe.

☐ In appreciation of GOD'S goodness to me and my family, I (we) wish to give love offerings this year of_____ weekly.

*"Upon the first day of the week let every one of you lay by him in store, as GOD has prospered him..."*  I Cor. 16:2

# Chapter 15

# The Facilities
# of the Local Church

One of the most critical phases of church planting is the acquisition of property and the erection of suitable facilities. Your location and building will influence the success or failure of your church for decades to come. Careful planning will enable you to avoid many of the pitfalls encountered by others in the past.

## Choosing a Building Site

Before purchasing any piece of property, do a feasibility study to determine these four factors:

**Is it adequate?** Is there ample room for off-the-street parking? Does it allow for future expansion as well as meet the present need? Is there sufficient space to develop Christian school facilities? If you purchase too little property, either the church will be forced to relocate later or will be limited in its outreach in the future. A minimum of three to five acres should be secured before any building is undertaken.

**Is it accessible?** Location is the single most important factor in determining a building site. It must be both visible and accessible. Do not purchase property in a housing development or behind other large buildings where it is hidden from view. If people cannot see the church or get to it easily, they will not come.

Consider property which has easy access to major highways or is located on a main street with a secondary street for easy access and exit. Corner property is ideal. Avoid congested traffic areas. Many people measure distance in minutes rather than miles. They want to be able to get in and out without a lot of fuss or waiting.

The property you select should be near the majority of your members or the community in which you are ministering. A middle-class working community is more desirable than wealthy or low-income rental communities.

**Is it affordable?** The cost of land varies greatly depending on location and availability. It can range from a few hundred dollars to over a hundred thousand dollars per acre. While you want to be a good steward of the Lord's resources, be careful about purchasing cheap property. Land is usually inexpensive because it is undesirable and no one is willing to purchase it. It is better to spend a few thousand dollars more to acquire the property you want than to accept a piece of land that will not meet your needs. Do not be "penny wise and pound foolish." On the other hand, do not place yourself under such a debt obligation for property that it hinders your present ministry or will keep you from building for many years to come. You should be able to pay for your property within a year or less. Otherwise, it is not affordable.

**Is it advisable?** Check on the zoning and building regulations for the property under consideration. Is the property zoned industrial (factories), commercial (business, stores) or residential (homes)? This not only affects the price, but in some communities will restrict the erection of church buildings. Building codes will regulate the size, materials and workmanship used in your church. You will not be allowed to occupy your building until these standards are met. Sometimes the requirements are so stringent or costly that they become prohibitive. Find out before you buy.

Consider the environment. Look for objectionable factors such as noisy thoroughfares, swamps, railroads, airports, stockyards, factories and substandard housing. What is the topography like? Does it have good soil and drainage? Is the land fairly level? Stay away from low-lying areas which flood or must be filled in. Avoid protruding rock formations.

Choose land near the conveniences you desire such as utilities (gas, water, sewer, electricity, telephone), schools and public transportation. Look into local fire codes: How far away is the nearest fire station? Are fire plugs nearby? This will affect the cost of your insurance as well as the cost of construction. Check the deed for easements, liens and restrictions which may limit the use of the property. Even if you find property which is adequate, accessible and affordable, be sure it is an advisable purchase before proceeding

Once you have located suitable property, hire a knowledgeable lawyer to handle legal matters for you. Insist on a title search to ensure that you will have clear title to the property. Accept only a Warranty Deed which guarantees that there are no restrictions or liens on the property. If possible, get a Title Guarantee. This is insurance that pays if it turns out that there is not a clear title.

# Developing the Building Funds

You must have money to build a church–lots of it. From the very beginning, establish a "Building Fund" for the purchase of property and erection of a building. Make this part of your regular budget by setting aside a minimum of ten percent of the general fund income for this purpose. In addition, you can take up special building-fund offerings on holidays or the fifth Sunday of the month. Provide your people with envelopes that allow them to designate a portion of their offering to the building fund.

When will the church be able to begin building? Usually a church can begin a building program when it has paid for its land, is free from all other indebtedness and has one third to one half of the estimated cost of the total building project in the building fund. The church should also be showing moderate monthly growth.

Additional construction funds can be secured from a number of sources. Sometimes a church family or a friend will lend or give a large sum of money to the church for this purpose. Churches in fellowship with the General Association of Regular Baptist Churches can apply for a grant from the Baptist Builders Club. Some mission agencies will co-sign for a construction loan for churches they are developing.

Many churches have sold bonds to finance their building programs. While they enable the church to raise money quickly, they are very expensive. Care must be taken to deal with a reputable bond company and not to overextend your ability to repay.

A conventional construction loan from a bank, insurance company or lending institution can also provide the additional funds needed for building. Most lenders require detailed information concerning the church's ability to repay the loan. This includes financial statements from previous years, a record of any real property belonging to the congregation, any indebtedness or current financial obligations and a copy of the operating budget of the church. Loans are generally limited to two-and-a-half times the annual income of the church.

A church can normally afford to carry a debt five times larger than the previous year's total income. For example, if the total income last year was $20,000, the limit of debts should not exceed $100,000. The debt payment should not exceed 25% of the budget income.[1] Loans should be limited to 75% of the appraised value of the church property and be repayable in fifteen or twenty years.

Search for the best method of financing your new building before making a final decision on building. Remember the words of Jesus: "For which of you, intending to build a tower, sitteth not down first, and counteth the cost, whether he have sufficient to finish it?" (Luke 14:28).

## The Building Program

All construction is expensive. A substantial portion of the total cost consists of consultation fees, development of the actual plans and the general contracting for construction. Develop a building program which eliminates unnecessary expenses.

You need to exercise tight cost control over your building program. Much of the waste can be controlled in the design stage if adhered to on the job site. Quality must never be sacrificed to obtain a good cost/value ratio.

There are three parts to every building program: planning, architecture and construction.

### • The Planning Stage

Although the planning phase takes the least amount of time and money, it is the most important part of the program. Planning properly is not easy. It takes a lot of research and study to make prudent decisions.

**Appoint a building committee.** The church should appoint a building committee to plan and oversee the construction of its new facilities. This committee should consist of five to eight church members and should include the pastor, two or three deacons and at least one lady. (Ladies can give valuable insight in the planning of bathrooms, nursery, kitchen, classrooms and interior decorating.)

The building committee is responsible to guide the church in making right decisions based on its research and study. It should be empowered to serve for the length of the building program and must have authority to make decisions within the basic design concept agreed upon by the congregation.

The building committee will need the help of specialists. It should recommend that the church engage such planning, financial and architectural services as are needed. Some hire the services of professional church building consultants. These companies can assist you in any or all phases of your building program. Check with two or three companies before selecting one. Their fees vary and can run as high as fifteen percent of the total cost of the building. If you have no knowledgeable builders in the church to advise you, their advice can save the church much more than their fees cost. Some mission agencies, such as Baptist Mid-Missions, have "mission builders" who serve as consultants for churches they are developing

**Do a feasibility study.** Form should follow function. The programs of the church should dictate the type and amount of space to be built. Analyze the church's past, present and future ministry. Every phase of church life should be reviewed.

How much do you expect the church to grow in the next five to ten years? For how many people should you build? How much space will you need? What new ministries do you expect to add? Should you build in phases or all at once? Is your building site adequate for future needs?

Next analyze your financial capability. What is the projected income for coming years? How much do you have in the building fund? How much of a debt load can you carry? How much can you spend on the building project?

Finally, determine what your facility requirements are. How much land do you need for present and future growth? What kind of building should you erect? Determine how much space you need for various programs. How can the space best be utilized? Zoning regulations and building codes should be studied to determine what can be built, what permits will be needed and the type and frequency of inspections required.

Once the building committee has completed its feasibility study, it should develop a master plan covering present and future development. A phased development can be planned which is both economically feasible and aesthetically pleasing.

This master plan and the committee's recommendations should then be presented to the church for its consideration and approval.


• The Architectural Stage.

Most communities have "building codes which classify churches as public buildings and require plans and specifications be prepared by a state licensed architect"[2] before building permits will be granted. The church's choice of an architect is crucial. This is the man who must transform the congregation's needs and desires into a functional and beautiful structure which is in balance with the church's financial ability. You can use the architectural services of the consulting firm that has been helping you or hire an independent professional. His fee is usually a specified percentage of the overall cost of the building.

In making this decision, ask these questions: "1) Has the man been able to satisfy others in situations similar to yours? 2) Have his former clients been happy to the point of using him when they build again? 3) Did he interpret their needs within their ability? 4) Has the relationship between the architect and past contractors been a good one? 5) Has the architect been successful in holding costs reasonably close to the first estimate? 6) Does he understand the needs of the fundamental church and does he have a personal relationship to Christ through salvation?"[3]

What kind of building do you want the architect to design? In most cases, the first phase of your master plan should call for an auditorium and education space for two hundred people. It is better to build twice than to have a large auditorium that is only half filled. It is recommended that a single-story structure be planned because it is less expensive, safer and more adaptable. (See the comparison of single and two-story buildings at the end of this chapter).

You want a building that is economical but beautiful. Plan one that fits into the architecture of the community and can be easily adapted to other uses should the church ever decide to relocate. The building should have an attractive exterior design and a functional interior plan. It should be designed to use space efficiently. "Space should be convertible, expandable and multipurpose."[4] Remember that form should follow function, not the other way around.

Every new church is deserving of its own original design concept. This eliminates "off-the-shelf" plans which seldom provide an adequate solution to the individual needs of churches. After evaluating the feasibility study, the architect will prepare schematic drawings for a building to meet your needs. These preliminary drawings should include floor plans, front and side elevations, a master plan showing how this first phase will fit into later stages of development and a water-colored perspective drawing.

Once these preliminary plans have been approved by the building committee and the congregation, the architect will proceed with the detailed design drawings. They include

1. A plot plan showing the dimensions of front, rear and side yards; off-street parking; location of walks, driveways, approaches, steps, terraces, porches, fences, retaining walls,

utility lines, easements, setbacks, boundaries and the location and dimensions of accessory buildings.

2. Detailed floor plans showing the layout of every section of the building along with wall sections and detailed elevation drawings showing what the building will look like outside from various vantage points.

3. The actual construction drawings with specifications for the builders.

4. Special engineering blueprints required for installation of electricity, plumbing, heating and air conditioning.

5. A detailed estimate of the total cost of the proposed building.

These plans should be reviewed in detail and approved by the building committee and then presented as a package to the church for its approval.

## The Construction Stage

Once architectural plans have been approved, you will need to submit them to local suppliers and reputable contractors for bids. It is wise to have at least four bids. The church then can vote to engage whichever contractor best meets their needs or seek additional bids. If all bids are unacceptable, you may have to reconsider either your financing or the size of your building.

If possible, the church should serve as its own contractor. It can then subcontract major portions of the work (something the contractor will do anyway) which it is incapable of doing for itself. Substantial savings can be realized by doing this, especially if the church has capable volunteers to help. Some mission agencies provide a "church builder" who will oversee the construction.

If you do not have experienced builders in your church or mission agency, it is best to hire a contractor to build the building for you. There are three basic types of building contracts:

First is the "turn-key job." The contractor agrees to build the church building for a specific amount. He does everything and simply presents the key to the church when the job is finished.

Sometimes a "cost plus ten percent" contract is agreed upon. In this case the contractor builds the church for whatever it costs him and receives an additional ten percent for his profit.

Still other times agreement is reached on a "contract plus percentage of savings." In this case the builder agrees to build the building for a certain amount including his profit. If he is able to build it for less, he receives his profit plus half of the amount he saved the church. Include a time limit in the contract which sets a date by which the work is to be finished. If the contractor does not complete the work by the date agreed upon, he becomes responsible for any expenses incurred thereafter.

"In some cases the church will let the contract for a portion of the building and use volunteer labor for the rest."[5] Be sure that both the church and the contractor know which parts of the building are going to be done by the church family.

As soon as the contract is let, the church should have a big ground-breaking day. Goals should be set and a record attendance should be present. Make it a day of joy and victory. Invite dignitaries such as a mission executive, mayor or congressman. The ground should be broken by the pastor, head deacon or leading member. Take pictures for publicity purposes.[6]

During the construction phase, you will need a business manager and an on-site supervisor. These services can be provided by the architect, an engineer, a church consulting firm, mission builder or knowledgeable church member.

The business manager will oversee the business aspects of the project. He awards the subcontracts and arranges for material purchases and their delivery. He takes care of necessary insurance, building permits and inspections. He also monitors and verifies all billings and payments while providing written progress and cost reports to the building committee. No payments are to be made without a signed waiver of lien from the contractor.

The on-site supervisor functions as the architect's representative and oversees the total project. He is there to ensure that the building is constructed according to the plans and specifications called for by the plans. He will follow up on post construction warranties and see that the work is guaranteed. "Final payments are not made until the work has been completed, passed inspections and lien waivers have been signed."[7]

When the project is completed, the dedication is over and all eulogies have been exchanged, both pastor and people must recognize that the building is not an end in itself, but a means to an end. The congregation must now go forth to reach the lost for Christ and fill the building.[8]

# Endnotes

[1] Marvin G. Rickard, *Let It Grow*. (Portland, OR: Multnomah Press, 1984), p. 69.

[2] Roy L. Thomas, *Planting and Growing a Fundamental Church*. (Nashville, TN: Randall House Publications, 1979), p. 132.

[3] A. Joseph Cheney, *Your Church Building*. (Schaumburg, IL: Baptist Bulletin, March 1968).

[4] Elmer Towns, *Church Aflame* . (Nashville, TN: Impact Books, 1971), p. 169.

[5] Jack Hyles, *The Hyles Church Manual*. (Murfreesboro, TN: Sword of the Lord Publishers, 1968), p. 46.

[6] *Ibid*, p. 46.

[7] Thomas, *op. cit.*, p. 134.

[8] Thomas, *op. cit.*, pp. 134, 135.

## The Single Story Building
### vs.
## the Two Story or Basement Building

• The single story building has many inherent advantages:

1. It follows today's trend in architecture.

2. It is the least expensive to construct.
   a. More donated labor can be used.
   b. The concrete slab floor is ideal for radiant panel heat.
   c. It allows for simple walls with much glass.
   d. It permits a lower ceiling, saving on materials and utility bills.
   e. It requires less foundation and will use only about half as much material for its walls.

3. Rooms on one level have multi-purpose uses: for Sunday School, social activities and overflow space.

4. It is safer, especially for small children.
   a. Hazardous stairways are eliminated.
   b. Doors can be placed wherever needed at little cost.
   c. Direct entrances from outside reduce need for corridors and eliminate traffic jams.

5. Rooms above ground are more cheerful. They usually have more light and color.

6. It is more adapted to the Sunday-school building.
   In multiple-floor buildings, one level sets the dimensions for another, while in single-level buildings each room can follow its own genius and be the size which is best suited to the purpose it serves.

7. The cost of remodeling and expansion is reduced.
   a. Adding to a multi-level building always presents problems and is usually expensive, while a one-story building can be indefinitely expandable.
   b. With single-story construction there is no excuse for large debts. A church can expand either its educational plant or sanctuary whichever is most needed. It can expand what it needs without expanding the other. There is never any unusable space.

  c. The church can build what it can pay for, then build more later.

 8. Modern heating systems are easily expanded as you build.


• Church basements have a number of inherent drawbacks:

 1. They add more to construction costs than benefits derived from them.
    a. Foundation walls only need to go down three or four feet in the coldest regions. To save this wall, it is necessary either to dig deeper or to put the first floor higher. This requires a thicker wall to carry the additional weight of the suspended floor. Floor-load requirements are usually at least two times greater than roof-load requirements.
    b. The floor over the basement has to be supported by beams and posts, while the single-story floor rests on the ground and does not need to be held up.
    c. The law requires two exits from each floor level, each leading directly out of doors. There must be some way to get from one floor to the other within the building. There must be two sets of steps the full height of the basement room. Stairways are costly and take away approximately ten percent of the floor area.
    d. The cost of stairways and floor supports cancels out what is saved on the roof.

 2. Getting in and out presents hazards.
    a. This is especially true for older folks and small children.
    b. Fewer people today want to climb steps to get into church. All levels must be accessible to handicapped individuals, resulting in additional costs.

 3. Basements often flood or have water problems.

 4. It is difficult and expensive to keep paint on basement walls. Moisture discolors whatever is on them.

 5. Usually there is not enough ventilation to prevent the contents from getting moldy in summer.

 6. Daylight is limited and rooms below ground are never as cheerful as above ground.

## Order of Service for Building Dedication

"Except the Lord build the house, they labour in vain that build it..." (Psalm 127:1).

Organ and Piano Prelude                                    (organist)
                                                           (pianist)

Hymn: "Faith is the Victory"

Prayer

Welcome & Greetings by the Pastor

Recognition of Honored Guests

Special Music

History of the Church  (One of the deacons)

Hymn:  "Great is Thy Faithfulness"

Scripture Reading:   II Chronicles 7:1-16

Act of Dedication (To be read by pastor and people responsively)

Prayer of Dedication  (Fellow pastor or a deacon)

Special Music (Song of Dedication)

Hymn: "To God be the Glory"

Message of Dedication   (Special speaker)

Hymn:  "Blest be the Tie that Binds"

Benediction

"I was glad when they said unto me, let us go into the house of the Lord...Peace be within thy walls, and prosperity within thy palaces...Because of the house of the Lord our God I will seek thy good...," (Psalm 122:1, 7, 9).

## The Act of Dedication

(To be read responsively by pastor and people)

**Pastor:**  We have built this building to honor and glorify the Lord Jesus Christ, who is the "King of kings, and Lord of lords," to whom be glory and power everlasting.

**People:**  To the worship of this Almighty God, Creator of heaven and earth,

**Pastor:**  To the proclamation of the Gospel of Jesus Christ, our Savior, in this place and unto the ends of the earth,

**People**: We dedicate this building.

**Pastor**:  To the instruction of youth, maturity and old age in the truths of the Bible, the Word of God,

**People:**  To the observance of the ordinances of the Church of Jesus Christ–Baptism by immersion and the Lord's Supper–do we dedicate this building.

**Pastor:**  As a monument to the faith of God's people and for the salvation of lost souls,

**People:**  As a place of prayer for all people,

**Pastor:**  As a rebuke to wickedness and an encouragement to righteousness in this community,

**People**: We dedicate this building.

**Pastor:** May no note of discord ever be heard within these walls and no unholy spirit of pride or worldliness find entrance here.

**People**:  May this building be a haven for rich and poor alike, in sorrow and distress, and a place of praise for the joyous.

**Pastor**: When we shall have gone to our heavenly home, may others take up the service until Jesus comes and His own are gath - ered home.

**Pastor & People:**  May the Lord ever be glorified herein; may His rich blessing rest upon all who sincerely worship here, upon all who faithfully preach or teach the Bible as the Word of God, and upon every service held here to the glory of His holy name. To this end do we DEDICATE THIS BUILDING!

# The Act of Dedication

(To be said responsively by pastor and people)

**Pastor:** We have built this building to honor and glorify the Lord Jesus Christ, who is the King of kings and Lord of lords, to whom be glory and power everlasting.

**People:** To the worship of thee Almighty God, Creator of heaven and earth.

**Pastor:** To the proclamation of the gospel of Jesus Christ, our Saviour, in this place and unto the ends of the earth.

**People:** We dedicate this building.

**Pastor:** To the ministration of the word and truth and help in the truths of the Bible, the word of God.

**People:** For the observance of the ordinances of the Church of Jesus Christ, baptism by immersion and the Lord's supper, we dedicate this building.

**Pastor:** As a monument to the faith of God's people and for the salvation of lost souls.

**People:** As a place of prayer for all people.

**Pastor:** As a tribute to wholesomeness and an encouragement to righteousness in this community.

**People:** We dedicate this building.

**Pastor:** May no note of discord ever be heard within these walls, and no unholy spirit of pride or worldliness find entrance here.

**People:** May this building be a house of refuge to all that need it, a comfort and distress, and a place of peace for the joyous.

**Pastor:** When we shall have gone to our heavenly home, may others take up the work and continue to save souls and lift the world to a higher plane.

**Pastor & People:** May the head over all spiritual house, and His rich blessed rest upon all who shall offer worship here; upon all who faithfully proclaim in this place the truth as the Word of God, and upon every serve, bend here to the glory of His holy name.

(Ascend the WEDDING TO THE BUILDER)

# Chapter 16

# The Fallacies
# in the Local Church

In the process of planting a church, you will find there are many trials, pressures and problems that must be overcome. These will either make you or break you depending on how you handle them. You have only three options: you can ignore them while they fester and get worse; you can run away from them to "greener pastures" in which case they will reappear; or you can face them honestly and seek to resolve them. Only those who exercise the last option will be successful in planting strong, indigenous churches.

## Discouragement

It has been said that "a depressed Christian is a contradiction in terms...a poor recommendation for the gospel."[1] While that may be true, discouragement is a reality the church planter must face. Many great men of the Bible encountered times of discouragement when they wondered whether God was really with them. We read of Moses ( Numbers 11:15), Joshua (Joshua 7:7), Elijah (I Kings 19:4), Job (Job 10:1), David (Psalm 42:6), Jeremiah (Jeremiah 15:10) and the disciples of Jesus (Luke 24:17).

There are many reasons why missionaries, pastors and church planters become discouraged. A number of factors may be involved including physical or spiritual weariness, wrong goals, a lack of response or recognition, frustration or failure of those in whom you trusted.[2] Dr. Lloyd-Jones summarizes causes of discouragement under four headings: First, temperament, some people tend to be introverts who are given to melancholy moods. Second, reaction to a great blessing such as in the case of Elijah after his Mount Carmel experience (I Kings 19). Then, there is the devil, the adversary of our souls, whose main desire is to depress Christians and cause the ungodly to scorn us. Lastly, the ultimate cause of all discouragement is unbelief.[3]

Discouragement must be dealt with without delay, or it will lead to depression, and depression to defeat. Recognize that you are involved in a spiritual warfare (Ephesians 6:12). Get alone with God and pour your heart out to Him, read in His Word the accounts of others who have become discouraged. Replace unbelief with faith by taking God at His word. The Psalmist kept declaring to himself, "Hope thou in God; for I shall yet praise Him for the help of His countenance" (Psalm 42:5). Get active, do something for God. Go soul winning, play tennis, go visiting at the hospital. Get your mind off yourself and onto someone or something else. Every church planter should read Dr. D. Martin Lloyd-Jones' book, *Spiritual Depression, its Causes and Cure*. It will greatly help you in dealing with depression, both in your own life and that of your church family.

## Burnout

Many a church planter has said: "I would rather burn out for Jesus than to rust out!" While that sounds noble, it is not very practical and does not glorify God. The Lord wants our lives and ministries to produce a steady glow, not a flash in the dark. Too many men have suffered from "burnout" and have ended up leaving the ministry prematurely. They "burn their candle at both ends" by trying to do everything. They see themselves as being indispensible: "The church cannot do without me." Because of this attitude, these men "bite off more than they can chew."

Sometimes the problem is a failure to delegate authority and responsibility to others. Some men just don't trust other people. Other times, the people refuse or fail to help the pastor and he ends up trying to do it all. But there just are not enough hours in the day to get everything done. He feels isolated and alone. No one seems to care or share his vision for the work. Eventually, the pastor "cracks" under the strain, and either ends up with a nervous breakdown or leaves the ministry in frustration.

The solution to the problem is simple: learn to delegate and to say "no." Refuse to do for the church that which it is capable of doing for itself. Meet with your people, share the problem and ask for their help in solving it. Just as Moses learned to delegate and share the responsibility of leadership with the seventy, so church planters must learn to develop realistic goals and expectations, both for themselves and their people. Church planting is a joint venture, not a one-man show.

## Laziness

Dr. Charles Wagner once said that there are three main perils in the ministry: "dine, whine and recline."[4] He went on to say, "Lazy pastors will develop into superficial pastors."[5]

It is easy for a pastor to be lazy, for he is generally his own boss. Unless he disciplines himself to a schedule, he will waste time. He must plan his work and work his plan. The solution to laziness? The pastor must recognize his problem. The Word of God has much to say about the wise use of time: Ephesians 5:16; Proverbs 6:6; 24:30,31 and Ecclesiastes 10:18. A daily schedule similar to the one in chapter two must be developed and followed.

## Quiet Time

One of the greatest problems a pastor must deal with is the neglect of his "quiet time" with the Lord. "The concern of the devil is to keep Christians from praying. He fears nothing from prayerless studies, prayerless work, prayerless religion. He laughs at our toil, mocks at our wisdom, but trembles when we pray."[6]

God places great value on the need to seek His face daily as is seen in Hebrews 2:3; Isaiah 55:6; Psalm 27:8; Isaiah 30:15 and Psalm 27:14. The failure to spend time with the Lord in prayer and meditation on His Word will result in a lack of power and effectiveness in your ministry. It will lead to spiritual stagnation, defeat and sin. There will never be any "free" time when you can have your daily devotions. You must make the time. It's a matter of priorities. It may involve getting up earlier or skipping some other activity. Carve out a set time every day when you read God's Word and pray. Use a book such as the "Spiritual Diary" published by Baptist Mid-Missions to help you.

## Family Problems

The church planter's family is a key ingredient in determining the success or failure of his ministry. Many a dedicated man has given sacrificially of his time and effort to build a church and has ended up losing his family due to neglect.

Learn to spend time with your family. Make one night a week "Family Night" when you do things together. Go shopping, attend a ball game, play with the children or visit the zoo. Take your wife out to eat occasionally. Buy her flowers or a little present to let her know how much you appreciate her. Your family needs to know that they are as important to you as other people in the church.

Don't expect your wife to be as active in the ministry as you are. Remember, she has a home to care for, clothes to wash, meals to cook and children to nurture. While she may be involved in the church work, do not expect her to carry the load of an "assistant" pastor.

Dr. Quentin Kenoyer has written an excellent little study book for church planters called *The Christian Family*. It is available from Baptist Mid-Missions in Cleveland, Ohio. You will find it most profitable.

## Church Problems

Every church planter will encounter problems in the church he is seeking to establish. It has been observed that most of these problems come from one of three sources: women, deacons and Bible-school graduates. While there may be some truth in this observation, a closer look will reveal that most problems can be traced to sin in someone's life, personality conflicts, policy and procedural differences or spiritual immaturity. Regardless of the source, problems must be faced head on when they arise or they will eventually undermine and destroy the work you seek to build.

Church problems are not always easy to resolve. Sometimes there will be a spirit of indifference or a lack of enthusiasm. Other times you may be the center of controversy and will find people strongly opposed to your policies. These times will take a heavy toll on you unless you learn to take the burdens to the Lord and leave them there. Avoid taking your problems to bed with you. Lay them aside when you off take your shoes. A sleepless night will not help you nor them.

Deal with problems in a biblical manner. Matthew 5:23, 24; 18:15-17 and I Corinthians 5 provide the basic format to follow. Meet with the individual(s) involved personally. Share your concern, listen to their side of the story. Do you have the facts straight? Many times the problem can be resolved with a single visit. If it cannot, continue to pray for them and to urge the parties involved to solve the problem in a scriptural manner. If the problem persists, then take the matter to the church for appropriate action.

## Success in the Ministry

How do you define success in the ministry? For many it can be defined with one word, RESULTS. If you have souls saved regularly, a growing congregation, large modern facilities and a staff, you are considered successful. If these things are lacking, you are a failure. Supporting churches often expect their church planter to produce results overnight. If he does not, his support may be transferred to a more "successful" man.

While some men may be unproductive because of laziness, or a lack of training, it must be recognized that many men have faithfully labored in extremely difficult places with little visible results. God does not measure success in terms of fruitfulness, but in terms of faithfulness. Faithfulness does not always result in fruitfulness. Noah and Jeremiah faithfully proclaimed God's message for years with little tangible results, and yet they successfully fulfilled their God-given roles.

Sometimes a church planter must labor for years, preparing the soil before significant results are obtained. If you are not seeing the results you desire, do not give up or consider yourself a failure. Visit aggressively, preach enthusiastically, faithfully continue the ministry God has given you and leave the results with Him. Do not measure yourself by what others are doing, and stop worrying about what people think. If you faithfully and fully carry out the task God has given you, you are a success in His book and will hear His "Well done, good and faithful servant."

## Communication with Supporters

If you receive outside financial assistance for your church-planting ministry, it is essential that you maintain good communication with those supporters. You cannot expect them to continue their backing if you do not inform them of your progress and needs.

Send each supporter a written progress report every two to three months. These should be positive, informative and well typed. Do not send messy or poorly mimeographed materials as these reflect on the quality of work you do. In addition, write a personal note to the pastor or individual involved. Express your appreciation for their faithfulness and help.

Express your needs in a positive manner. Do not complain or be negative. Include prayer requests, but keep them to a minimum, using the majority of the report to tell of some positive development.

Supporting churches sometimes forget that you are actively involved in your field of service. A church planter cannot simply drop what he is doing to go speak in a supporting church. When such requests come, try to work out a mutually agreeable date which will allow you to be away without interfering too much with the work. Keep such absences to a minimum. If it is simply impossible for you to leave, honestly explain the problem to the supporting pastor and try to arrange a more suitable date. Most will work with you in this area, especially if you have maintained good communication with them.

## Endnotes

[1] Dr. D. Martin Lloyd-Jones, *Spiritual Depression , Its Causes and Cures.* (Grand Rapids: Eerdmans Publishing Co., 1966), p.11

[2] G. Carl Barton, *A Handbook For Missionaries.* (Cedarville, OH: 1984), pp. 55-61.

[3] Lloyd-Jones, *ibid,* pp. 14-20.

[4] Quoted by Dr. Charles U. Wagner in his book, *The Pastor, His Life and Work.* (Schaumburg, IL: Regular Baptist Press, 1976), p. 229.

[5] *Ibid.* p. 230.

[6] Cameron V. Thompson,*The Master Secrets of Prayer.* (Lincoln, NE: Back to the Bible Publishers, 1960), p. 9.

# The Finished Job—
a Local Church

Every church planter's goal is the same: to establish a local New Testament church which can fully function without outside assistance. He begins with an aggressive visitation schedule, seeking to contact and win the lost to Christ. As people are won and interested families are located, a core group or nucleus develops. This group is then organized into a local church with the church planter serving as pastor.

As the work progresses and the church grows, it will be able to assume more and more of the pastor's salary, purchase property and erect a building. When this occurs, "graduation" day will be near. This term is used commonly by missionary church planters to describe the time when the mission church is ready to assume full responsibility for its own ministry.

## How to Determine Maturity for Graduation

Four basic areas must be considered when determining if the church is ready for graduation. This decision should be made only after prayerful consultaion with the deacons and the mission agency under which the missionary serves.

• Membership

As Jackson pointed out in his definition, the local church is an organized body of believers "banded together for work, worship, the observance of the ordinances and the worldwide proclamation of the Gospel." [1]

This purpose can hardly be carried on by two or three individuals who meet together occasionally and call themselves a "church." The Scriptures do not establish a minimum member-ship requirement. However, it should be a sufficient number to support the church and to enable it to carry out its established program.

## • Finances

Is the church able to support its pastor fully meet its mortgage and bond payments, pay its normal operating expenses and support a missionary program? If not, then it is not ready to graduate.

Church planters must clearly teach the responsibility of Christian stewardship. The Lord Jesus Christ emphasized this subject in training His disciples. God has entrusted us with material possessions which are to be used for His honor and glory.

Paul was an effective church planter. He worked very hard to establish an independent church in the city of Corinth. Later, however, he wrote to ask them to forgive him for failing to instruct them thoroughly in the area of finances. His words were, "For what is it wherein ye were inferior to other churches, except it be that I myself was not burdensome to you? Forgive me this wrong" (II Corinthians 12:13). Paul had chosen to support himself rather than teaching the church to assume the financial responsibility of supporting their missionary pastor. As a result, they had not experienced the blessings God had in store for them (II Corinthians 6:6,8).

God will provide for the needs of the local church if the people are taught to give. This was proven to the members of the church at Philippi. Philippi had been Paul's first supporting church. They had sent him as a "home missionary" to Thessalonica (Philippians 4:15,16). Due to his imprisonment, they discontinued his support. Later it was reinstated and Paul wrote: "Now at the last your care of me hath flourished again...but my God shall supply all your need according to His riches in glory by Christ Jesus" (Philippians 4:10,19).

Is God's program through the local church being adequately supported by your people? It will be if you faithfully teach tithing and develop a stewardship program based on biblical principles. A church yielded to God and desirous of carrying out the Great Commission will experience God's provision.

## • Leadership

Leadership is essential to any organization. For the local church to be self-governing, it must have within its membership mature Christians who are able to lead the congregation in carrying out the Great Commission, beginning in its own "Jerusalem."

Part of your ministry is to "equip the saints for the work of the ministry" (Ephesians 4:12). This involves discipling, or training men and women to be leaders in the church. Do you have spiritually mature men who are qualified and experienced deacons? Is there a solid core of Sunday-school teachers? Do you have spiritually mature individuals to handle the finances? Do your people exercise leadership in winning and discipling new converts?

Your people will have differing spiritual gifts which must be discovered, developed and deployed in leadership positions before the church is ready for graduation (Romans 12:4-11). Be careful not to confuse spiritual gifts with human talent. A spiritual gift is from God. It is a supernatural enabling to accomplish a spiritual task. A talent is simply a natural ability. Never assume that a natural ability can be used to communicate spiritual truth effectively.

The local church should seek God's direction in assigning leadership responsibilities. Sunday-school teachers should be exemplary Christians who are able to expound effectively and apply the Word of God in teaching and discipling situations. Deacons must meet qualifications set forth by Scripture (I Timothy 3:12,13). The church clerk, treasurer and other officers should have clear Christian testimonies and manifest abilities in their areas of assigned responsibility.

Leadership is the exercise of supernatural ability combined with human talent in the completion of the task assigned by the Lord and recognized by the church. To graduate a church without adequate leadership would be tantamount to inviting disaster. Your mission is not accomplished until there is evidence of solid, committed leadership among your members.

## • Facilities

The church may begin in a home, school, bank, community center or other rented facility. Generally, a church is not considered ready for graduation until it has a permanent location that enables it to develop a comprehensive program with adequate facilities for its training and worship. However, in some cases where property is extremely expensive and the church is able to pay the pastor's salary and other operating expenses, the church may graduate earlier. In this case the missionary church planter steps down and a full-time pastor is called who then leads the church into the building program.

## Calling A Pastor

If after considering the preceding four points, you, your deacons and the mission administration feel that the church is sufficiently mature, it will be time to recommend graduation. The next step would be to recommend that the church seek God's will concerning its first full-time pastor.

In some cases the church planter will stay on after the church has reached the self-support level. In this case, he resigns from his mission agency and gives up the outside support he has been receiving. Church planters who are not affiliated with a mission agency usually continue on as the pastor of the church they have founded when it achieves maturity.

If the church planter is not going to remain as pastor of the church, then the church should follow the procedure for calling a pastor outlined in the constitution which it accepted at the time of organization. This involves the naming of a pulpit committee comprised of the deacons and church planter.

Edward T. Hiscox's *New Directory for Baptist Churches* published in 1894, has long been the standard for Baptist polity. At the end of Hiscox's chapter on church officers, he adds seven notes which are worthy of consideration by the church and pulpit committee. These seven points can be summarized as follows:

Note 1. Great care is needed in the selection of a pastor. Grave interests are committed to his charge, as the religious teacher, leader, and example for the flock. So vital an act should be preceded by earnest and protracted prayer for divine direction in the choice.

Note 2. In calling a man to the pastorate, the church should take deliberate care to know his record, what he has done elsewhere, and how he is esteemed and valued where he has previously lived and labored. A man of deep piety, thoroughly in love with the Word of God, is much to be preferred to the brilliant platform declaimer.

Note 3. If a young man without a record is called, his reputation for piety, sound sense and pulpit ability should be carefully considered. If he be of the right spirit and the right material, he will grow into larger usefulness through study, the endowment of the Spirit and the prayers of the people.

Note 4. In giving a call, the church usually appoints a meeting for that express purpose, notice being publicly given two Sundays in succession. A three-quarters vote of all present at such a meeting should be deemed essential to a call. The candidate should be informed exactly how the vote stands, and what the feeling toward him is, concealing nothing. Let there be transparent honesty in so delicate and important a matter, and no deception practiced.

Note 5. The connection between pastor and people is sometimes made a specified and limited time. But more generally–now almost universally–for an indefinite time, to be dissolved at the option of either party, by giving three months' notice; or otherwise by mutual agreement. Permanency in this relation is greatly to be desired, as tending to the best good of all concerned.

Note 6. The too common practice of hearing many candidates preach on trial cannot be approved, and usually works evil to the church which indulges in it. A few sermons preached under such circumstances form no just criterion of a man's ministerial ability, pastoral qualifications, or personal worth.

Note 7. Is it right for one church to call a pastor away from another church? Merely to call a man would be neither wrong nor dishonorable. Let the responsibility, then, rest with him of accepting or declining the call. But if one church should use other means to unsettle him by arguments, persuasions, and the offer of special inducements, it would be both unchristian and dishonorable. [2]

Additional information can be found in Dr. Paul R. Jackson's book, *The Doctrine and Administration of the Church.*

The pulpit committee has the responsibility to recommend candidates to the church. Before such a recommendation is made, the committee should seek to learn as much as possible about the man. If he is pastoring a church, a member or a delegation from the pulpit committee may be sent to visit the church where he is preaching. This would provide an opportunity to observe not only his ability to handle the Word from the pulpit, but also the work that he has accomplished in his present location. The potential candidate may be invited to the church as a pulpit supply. Before recommending him to the church, the committee should have determined his position regarding

1. Doctrine. (Does he agree with the doctrinal statement without mental reservation?)
2. Church covenant. (Has he read and does he agree with each covenant statement?)
3. Church constitution. (Has he read and does he concur with the constitution of the church?)
4. Spiritual gifts. (What does he consider as his spiritual gifts, i.e. his strengths in the ministry?)
5. His family. (Does he have a good relationship with his wife and family? (I Timothy 3)
6. Finances. (How does he handle his money? Is he prompt in paying his debts? Does he have any large indebtedness?)
7. Morals.
8. Contemporary theological issues.
   a. Divorce and remarriage
   b. Charismatic movement
   c. Neo-evangelicalism
   d. Bible translations
   e. The Atonement

Only after the pulpit committee is satisfied that the man meets the qualifications should they recommend the church invite him as a candidate. It is suggested that the candidate and his family meet with the church for a weekend, that is Friday through Sunday. The Friday-evening meeting would be more or less informal, a "get-acquainted" time, perhaps combined with a fellowship supper. Saturday would provide an opportunity for church families to invite the candidate and his family to their homes. The candidate should have maximum exposure on the Lord's day. In addition to preaching in both services, he should teach the Adult Sunday School class.

The voting members of the church should meet with the candidate and his wife on Sunday afternoon or following the evening service. This will provide an opportunity for members to ask questions. It should be remembered that the candidate and his wife should also be accorded the privilege of asking questions of the church family. Not only does the church need to make a decision, but the candidate must also decide whether or not to accept a call if it is extended to him.

Candidates should not be viewed as competitors for a job vacancy. Consider only one candidate at a time. To vote on two candidates in one meeting could easily result in a church split. After the vote by the church, the candidate should be informed immediately whether or not he has been called by the church. If the call is in the affirmative, he should be provided with a letter stating the pastoral salary, vacation time and other benefits which have been discussed during the interview. If a candidate is rejected or refuses the call, the pulpit committee should seek another candidate in the same manner.

After acceptance by the candidate, all that remains for the graduation is to establish a timetable for his installation as the first full-time pastor of the church. The missionary should make plans to move on to his new assignment. The church-planting agreement between the mission agency and the mission church has now served its purpose and should be considered null and void.

A special graduation service should be planned when the new pastor assumes his responsibilities. Often, the church planter and a member of the administrative staff from his mission agency are present to participate. A "graduation certificate" is presented to the church, thereby signifying "Mission Accomplished."

### Endnotes

[1] Paul R. Jackson, *The Doctrine and Administration of the Local Church.* (Des Plaines, IL: Regular Baptist Press, 1968), p. 27.

[2] Edward T. Hiscox, *The New Directory for Baptist Churches.* (Valley Forge, NY: The Judson Press, 1894), pp. 117-118.

## The Graduation/Installation Service

Organ & Piano Prelude                                    (organist)
                                                         (pianist)

Hymn: "Praise Him, Praise Him"

Prayer of Invocation (Founding Pastor)

Welcome and Greetings

Recognition of Honored Guests

Hymn: "The Church's One Foundation"

History of the Church (Founding Pastor or Deacon)

Scripture Reading: Acts 14:21-28

Special Music

Graduation Message (Mission Representative)

Installation of the New Pastor

Charge to the Church (Visiting Pastor or Church Planter)

Acceptance of the Charge (Chairman of the Deacons)

Charge to the New Pastor (Visiting Pastor)

Acceptance of the Charge (New Pastor)

Presentation of Graduation Plaque (Mission Representative)

Reception of Graduation Plaque (New Pastor or a Deacon)

Hymn: "To God be the Glory"

Benediction

Postlude

"And He gave some, apostles; and some, prophets; and some, evangelists; and some, pastors and teachers; for the perfecting of the saints, for the work of the ministry, for the edifying of the body of Christ" (Ephesians 4:11,12).

PRESENTED TO
the members of

who, in obedience to the Word of God, have faithfully cooperated with Baptist Mid-Missions in the establishing of this independent Baptist Church.

"Go ye therefore, and teach all nations, baptizing them in the name of the Father, and of the Son, and of the Holy Ghost: teaching them to observe all things whatsoever I have commanded you: and lo I am with you alway, even unto the end of the world. Amen."
Matthew 28:19-20

PRESENTADO
a los miembros de

quienes, en obediencia a la palabra de Dios, han cooperado fielmente con Baptist Mid-Missions, estableciendo esta iglesia Bautista independiente.

"Por tanto, id, y haced discípulos a todas las naciones, bautizándolos en el nombre del Padre, y del Hijo, y del Espíritu Santo; enseñándoles todas las cosas que os he mandado; y he aquí yo estoy con vosotros todos los días, hasta el fin del mundo. Amén."
Mateo 28:19-20

# Bibliography

Allen, Arthur, *Planting Baptist Churches.* Minneapolis: Minnesota Baptist Association, n.d.

Allen, Roland, *Missionary Methods: St. Paul's or Ours?* Grand Rapids: Eerdmans, 1962.

_____, and Borror, Gordon, *Worship-Rediscovering the Missing Jewel.* Portland, OR: Multnomah Press, 1982.

Amberson, Talmadge R., ed., *The Birth of Churches: The Biblical Basis for Church Planting.* Nashville: Broadman Press, 1979.

Amstutz, Harold E., *Church Planter's Manual.* Cherry Hill, NJ: Association of Baptists for World Evangelism, Inc., 1985.

Bailey, Keith M., *The Church Planter's Manual.* Harrisburg, PA: Christian Publications, Inc., 1981.

Barlow, Fred M., *Special Days in the Sunday School.* Des Plaines, IL: Regular Baptist Press, 1971.

Barton, G. Carl, *A Handbook for Missionaries.* Cedarville, OH: 1984.

Beals, Paul A., *A People for His Name.* Pasadena, CA: William Carey Library, 1985.

Belew, Wendell, *Churches and How They Grow.* Nashville: Broadman Press, n.d.

Benson, Donald, *How to Start a Daughter Church.* Quezo City, Philippines: Filkoba Press, 1972.

Bisagno, John R., *How to Build an Evangelistic Church.* Nashville: Broadman Press, 1972.

Brock, Charles, *The Principles and Practice of Indigenous Church Planting.* Nashville: Broadman Press, 1981.

Brown, L. Duane, *Biblical Basis for Baptists*. Schaumburg, IL: Regular Baptist Press, 1969.

Chaney, Charles L., *Church Planting at the End of the Twentieth Century*. Wheaton, IL: Tyndale House, 1982.

Cheney, A. Joseph, "Your Church Building," Schaumburg, IL: Baptist Bulletin, March 1968.

Chapman, Kenneth, *How to Plant, Pastor and Promote a Local Church*. Lynchburg, VA: James Family Christian Publishers, 1979.

_____, *The Successful New Church*. Alta Vista, CA: Alta Vista Press, 1981.

Clark, Carl A., *Rural Churches in Transition*. Nashville: Broadman Press, 1959.

Cover, Kenneth L., *Shaping the Church's Educational Ministry*. Valley Forge, PA: Judson Press, 1971.

Currin, James H., *Starting New Missions and Churches*. Nashville: The Sunday School Board, 1971.

Dersham, James F., *Enlisting Teachers*. Schaumburg, IL: Regular Bapist Press, Winter, 1981.

Dollar, Truman, *How to Carry Out God's Stewardship Plan*. Nashville: Thomas Nelson Publishers, 1974.

Green, Hollis L, *Why Churches Die*. Minneapolis: Bethany Fellowship, 1972.

Greenway, Roger S., *Guidelines for Urban Church Planting*. Grand Rapids: Baker Book House, 1976.

Gunther, Peter F., *The Fields at Home*. Chicago: Moody Press, 1963.

Hakes, J. Edward, *An Introduction to Evangelical Christian Education*. Chicago: Moody Press, 1967.

Helton, Max, *The Making of a New Church*. Hammond, IN: Helton Publications, n.d. (series of six cassette tapes)

Hesselgrave, David J., *Planting Churches Cross-Culturally*. Grand Rapids: Baker Book House, 1980.

Hiscox, Edward T., *The New Directory for Baptist Churches*. Philadelphia: Judson Press, 1894.

Hodges, Melvin L., *A Guide to Church Planting*. Chicago: Moody Press, 1973.

_____, *Growing Young Churches*. Chicago: Moody Press, n.d.

Howse, W.L., *A Church Organized and Functioning*. Nashville: Convention Press, 1963.

Hyles, Jack, *How to Boost Your Church Attendance*. Grand Rapids: Zondervan Publishing House, 1958.

_____, *Let's Build an Evangelistic Church*. Murfreesboro, TN: Sword of the Lord Publishers, 1962.

_____, *The Hyles Church Manual*. Murfreesboro, TN: Sword of the Lord Publishers, 1968.

Jackson, Paul R., *The Doctrine and Administration of the Local Church*. Des Plaines, IL: Regular Baptist Press, 1968.

Jones, Ezra Earl, *Strategies for New Churches*. New York: Harper and Row, 1976.

Kenoyer, Quentin D., *A Spiritual Diary*. Cleveland: Baptist Mid-Missions, 1984.

_____, *The Christian Family*. Cleveland: Baptist Mid-Missions, 1981.

Knight, Walker and Touchton, Ken, *Seven Beginnings*. Atlanta: Home Mission Board, Southern Baptist Convention, 1977.

Lilly, Tom, *Building A New Church*. Nashville: Free Will Baptist Home Missions Department, 1971.

Longenecker, Harold L., *Building Town & Country Churches*. Chicago: Moody Press, 1961

Lloyd-Jones, D. Martin, *Spiritual Depression, Its Causes and Cures*. Grand Rapids: Eerdmans Publishing Co., 1966.

MacNair, Donald J., *The Birth, Care and Feeding of a Local Church*. Washington, D.C.: Canon Press, 1971.

McGavran, Donald A., *How Churches Grow*. New York: Friendship Press, 1955.

_____, *Understanding Church Growth*. Revised Edition, Grand Rapids: Eerdmans, 1970.

_____, and Arn, Win., *How to Grow a Church*. Glendale, CA: Regal, 1973.

_____, and Hunter, George G. III., *Church Growth Strategies That Work*. Nashville: Abingdon, 1980.

Mears, Henrietta, *Ways to Plan and Organize Your Sunday School*. Glendale, CA: International Center for Learning, 1971.

Minnery, Thomas, "Success in Three Churches: Diversity and Originality," Leadership Magazine, Winter Quarter, 1981.

Mooneyham, Lamarr, *Starting a Church From Scratch*. Hillsborough, NC: Lamarr Mooneyham Productions, 1981. (Two taped lectures)

_____, *Specifics in Church Planting*. Hillsborough, NC: Lamarr Mooneyham Productions, 1981. (Two taped lectures)

Moorhouse, Carl W., *Growing New Churches; Step-by-Step Procedures in New Church Planting*. Cincinnati: Standard Publishing, 1975.

Nevius, John, *Planting and Development of Missionary Churches*. Philadelphia: Presbyterian and Reformed, 1899.

Orjala, Paul R., *Get Ready to Grow*. Kansas City, MO: Beacon Hill Press, 1978.

Parrott, Leslie, *Building Today's Church*. Grand Rapids: Baker Book House, 1973.

Parvin, Earl, *Missions USA*. Chicago: Moody Press, 1985.

Pearson, Dick, *Missionary Education Helps for the Local Church*. Palo Alto, CA: Overseas Crusades, Inc., 1966

Perkins, Ernie, *Guidelines for the Pioneer Pastor*. Fairborn, OH: Encounter Publishing Company, 1971.

Redford, Jack, *Guide for Establishing New Churches and Missions*. Nashville: Home Mission Board/Southern Baptist Convention, n.d.

_____, *Planting New Churches*. Nashville: Broadman Press, 1979.

Reese, J. Irving, *A Guide for Organizing and Conducting a Baptist Church*. Elyria, OH: F.B.H.M., 1962.

Rice, Grant G., *Church Planting Primer*. Louisville, KY: Tabernacle Press, 1985.

_____, *Church Planting Pre-Planning*. Rockvale, TN: Grant Rice, n.d.

Rickard, Marvin G., *Let It Grow*. Portland, OR: Multnomah Press, 1984.

Schmidt, Richard F., *Legal Aspects of Church Management*. Los Angeles: Christian Ministries Management Association, 1984.

Seibel, Roy W., *Shepherding New Flocks*. (self-published mimeograph notes)

Shippey, Fredrick A., *Church Work in the City*. New York, Abingdon, Cokesberry Press, 1952.

Snyder, Howard F., and Wiersbe, Warren W., *When the Pastor Wonders How*. Chicago: Moody Press, 1973.

Spurgeon, C.H., *Lectures to my Students*. Grand Rapids: Zondervan, 1954.

282

Starr, Timothy, *Church Planting: Always in Season*. Willowdale, ON: Fellowship of Evangelical Baptist Churches of Canada, 1978.

Steward, Kenneth N., *Strategy for an Effective Church Missionary Program*. Grand Rapids: Grand Rapids Baptist Seminary, 1973.

Thiessen, John Caldwell, *Pastoring the Smaller Church*. Grand Rapids: Zondervan Publishing House, 1962.

Thomas, J.V., *How to Start New Mission/Churches: A Guide for Associational Mission Leaders*. Dallas: Baptist General Convention of Texas, 1979.

Thomas, Roy L., *How to Start a Church from Scratch*. Nashville: Free Will Baptist Home Missions Department, 1972.

_____, *Planting and Growing a Fundamental Church*. Nashville: Randall House Publications, 1979.

Thompson, Cameron V., *The Master Secrets of Prayer*. Lincoln, NE: Back to the Bible Publishers, 1960.

Towns, Elmer L., *Getting A Church Started*. Elmer L. Towns, Lynchburg, VA: Privately published by author, but available from Fuller Bookstore, 1982.

_____, *Getting a Church Started in the Face of Insurmountable Odds with Limited Resources in Unlikely Circumstances*. Nashville: Impact Books, 1975.

_____, *Church Aflame*. Nashville: Impact Books, 1971.

Underwood, Charles M., *Planting the Independent Fundamental Church*. Greenville, SC: Bob Jones University, 1972.

Vedder, Henry C., *A Short History of the Baptists*. Valley Forge, PA: Judson Press, 1907.

Wagner, Charles U., *The Pastor, His Life and Work*. Schaumburg, Illinois: Regular Baptist Press, 1976.

Wagner, C. Peter, *Frontiers of Missionary Strategy*. Chicago: Moody Press, 1971.

_____, *Your Church Can Grow*. Glendale, CA.: Gospel Light Publications, 1976.

Watermann, L.P., *New Church Manual*. Wheaton, IL: The Conservative Baptist Home Missions Society, n.d.

Wilson, Ron, *Multimedia Handbook for the Church*. Elgin, IL: David C. Cook Publishing Co.,1975.